Tree

Simon & Su ...lly

www.capallbann.co.uk

Tree Seer

ISBN 186163 084 0

Cover design by Paul Mason
Cover and internal illustrations Simon Lilly

Published by:

Capall Bann Publishing
Auton Farm
Milverton
Somerset
TA4 1NE

Dedication

For Bethan and Joshua - the next generation

By the same authors, also published by Capall Bann:

Crystal Doorways
Tree: Essence, Spirit and Teacher
Tree: Essence of Healing
Healing With Astrology (Sue Lilly)

Contents

Introduction   3
Chapter 1 "Becoming Rooted"   7
    Earth Breath   11
    Tree Roots   12
    Axial Breath (Centre-line breathing)   14
    Tree: Roots and Branches   15
    Variation One: 17
    Variation Two: 17
    Variation Three: 17
    Variation Four: 17
    Variation Five: 17
    Earth Star Anchor   19
    Tree Roots and a Secret Chamber   21
    Mindless Grounding   22
    Grounding Layout with Smoky Quartz   24
    A Tree at the Earth's Core   26
    The Fountain Tree   28
    Complete Rootedness   30
    Becoming Centred - Becoming Yourself   32
    Using the Breath to Centre   33
    Bee Breath   33
    Alternate Nostril Breathing   34
    Cool Breath   35
    Centring with Sound   35
    Centring on the Voice   36
    Energy Balancing for the Ground State   36
    Tapping In   37
    Cook's Hook Up   38
    Meridian Massage   40
Chapter 2 Developing a Protocol for Working with Tree Spirits   44
    Internal Balance   45
    Balance in the External Elements   45
    Offering Breath   45
    Focusing on Intent   46
Chapter 3 Protection and Support   52
    The Varieties of Stress Factors   55
    Other Spirit Presences   57
    Cosmic Influence   60
    Support Using Grounding   61

Support Using the Sense of Sound 63
Support Using the Sense of Smell 63
Support Using the Sense of Sight 64
Other Support Processes 66
Chapter 4 The Dendrochronology of a Land 67
Chapter 5 Climbing the World Tree – Shamanic Technology 96
The World Tree 98
Entranced and Entrained 99
Drumming Up Support 102
Protocols for Drumming 104
Preliminaries – Clearing etc 105
Signals - Call-back 107
Meeting Power Animals 107
Solo Calling of the Animals 111
Group Calling the Animals 112
Journeying to Find a Power Animal 113
The Nature of Power Animals 114
Using Discretion 115
Beginning to journey to the Lower World 117
First Journey into the Lower World 118
Journeys to the Lower World 120
Journeying to the Upper World 121
First Journey to the Upper World 122
Middle World Journeys 123
Allies From The Four Directions 125
Journeying Between the Elements 125
Working at a Place 127
Tips for Trips - Advice for Making Journeys More Effective 128
Chapter 6 Healing Techniques 133
Wooden Pendulums as Healing Tools 133
Pendulum Over Palm Techniques 134
Five-Line Clearing 137
Options For Five-Line Clearing 140
Breath Spirit Healing 141
Elemental Balancing 143
"Two Wheels" Elemental Balance 144
"Three Tree Healing" 146
Tree Essences and the Nature of Flower Essences 150
Using Essences in Sequence 157
The Tao of Trees 159
Establishing Communion 162
Patterns of Energy flow 165
Chapter 7 Tree Teas 168
Protocol for Taking Tree Teas 171

Chapter 8 Tree Initiations and Other deep Contact   201
    The Yew Initiation   203
    The Elm Initiation   205
    The Ivy Doorway   206
    Oak Initiation   207
    Holly Initiation   208
    Maple Initiation   210
    Birch Initiation   212
    The Lime Initiation   214
    Cherry Initiation   215
    Strawberry Tree Initiation   216
    Poplar Initiation   217
    Other Deep Contacts   219
Chapter 9 New Tree Essences   223
Chapter 10 Tree Attunements   295
    Attunement to the Spirit of Aspen   302
    Attunement to the Spirit of Atlas Cedar   303
    Attunement to the Spirit of Bird Cherry   304
    Attunement to the Spirit of Blackthorn   305
    Attunement to the Spirit of Black Poplar   306
    Attunement to the Spirit of Box Tree   307
    Attunement to the Spirit of Catalpa   308
    Attunement to the Spirit of Cedar of Lebanon   309
    Attunement to the Spirit of Cherry Laurel   310
    Attunement to the Spirit of Cherry Plum   311
    Attunement to the Spirit of Copper Beech   312
    Attunement to the Spirit of Douglas Fir   313
    Attunement to the Spirit of Eucalyptus   314
    Attunement to the Spirit of Field Maple   315
    Attunement to the Spirit of Fig   316
    Attunement to the Spirit of Foxglove Tree   317
    Attunement to the Spirit of Ginkgo   318
    Attunement to the Spirit of Glastonbury Thorn   319
    Attunements to the Spirit of Gorse   320
    Attunement to the Spirit of Holm Oak   321
    Attunement to the Spirit of Hornbeam   322
    Attunement to the Spirit of Italian Alder   323
    Attunement to the Spirit of Judas Tree   324
    Attunement to the Spirit of Juniper   325
    Attunement to the Spirit of Laburnum   326
    Attunement to the Spirit of Larch   327
    Attunement to the Spirit of Leyland Cypress   328
    Attunement to the Spirit of Lilac   329
    Attunement to the Spirit of Liquidamber   330

Attunement to the Spirit of Lombardy Poplar   331
Attunement to the Spirit of Lucombe Oak   332
Attunement to the Spirit of Manna Ash   333
Attunement to the Spirit of Medlar   334
Attunement to the Spirit of Midland Hawthorn   335
Attunement to the Spirit of Mimosa (Silver Wattle)   336
Attunement to the Spirit of Norway Maple   337
Attunement to the Spirit of Norway Spruce   338
Attunement to the Spirit of Olive   339
Attunement to the Spirit of Osier   340
Attunement to the Spirit of Pear   341
Attunement to the Spirit of Pittospora   342
Attunement to the Spirit of Privet   343
Attunement to the Spirit of Red Oak   344
Attunement to the Spirit of Robinia   345
Attunement to the Spirit of Sea Buckthorn   346
Attunement to the Spirit of Silver Fir   347
Attunement to the Spirit of Spindle   348
Attunement to the Spirit of Strawberry Tree   349
Attunement to the Spirit of Sweet Chestnut   350
Attunement to the Spirit of Tamarisk   351
Attunement to the Spirit of Tree of Heaven   352
Attunement to the Spirit of Viburnum (V. Tinus)   353
Attunement to the Spirit of Walnut   354
Attunement to the Spirit of Wayfaring Tree   355
Attunement to the Spirit of Western Hemlock   356
Attunement to the Spirit of Western Red Cedar   357
Attunement to the Spirit of White Willow   358
Attunement to the Spirit of Wild Service Tree   359
Attunement to the Spirit of Willow - Leaved Pear   360
Attunement to the Spirit Wych Elm   361
Attunement to the Spirit of Yellow Buckeye   362
References and Sources   363

Introduction

This is the third book in the Tree Seer series. Volume One, *"Tree: Essence, Spirit and Teacher"*, explored many ways to begin to work with trees and tree spirits. Volume Two, *"Tree: Essence of Healing"* focused on how trees, and particularly flower essences gathered from trees, could be used to bring healing energy into our lives.

"Tree Seer" is a continuation of these themes with a re-examination of some of the core material plus a lot of brand new material. We have given emphasis to essential procedures such as grounding and protection. These are so vital to success and health in tree seer work, as well as in every other area of life, that we felt it worthwhile reiterating their importance. Even with Earth-based practices and Earth-based philosophies it is easy to get carried away by the glamour, rather than the reality, of one's experience. The first three chapters also present some of the most useful meditations and visualisations in a way that is, hopefully, easier to follow on the page.

Chapter Four, The Dendrochronology of a Land, is a survey of the tides of tree species that have washed over Britain during the last few thousand years. Hopefully it will help to redress the balance by bringing to attention the variety and legitimacy of the majority of British trees not regarded as 'native species'. We live here, now, not in some imagined mythical past. Tree seer work is all to do with awareness. If we cannot see clearly the larger viewpoint then the value of our work will be seriously diminished. A seer is one who sees clearly, not one who simply accepts what the majority is saying.

4

Chapter Five is a detailed exploration of shamanic processes. In *"Tree: Essence, Spirit and Teacher"* these methods were briefly discussed, but at the time plenty of good books were available for those who wanted to take their explorations further. Over the last few years some of the classic texts on shamanic practice have been out of print, and although they may re-appear in the future, we felt that it was worthwhile to present the information in a way relevant to tree seer work.

Chapter Six explores methods of healing using trees and tree spirits. There are some new processes here that have proved to be very effective. The key to healing effectively will always be the applicability of the techniques to the individual. There is still a worrying trend amongst some complementary therapists to view the pathways of disease in a similar way to the orthodox allopathic medical profession. Although they may speak the jargon of holism, our education (splitting things down into different areas of study and expertise), and the desire to be seen as professional (ie. rational and 'scientific'), can often cloud the issues. For those interested in the background information and theory we refer the reader to the relevant chapters in volumes one and two.

Chapter Seven presents information that may also be of use in healing work, as it gives a brief survey of herbal and traditional uses of trees. However, the main aim of 'tree teas' is to integrate the energy of the tree at a more profound level, so that the practitioner feels really at home with the trees and tree spirits being worked with.

The final three chapters are largely new information gathered since the publication of the previous volumes. 'Tree Initiations and Other Deep Contact' reviews those initiations found in volume one, but also includes many new tree initiation processes that we have been teaching over the last few years. Chapter Nine presents twenty new tree essences, so that with the information in *"Tree: Essence of Healing"*, there is now available in detail all the tree essences contained in the range of "Green Man Tree Essences". This information is, of course, relevant to every form the tree energy might occupy, not just the flower essences but also the wood, the tea, the spirit signatures, the attunements and so on.

Finally, Chapter Ten introduces over fifty new tree attunements so that the student is able to choose to work with a larger range of British trees. (North America and the Far East are now better represented in the selection of trees we have looked at).

After more than ten years of exploring with trees and tree spirits, and of teaching others to access and become aware of tree energies, we are still amazed by the potential for revelation and paradigm shift, as well as individual healing, that working with tree spirits allows. We hope that this third volume "*Tree Seer*" will further this work.

Ungroundedness is endemic in most of humanity because we are continually 'looking forward to' things and events that may make things 'better' for us in the future. Make no mistake, hope is a really essential psychological food - without it the will to exist falters, and the immune system itself begins to be compromised. But investing too much energy in what may or may not happen depletes and unbalances us.

Personal power, the ability to control our own circumstances, is the second essential psychological need. Take away hope and an individual's ability to exert some control (or even the belief of hope and control) and every system will gradually close down.

Chapter 1

"Becoming Rooted"

Above all things in this field is the necessity to be grounded and centred. Being grounded, centred or earthed means that we have available to us the maximum energy, strength and stability. Grounding is any process that enables us to access the source of our personal power – the energy of the planet itself.

It is not possible, ever, to be too grounded. There is a general misapprehension that being grounded equates in some way with being trapped in 'dense' material vibrations – that being grounded is the opposite of being spiritually sensitive. This is a great mistake, possibly the greatest mistake a human being can ever make.

To use an analogy, it is possible to play an electric guitar completely unplugged – it is not very loud and the sound is brief and tinny but one could convince oneself that this is the natural quality of the instrument. One could even develop elegant theories and eulogise the subtle characteristics of the near-silent guitar – that it is so superior to all those other brash, loud musical instruments those with little taste or discrimination always seem to favour. And then someone suggests that, in fact, the electric guitar has been specifically designed to work plugged into an amplifier within an electric current. Now the range of sounds, moods and power beggars the paltry un-plugged twangings. Such is the difference between a human having a true connection to its power source, the Earth, and a human who has a core belief (conscious or unconscious) that this world is not the place for them.

Grounding is largely an act of intention and attention. Effective grounding techniques move energy from an unbalanced concentration in the head outward into the rest of the body and even extend beyond into the environment perceived by the senses and sense organs.

Grounding establishes us as part of the system of the planet giving us access to the resources of the whole system.

The deeper our energies are rooted into the immediacy of planetary reality the greater our ability to explore and experience the full range of existence.

There will be those who have had from childhood an unusual range of sensitivities and there will be others who have trained themselves to access certain subtle sensing skills. However, unless these skills are founded upon a truly integrated, grounded state where an open flow of energy sustains them from the Earth, serious imbalance will be inevitable on one level or another – physical, emotional, mental or spiritual. What often happens with these individuals, if they can be convinced at all to practice regular grounding procedures, is that they will appear to lose some of their skills and sensitivities. At this point they often tend to give up and return to the more familiar feelings of vague spaciousness and a sense of 'secret specialness' that their 'powers' bring to them.

When psychic phenomena and sensitivities diminish or disappear as we are more grounded, this simply is a clear indication that there existed a false equilibrium, putting strain and stress on our energy systems as a whole. Continuing with a practice of grounding and balancing will eventually ensure that all these skills and more, will return to us in an integrated, balanced and life-supporting way.

Grounding practices ensure that we become aware of our place here and now. By encouraging our awareness to escape from continual judgmental chatter of the conscious mind and pay more attention to the senses and the 'outside' world we are able to notice more of what is happening, at all levels, around us.

A great many of the techniques described in 'Tree Seer' rely on, firstly being well grounded, and then being able to turn our attention to very particular sense experiences. We don't need to go anywhere or do anything much to begin to be aware of the presence of spirit energies. The indications, signs, songs and voices are there at all times. Hopefully the exercises presented here will help you to learn how to recognise what has been around us unnoticed, ignored or misinterpreted.

Effective grounding is experienced as an increase in solidity, presence and security. There is a greater mental focus and internal stillness. These signs arise because grounding automatically helps to 'earth' energies that are not able to dissipate any other way. A build-up of inappropriate energy – of any kind – simply adds 'noise' and stress to the body. This excess clogs the flow of normal energy and often leads to symptoms such as the inability to be still, nervousness, a sense of unease, confusion, an inability to maintain a focus of attention, waves of strong emotion, constant feelings of tiredness.

A tree's roots may be out of sight, but without them the tree would not exist. Grounding practices give our own energy system the roots to be able to sustain and understand the world in a more profound way.

10

Each exercise here uses slightly different ways to achieve an effective ground-state. Some will naturally be more suited to you than others. If you become familiar with a wide range of techniques then whatever your circumstances, you will be able to achieve a stable, grounded awareness.

Being grounded means being protected yet open to a wider range of information. Once you are grounded there is a link established between the individual and the planet. The better this link is, the more persona and planet become integrated into one. The Hermetic maxim 'As Above, So Below' refers to the concept of the microcosm – the body of a human – echoing the macrocosm – the greater universe. The same system exists in the planet Earth itself. Within it is a reflection of and access to all possible states and realms. By aligning more closely with the core of planetary energy we are not cutting ourselves off from 'out there', we are creating a firmer, more secure bridge to everywhere and everything else. At the same time we ensure that we have sufficient energy resources and flexibility to cope with whatever is experienced.

Earth Breath

This is a very simple process that can be done in any circumstance. It forms the basis of many more elaborate grounding techniques.

1. Whilst breathing remains normal and steady through the nose, visualise the following:

2. On the inbreath, you pull the air into your lungs from the Earth below your feet.

3. On the outbreath you visualise pushing the air out of the lungs down your body, through your feet and out into the ground.

4. Simply keep this process going until you feel sufficiently stable and calm.

5. Breathing in from the Earth opens the flow to the supporting and nurturing energy of the planet.

6. Breathing out into the Earth helps to make a path to release any excess energy experienced as instability or tension.

7. Don't be surprised if you feel a little more weighty and solid – it is simple a by-product of increased body-awareness.

In times of stress or fear Earth Breath quickly brings the system to equilibrium. Focusing awareness away from the head and its noisy speculative activity effectively cuts the loop of self-perpetuating 'what if' panic.

Tree Roots

This is a powerfully simple way to reinforce your intention to ground your energies. It helps to reduce thought and mental activity and connects you at a deeper level to your surroundings.

1. Settle in your seat so as to become comfortable. Have your feet uncrossed and firmly placed on the floor.

2. Take a few slow, deep breaths and allow yourself to relax further into your seat.

3. Place your attention gently on your physical body. Feel its solidity and weight. Become aware of the pull of gravity downward. Let your mind settle on the feel of that pull.

4. Follow that sense of weightedness down to your feet. Feel the weight of the soles of your feet. Focus on the feel of that pull.

5. Now, allow your awareness to flow downward below your feet. Begin to see or feel the energy as a structure of roots growing and extending downward into the Earth. See them reaching out in a widening circle around you.

6. Feel these roots of energy as they search deeper and deeper, establishing you firmly and securely upon the surface of the planet.

7. With each breath you breathe, allow gravity and the magnetic attraction of the Earth's Heart to draw your roots deeper and wider.

8. When you feel that you are secure and well-rooted, begin on your inbreath to draw sustaining energy back along your root paths into your body.

9. Feel the nutritious and life-giving energy of the Earth slowly fill the whole body as it travels upwards from the very root-tips of your earthed awareness.

10. Continue to draw the energy upwards with your inbreath. On the outbreath allow this root system to strengthen and spread deeper and farther outward from your place.

11. Remain in this easy flow of breathing in the energy of the Earth and breathing out, deepening your connection and integration.

12. When you are ready allow the imaginings to fade slowly. Become aware of the edges of your physical body: your hands, your feet, how you are sitting, what is going on around you in the room and outside. Move your fingers and toes gently. Take

several deep breaths. When you feel ready, slowly open your eyes. Take a good minute or two to return fully to a normal state.

With practice you will be able to successfully hold this visualisation when standing or moving around. Don't let your logical brain create difficulties with concrete floors, being several storeys off the ground or other situations where part of you doesn't feel a real Earth contact. The mind being non-physical, is free of the limitations of time and space. Intention, and the power of your feeling or imagination will bring success.

Axial Breath (Centre-line breathing)

This technique creates a stable energy link between the Earth and cosmos, with the individual becoming a conduit for the flow of universal energy. Initially its emphasis should be on the downward, grounding link to anchor personal awareness securely into the planet before any 'upper' links are made.

1 Imagine a line extending through your body from below your feet to the top of your head, positioned just in front of your backbone.

2. In your mind's eye, now extend that line of energy down into the Earth as deep as it will go.

3. With each breath imagine pulling energy up this line and into your body.

4. As you exhale let the breath pass into the Earth. With each outbreath push the line a little deeper towards the centre of the Earth.

5. Continue this until you feel a secure integration with the energy of the Earth.

6. Take you attention now, to the top end of the line.

7. When you have drawn breath from the Earth, now breathe it out into the universe through the top of your head.

8. At the next inbreath, draw in this universal energy into your lungs and exhale it down into the Earth.

9. Continue this new cycle for a few minutes so that you are alternately breathing from the Earth out into the universe, then in from the universe and out into the Earth.

10. When time to stop, simply relax and allow the imagery to fade and your energies to settle. Take a good few minutes to be still before resuming normal activities.

You may find that your breathing automatically settles into a slightly different pattern. Don't be concerned if this should happen. The main purpose is to focus easily on your midline whilst harmonising a flow of energy with the breath. Keep relaxed and don't strain to visualise. A feeling of what is required will be sufficient to begin with.

Tree: Roots and Branches

This takes the basics of 'axial breath' and adds the visualisation of a tree's form. Because of the nature of the imagery this version of the technique is more likely to establish a broader awareness and connection with the surrounding environment.

1. Begin in the same way as in the basic 'Tree Roots Meditation'. Relax your body. Allow your awareness to sink downward to your contact with the ground.

2. Extend you awareness beyond the physical body making it into searching roots that spread deeper and wider with each

exhalation. Continue this process until you feel really secure and well-rooted.

3. Clearly intend that your sense of rootedness will maintain itself without your extra attention. Now focus on the area of your upper body.

4. Become conscious of the space above the top of your head. Feel the energy of the sun and the vast spaciousness of the universe gently drawing your energy upwards.

5. Mould that upward-moving, expanding energy into the form of boughs and branches growing in an ever-widening dome, upwards and outward.

6. Once you have a clear sense of these spreading branches, begin to hold in your awareness both the branches above your head and also the root system spreading below your feet. To help, you can visualise your physical body as the trunk of a tree holding in place and focusing the energy of root and branch.

7. When this imagery is comfortable with you, and stable, begin to sense an integration, a mixing, of the energies that each expansion of your awareness is receiving and releasing into its surroundings.

8. When you want to stop, simply relax the visualisation and rest calmly until you feel ready to open your eyes.

There are a great many variations possible with this technique. It is a good idea to become familiar with them, as each has a different energy characteristic.

Variation One:

With the inbreath take Earth energy in through your roots. With the outbreath, extend you roots deeper and more securely. On the next breath, breathe energy in from the universe through your branches and then breathe out, extending your awareness outward amongst the sun and stars. This variation alternates breathing in and out downward, with in and out upwards.

Variation Two:

Take your inbreath through the roots filling the whole body with energy. Send each outbreath up through the branches into the cosmos. This variation is a one-way flow from the Earth to the universe.

Variation Three:

The inbreath rises from your roots and you breathe out into the cosmos. On the next breath, inhale from the cosmos and breathe out into the Earth. This variation makes a cycle from below to above and back again.

Variation Four:

Begin by taking the inbreath from the cosmos down through your branches and exhale through your roots deep into the Earth. This variation is a one-way flow, grounding universal energy into the Earth.

Variation Five:

On the inbreath simultaneously draw energy through both roots and branches filling your centre – your hara or your heart – or any other area that you feel needs some extra energy. Breathe out through both roots and branches. This variation can be thought of as expanding and then contracting spheres of breath.

With visualisation exercises the more involved the imagery, the greater the potential for the mind to drop its normal compulsive thought conversation allowing the possibility for greater clarity. However it usually needs steady, patient practice to work with a complex picture. Begin by being content to have the general 'feel' of the process. Never try to form clear, steady visual images in your mind. They will occur quite naturally with a little practice. Never strain.

Earth Star Anchor

The energy centre, or chakra, at the base of the spine gives us the ability to hold on to, and work with, physical reality. It integrates the planetary with the individual and acts as a stabiliser – like a microcosmic gravity. Minor chakras at the groin, knees and soles of the feet help to maintain this energy link. Because we are greater than our physical bodies there are also many chakras located outside the body. One of the most important is found about three feet (one metre) below the soles of the feet, sometimes called the Earth Star. This is a non-dimensional point that directly correlates to the central core of the planet.

Resonating with the planetary core the Earth Star chakra enables us to access identical energy patterns. The actual structure of the inner core of the Earth is assumed to be an iron-nickel mix, some believe it is solid, others liquid. Investigations by remote viewers and out-of-body journeyers - the only way humans can actually experience the inner core - suggest the inner core is of massive crystalline structure of octahedral shape, like two pyramids put base-to-base. Because of axial shifts in the poles over its four billion-year existence, re-crystallisation has created a multifaceted crystal whose many terminations are reflected on the Earth's surface crust as 'power points' or energetically anomalous regions. Far from being a densely physical 'dead-end', the extremely strong gravimetric forces and tides focused on the core have profound effects on all consciousness and can act as doorways to anywhere in the universe. An important lesson that keeps recurring in Tree Seer work: the fact that something can appear physically and implacably solid at one level of awareness will reveal itself completely otherwise when seen with a different level of awareness.

1. This exercise can be done standing or sitting, but to begin with it is probably easier to do it standing up.

2. Stand with your legs about shoulder-width apart, knees unlocked and balanced evenly on your feet.

3. Take a couple of deep breaths and allow your awareness to focus on the Base chakra at the bottom of your spine.

4. Now be aware of the two small energy centres in the sole of each foot. Visualise the triangle that these three points make with each other – the soles of the feet and the base of the spine.

5. Once you can sense this relationship in space, reflect another, identical triangle downward into the ground. This makes an elongated diamond shape with one point at the base of the spine widening out to the soles of the feet and then converging at a point the same distance beneath the ground as your base chakra is located above the ground.

6. Hold this image as clearly as you can and become aware that the point below the ground represents your Earth Star Anchor. Allow its energy and stability to flow into your body, increasing its life-force, strength, flexibility, assuredness and purpose.

7. After a minute or two, whilst still standing, let go of the visualisation, relax your mind and simply feel the energy balancing within your body.

8. When you feel ready, resume your normal activities.

A sense of real connectedness to the planet as a universal being is one benefit of working with the Tree Kingdoms. Profound insecurity and debilitating non-specific illnesses can be greatly alleviated using such techniques. Using the wood or essence of Persian Ironwood will help to clarify the experience.

Tree Roots and a Secret Chamber

Using the familiar tree roots visualisation as a basis, this exercise allows the awareness, once fully grounded, to open itself to the possibilities of receiving new information that can further your work with trees and tree spirits. It can be carried out with a specific purpose in mind, or can be done simply as a 'look around' exercise. Because grounding tends to integrate self with non-self, subjective with objective (or more accurately, dissolves the false mental distinctions we make between 'inner' and 'outer'), the limitations to effective explorations are reduced.

1. Settle down, breathe deeply and relax. Become aware of your relaxed and heavy body.

2. Allow awareness to gradually sink down below your feet and into the ground.

3. Feel your energy and awareness growing, spreading out as if they are roots. Each one searches for a secure hold, reaching out and contacting all the sources of nutrition and energy that you need to grow and thrive.

4. As you breathe in, breathe in that nutrition from the Earth. As you breathe out, relax, allow yourself to settle even more firmly and deeper into the supporting energies of the Earth.

5. For the next few minutes focus upon your awareness roots.

6. Now, gently begin to look for a special place, deeply hidden within the heart of your rooted awareness.

7. It may appear as a small, bright space, or as some kind of room or chamber. It may seem to be a cave or some sort of clearing that is surrounded and protected by your root energies.

8. Take time to tune your perceptions into this space. Carefully begin to explore what is there. It may contain objects or it may be inhabited by some beings. Everything there represents some aspect of your relationship with the world- an offering, a gift, some advice or help that will allow you to integrate further towards your full potential.

9. Feel the quality of the space. If you are offered a gift of some kind you will find that you also have something with you that can be exchanged as a parting gift.

10. When it is time to return to your everyday awareness, simply allow the image to slowly fade and once more become aware of you body and its surroundings.

You can reach for and enter this secret space whenever you feel the need to retreat into yourself for healing and rest. It is a safe, secure and healing environment where teaching can also be received. If a particular tree is your current focus of work, you can follow this pattern of imagery to come to a state where it will be possible to communicate with the spirit form of that tree.

Mindless Grounding

Sometimes we can be so off balance, so spun out, so confused that the mind is incapable of holding a focus to carry out a mental grounding exercise. In these instances it is better first to begin with grounding techniques that do not require any mental focus at all.

Any activity that takes attention from the mind to the physical body is grounding. Contact with the soil is also, naturally, grounding. Energetic walking, jumping, stamping, digging, gardening, are all useful. Physically focused disciplines like hatha yoga, chi gung and tai chi also ground and balance awareness in the body. Banging on a drum, so long as you are in a situation where it is possible to let go and make as much noise as you like, is an excellent grounding activity.

High carbohydrate and high protein foods focus the body's attention on the processes of digestion and will give an energy boost that effectively counters 'spacing out'. High sugar from chocolate and sweets is a useful first aid grounding tool but will unbalance the body energies after the initial 'sugar rush' and may prevent any further useful work for an hour or two.

Certain crystals can be really useful to ground your energies. Experimentation will reveal the most effective stone for each individual, but in general grounding stones tend to be red, focusing energy on the physical systems of the body, energy maintenance and the base chakra, or they are dark brown and black – integrating and quietening down overactive, unfocused patterns into orderliness. Effective grounding stones do not need to be large or of gem quality. A sea-worn pebble of black basalt may serve as well as a fine smoky quartz crystal, or a prism of black tourmaline. The dark, metallic ores, like the iron-rich haematite and lodestone (magnetite) are almost universally effective. Haematite especially will ground the most errant energies in a matter of minutes. There are a few people, however, who will have the opposite response, so be forewarned!

Holding a tumbled stone of haematite or wearing haematite jewellery will be sufficient to keep grounded in most energetically boisterous situations.

Lodestone, an earthy metallic, magnetised form of the mineral magnetite, grounds not only by its weight and solidity, but because it restores the integrity of the bioelectro-magnetic field within which we function. Stress and emotional surges create storms of hormonal and nerve impulse activity, changing the polarity of the body's electromagnetic system. In an environment soaked with other forms of electrical energy – biological or manmade - such upsets can continue or even accelerate without active inter-vention. Lodestone is inexpensive, but as it is not intrinsically attractive, can be a little difficult to track down.

Smoky quartz is a form of the common mineral quartz ('rock crystal'), that has a range of colours from black to golden brown to the palest of smoked glass tones. It is usually not as forceful in its effects as haematite.

Grounding Layout with Smoky Quartz

1. Place a small smoky quartz crystal, point downward at the thymus, near the top of the breastbone.

2. Put a second small smoky quartz crystal, point down the body, somewhere between the legs, either near the base of the spine or between the knees or feet.

This placement will effectively ground and quieten all the body systems in a couple of minutes.

Black tourmaline ('schorl') crystallises in long thin striated prisms that have a triangular cross-section. It is a common crystal found in association with quartz. Black tourmaline is one of the most useful and versatile of crystals. Placing a

24

small piece in the centre of the forehead will rapidly quieten thought processes and emotional extremes. As it helps to protect against strong outside influences, black tourmaline is also one of the best stones for maintaining personal energy integrity in difficult, dangerous or sticky situations. Tourmaline can be carried or worn and will prove most effective when it is near those areas of the body where you are most susceptible to upset in stress situations.

Tree essences, especially those with a red energy vibration like yew, ironwood, oak and bay will also ground energy rapidly.

In the end, though, if you find that you are always reliant on external support to keep you grounded, it is vital that you take time to establish a regular practice to train your energies to maintain their own stability. Health, sanity and effective perception of reality demands that you exist where you are – here on this planet.

A Tree at the Earth's Core

Becoming energetically linked to the energies of the heart of the earth can be of vital (literally 'life-giving'), importance in situations of extreme danger and threat or when the entire energy system has been seriously thrown off balance. Such times do not always arise when there is obvious external danger. If we are already off-balance and have lost our centre of gravity, a slight push in the wrong direction can send us spinning away into chaos. This happens more frequently than most of us are able to recognise. Somersaulting in oblivion can seem like normality if it goes on for long enough. The more grounded and centred we learn to become, the easier it is to recognise when we have really lost our energy integrity. At such times an exercise like the one that follows can rapidly restore clarity.

1. Begin as usual by settling into a comfortable position. Relax into the weight and gravity of your physical body.

2. Allow your focus of awareness to sink downward into the ground. See it extend outward as searching roots.

3. Together with the general downward and outward expansion, intend that a vigorous taproot of your consciousness dives strongly, straight downward towards the very centre of the earth.

4. As your roots become a strong and secure image in your mind, turn your attention more to really focus on that deep, thrusting taproot.

5. This taproot dives through soil. It dives through subsoil and rock. It is strong and sure of the pull to the earth's core.

6. As your awareness dives towards the heart of the planet it may pass through different areas of perception. There may be scenes, landscapes and many states of matter. Allow these images to come and go as you move through them.

7. When you reach the central core of energy allow as much as you require to flow into your body. You are of the earth's body. Made of its energy. Be aware of the unbreakable bond with the planet. Allow your awareness to settle completely and take comfort from belonging.

8. Rest in this state for as long as you are able. Gradually the images and sensations will begin to fade. Allow yourself to become aware of your place and surroundings. Return to the here and now.

The Fountain Tree

This is a visualised process that can both ground personal energies and create a cleansing effect within the self and the surroundings. It is protective and purifying and will also help to integrate a harmonious flow of energy. The technique arose spontaneously whilst leading a group through a more basic tree roots meditation.

1. Sit comfortably, quieten your energy and allow yourself to take a couple of slow, deep breaths.

2. Move your attention to the body's contact with the ground and allow your awareness to travel downward and out, as if it were forming roots.

3. Allow these roots of energy to grow, finding strength and security, locking firmly within rock and soil.

4. With every breath you take in, draw upwards the sustenance that your roots have absorbed from their surroundings.

5. Notice that your body is now filling with powerful surges of life-giving energy at each breath. At the same time, as you breathe out, your root system expands even further downward and in a wider circle, gathering in strength and power.

6. Each time you breathe in, the power builds in your body. Every part of you, every cell, every organ, every structure, every channel, fills with life-giving energy.

7. There will naturally come a point in time when you feel the pressure of this energy build-up, when you feel you can absorb no more.

8. When you reach this stage, allow the force of energy to column upwards through your body in a continuous stream.

See the energy rise high above the top of your head.

9. The stream of energy continues to flow forcefully through all your body. Somewhere, way above your head, that column of energy spreads out and fountains down, back to the ground in a continuous rain of gentle energy.

10. The fountain falls to earth around you and upon you. It is absorbed into the ground where your roots draw it up again.

11. A cycle is created. Cleansing and feeding energy moves upwards through your body. It rises in a strong column above your head. It fountains back down to the ground in a protective, rejuvenating, enlivening cycle. Rising and falling, absorbing and releasing, filling and emptying, breathing in and letting out the breath.

12. When you wish the process to come to a close, just focus again for a moment or two on the strength and endurance of the root system that you have established in the Earth, then gradually allow all imagery to fade away. Become aware once more of your surroundings.

Complete Rootedness
This exercise is very useful at times when the head and its 'logical' thought processes are too much in evidence, or when there is a distracted scattering of personal energies that seem difficult to bring under control. It has the virtue in these circumstances of being very easy to initiate and , once started, it tends to develop automatically.

1. Begin in the usual way, taking a moment to relax your breathing and your body position.

2. Allow your awareness to move downward following the pull of gravity.

3. As you begin to visualise roots extending from the soles of your feet, simultaneously begin to extend roots from all parts of your body.

4. Feel that roots are growing downward and outward from your toes and feet.

5. Roots flow downward from the base of your spine and from your fingertips.

6. Roots extend downward into the ground from your arms and legs, from your back and chest.

7. Roots flow from your chin and jaw, from your ears, eyes, from your mouth and from the top of your head.

8. Awareness from the whole of your body extends and reaches down and around. You create a total and complete rootedness, grounded into the heart of the Earth.

9. Take time to focus on those parts of the body where it seems most difficult to visualise roots extending downward.

10. As your whole body becomes rooted, now allow your thoughts, your consciousness, your mind to flow rooted into the ground.

11. Stay quietly in that silence until every part of you fully relaxes and melts into complete rootedness.

12. As you return to awareness allow the roots to easily melt away, beginning with the top of the head. As if in a downward-moving spiral, your body re-appears, your senses refresh themselves and you gradually become aware of your surroundings and your slow, steady breathing.

13. Take a couple of deep, slow breaths, stretch and, when you are ready, slowly open your eyes.

Becoming Centred - Becoming Yourself

Being centred is the second prerequisite for any work with trees and tree spirits. Whilst being grounded allows a free flow of energy and a connectedness to the planetary energies, being centred refers to a state where the awareness is alert, present and calmly focused.

In practice, it is not so easy to distinguish being grounded from being centred as one is concomitant on the other – one cannot be fully present without being grounded, and one cannot be properly grounded without a sense of being centred.

The primary characteristic of being centred is the equivalent of reaching, or being aware of, one's personal 'ground state'. The ground state is not a universal constant. Essentially, at best, it represents a completely neutral, disengaged mode of function where body, emotions and mind are simply 'ticking over' in an optimal but non-focused way. Practically speaking, as such a neutrality is rather alien to most of us, the ground state simply becomes the awareness of how we are thinking, feeling, reacting and sensing right at this moment.

Such awareness is of essential importance to any work with spirits and other subtle energies. Until we can clearly identify what is going on inside us now, in contrast to how we felt a moment ago, we have no means of gauging whether we are having an 'experience' or not.

The greatest obstacle we face is always going to be our own inability to notice the communications from tree spirits. Becoming centred and grounded helps to set all our dials to as close to zero as possible so that any flow of current, any message in whatever form, can be seen in a flick of those needles of awareness.

Grounding focuses on the flow, the relationship between individual and Earth. Centring focuses internally on the state of the awareness within the body.

Centring exercises generally work by putting the attention on the internal body feeling of a single, simple, sense input – such as a process like breathing, listening to a single note, gazing at an object, and the like. The key to becoming centred is to become momentarily wrapped up in a single sense experience. Once the experience fades we are left in a more spacious, calm, alert yet relaxed state. As they tend to be uncomplicated and short procedures a centring technique can be easily repeated until you have achieved a satisfactory quiet neutrality of body and mind.

Using the Breath to Centre

The breath is one of the easiest and most natural processes to use in order to become centred. Try out the following methods and see which are the most effective for you.

Bee Breath

1. Sit in a comfortable position, perhaps with a cushion under the base of the spine or in the small of the back so that your back is upright and unsupported.

2. Tuck in your chin and feel a slight stretching of the back of the neck.

3. Rest your hands on your thighs or knees, palms upwards, and relax the shoulders.

4. Breathe out slowly and completely as possible.

5. Take a slow, steady breath in.

6. As you breathe out, keeping your mouth shut, make a humming sound, like a bee, until you have no breath left.
7. Repeat as often as is needed.

This process gently vibrates all the bones and organs of the body, particularly those of the head and neck. Bee breath can thus be useful in relieving breathing difficulties, blocked sinuses and so on.

Alternate Nostril Breathing

1. Sit comfortably with spine straight, chin tucked in, hands resting on tops of legs.

2. Bring your right hand to the nose so that you can close your right nostril with the right thumb and your right ring finger can close your left nostril.

3. With your ring finger closing off the left nostril by pressing on the fleshy part, slowly inhale through the open right nostril.

4. As you want to exhale, close the right nostril with your right thumb, and release the left nostril so that you can exhale through it slowly and completely.

5. Keeping the right thumb on the right nostril, take the next inbreath through the left nostril.

6. At the end of the inbreath, use your ring finger to close the left nostril.

7. Release your thumb so that the outbreath can be slowly exhaled through the right nostril.

8. Repeat the entire sequence for about five minutes or until you feel a quiet equilibrium of body and mind.

Cool Breath
This is perhaps the simplest of all breath-related methods of centring.

1. Sit comfortably so that your body is relaxed.

2. Slightly open your mouth and breathe slowly and naturally through your mouth.

3. If you turn your attention to the roof of your mouth, towards the back of the palette, you will notice that the air you breathe in feels cool, but that there is no sensation when you exhale. Simply stay with this experience for a minute or two. Placing your awareness like this on the roof of the mouth calms the mind and also naturally helps to balance the energy flow within the meridian system and the deep energy channels of the body. This area of focus is also close to the location of the pituitary gland, one of the key control centres of the body.

Centring with Sound
Listening to a single resonant tone is a very rapid way of centring your energies.

1. Sit in a relaxed, easy way and close your eyes for a moment.

2. Strike a resonant note on a bell, bowl, tuning fork, wind chime or gong and simply listen to the sound until it dies away and you can no longer sense any vibration.

3. Repeat the process a few times until your body and mind feel clear and quietly energised

Any object that has a long resonance when struck can be used here. It is the following of the diminishing vibration that leads the mind to a quieter space.

Centring on the Voice

The simplest sound that can be made by the human voice is 'Aaaah'. No strain is placed on the vocal cords or mouth because the sound simply arises from exhaled air passing over the slightly vibrating larynx.

1. Take a few slow, deep breaths and relax.

2. As you exhale again begin sounding an 'Aaaah'. The volume and tone are not important, though the loudness will affect the degree to which the sound vibrates through bones and tissues.

3. As you make the sound, simply focus on the sound and its vibration for as long as it can be sustained.

4. You will be able to extend the sound longer if you send the air up via the back of your throat into your nasal passages as well as out of the mouth. This slows the exit of air considerably without affecting the sound itself.

5. Repeat the process as many times as you want, but remember to relax for a minute or two between each vocalisation. This will allow you to experience the lively quality of silence and centring.

Energy Balancing for the Ground State

Techniques like axial breathing (centre line breath) will automatically tend to combine grounding and centring processes. There are also a group of energy balancing exercises, mostly drawn from the wide field of kinesiology, that are always useful to maintain a balanced ground-state. These work by bringing the meridian system into a state of equilibrium. This is effectively the same as turning all your dials to zero or ticking over an engine in neutral. It is well worth getting into the habit of automatically and routinely using one of these techniques before doing any work with trees, essences or spirits, and better still if you make it part of a daily routine.

Tapping In

Tapping in brings all the main meridians into balance and keeps them in balance for about twenty minutes. It is such an easy procedure that any stressful or confusing situation can be eased in a moment.

1. Locate with your fingertips the area of your upper chest just below where your collar- bones (clavicle) meet the breastbone (sternum), a couple of inches below the throat. This is the approximate location of the thymus gland, central to the body's ability to generate and use life-energy.

2. Hold the fingertips of your hand close together, slightly overlapping.

3. Tap firmly but lightly in a small circle, anticlockwise, about three to six inches (7 – 14 cms) away from the central thymus point. (Looking down onto your chest the tapping is anticlockwise).

4. Tap your fingers in the circle so that each tap is fairly close to the last and repeat the circle about twenty times.

An alternate tapping procedure, which has the same balancing effect is to tap around the navel in the same manner but in a clockwise direction.

These two taps, the thymus anticlockwise tap and the navel clockwise tap, can be combined into one procedure making a figure-of-eight between the two points.

Cook's Hook Up

Disorientation, confusion and lack of coordination are common symptoms of being ungrounded and off-centre. This can often result from a disruption of communication and energy between the two hemispheres of the brain brought on by stress, emotional upset or illness. Even a slight lack of water in the body can impede the natural flow of nerve impulses through the brain. As the left hemisphere controls the right side of the body and the right hemisphere controls the nerve pathways on the left side, any breakdown in communication rapidly leads to a situation where the right hand, quite literally, has no idea what the left hand is doing. Kinesiologists have, over the years, devised many simple correction techniques that remind the nervous system to function as a whole. These exercises always contain an element of crossing over the midline of the body, helping to reintegrate impulses from opposite sides of the brain.

Cook's Hook Up energetically links up left and right, restoring natural energy flow so that the body, mind and emotions are balanced in a few moments. Cook's Hook Up is best done seated in a chair but can also be done lying down and, with more difficulty, and less discretion, standing up.

1. Cross your ankles, right over left. (If you are left-handed reverse all the procedures – so for you your left ankle would cross in front of your right.)

2. Bring your wrists together in front of you, right over left, pulse points to pulse points.

3. Now roll your hands downward so that the palms are facing each other.

4. Interlace your fingers and relax your arms so that your hands rest on your lap. If you are lying down, your hands can rest on your abdomen or you can bring them up to rest on your chest by rolling your lower arms inwards and upwards.

5. Close your eyes, take a deep breath and relax your body. If you are under emotional pressure it may initially seem to increase. Allow it to arise without putting any extra energy into it. This is part of the release process as balance returns to your energy systems. Discomfort will gradually subside.

6. When all tension has eased and you feel centred once more, unclasp your hands and uncross your ankles.

7. The final stage of Cook's Hook Up locks the state of balance more robustly into your system. If you are sitting, place both feet squarely on the floor.

8. Open your hands and gently bring them together with your fingers splayed so that all fingertips are touching – as if a small ball is being held between your palms. Hold this for half a minute.

The more regularly you practice this and other balancing processes the easier it will be for you to maintain equilibrium. Eventually, with Cook's Hook Up, simply bringing your fingertips together will remind the body to readjust itself.

Meriðian Massage

Whereas Cook's Hook-up primarily works with the hemispheres of the brain and their respective nerve functions, meridian massage works upon the meridian system of subtle energies running close to the surface of the skin. The massage is in reality an aura sweep, as the hands are held an inch or two away from the surface of the skin. It reinforces the general flow within the system and will effectively and quickly restore quite significant energy imbalances in a couple of minutes.

It does take a little while to get to grips with the movements, but it will be helpful to remember that it is all a symmetrical sequence where a sweep on one side is followed by one on the other side of the body. Begin slowly and with a focus of intention. When you get used to the process it can be done very rapidly, and will even work just as effectively going through the process only in your mind.

1. Hold your left fingertips to the heart centre in the middle of your chest.

2. Move your hand from heart to the front of your right shoulder an inch or two away from your body.

3. Sweep your left palm down the inside of your right arm to your right fingertips.

4. Now repeat the action on the left side of the body: hold your right fingertips to the heart centre and sweep to the inside of the shoulder and down along the inside of your left arm to the left fingertips.

5. Now the next movement is : take your left hand to where you finished at the right fingertips and now sweep up the outside of your right hand, up the right arm, around the back of the shoulder, the side of the neck, and then back to the heart.

6. Repeat this on your left side: take your right hand from the tips of your left fingers, up the left hand and left arm, over the

shoulder and back to the heart.

7. Now bring the hands together at the heart and sweep them simultaneously up the midline: chest, throat, face, forehead, top of head and as far down the back of the head and neck as possible.

8. To complete this movement you now need to reach up behind your back and imagine pulling that line from where you left it, drawing it down your back, over each buttock and down the backs of your legs.

9. Reaching your feet, move each hand around the outsides of your feet to your toes and then continue to sweep up the insides of the feet and the insides of the legs, thighs, up the centre of the abdomen, back to the heart.

10. This is one complete circuit. Repeat as much as you need – at least ten times, then finish off the whole process with two extra sweeps.

11. 'Zip up' the front of the body from groin to centre of lower lip. Repeat four or five times.

12. 'Zip up' the back of your body from the base of the spine upwards, over the top of the head to end at the centre of the upper lip. Repeat this four or five times. You will need to do this zipping up the back in two stages by 'throwing' the energy line from behind when you have got as far up the back as possible, and then 'catching' it from over the head the rest of the way to the upper lip.

Chapter 2

Developing a Protocol for Working with Tree Spirits

Every spiritual tradition, every tradition that recognises the reality of spirits, has developed one or more preparatory procedures that are carried out almost automatically before any other work is done. A skilled and experienced practitioner may sometimes seem only to be carrying out the most perfunctory actions or may not appear outwardly to be doing anything at all. Whatever the appearance, it is absolutely essential for you to establish your own opening procedures. It's no good sitting down to see your favourite television programme with beer and crisps unless you have first put the plug in!

Preliminary exercises are not something that can ever be bypassed. They are the key to the door that accesses the different levels of perception. They also set the scene internally for you. Do not be put off by the repetitive, even lengthy, nature of preliminaries. They will only seem to be tedious and awkward until you really begin to understand what they are about. At that point, it will become a completely new experience where every stage can be felt actually taking you deeper into contact with the spirit realities.

Different ways of working with tree spirits may require slightly different approaches but the pattern of the practice should usually have the same sequence of elements. This gives you a structure upon which your conscious awareness can rely and rest upon, even during the most abstract or most bizarre of encounters.

Internal Balance

Broadly speaking, the first preliminary action should be structured to harmonise internal energies. Grounding and centring in a way you find personally effective and economical establishes this sort of internal orientation.

Balance in the External Elements

Now balanced within the self, the next step is to align yourself to the space around you. The simplest way to do this is to acknowledge the cardinal directions (North, South, East and West), or the Elements (usually four or five in most traditions: Fire, Earth, Air, Water, Space). Very often Elements and Directions are linked together, but these and other correspondences vary a lot from culture to culture. No one set of associations is better than another. Bear in mind the process is one of symbolically acknowledging all aspects of the world around you and locating yourself and your actions within that greater context.

Offering Breath

Offering breath to the Elements or to the Directions is one of the simplest methods. As your breath is exhaled, visualise it travelling out in one direction after the other, or see it feeding each of the Elements in turn. This process can also help to slow and steady the breathing and naturally focuses the mind and quieten down unnecessary activity.

Focusing on Intent

The third stage will be an initial contact with the target of your attention. Again, a useful sequence is to formulate your intention as clearly as possible in your own mind, and to also include your senses and emotions in this imaginative process. When this is done to your satisfaction, open your awareness. If your work is to interact with a spirit or other sentient being it is important that you open yourself to that energy – a gesture that simply signifies "I am here" and that allows an exploration of your previously framed intent (at whatever level of perception that spirit can comprehend). This can be simply waiting quietly for a moment.

Next, ask permission to continue. Do it simply and honestly, then wait with your senses open. Usually a sense of "Go away", "No!" or "More information, please", can be felt quite clearly. If this does seem to be the response that you are getting then ask if you are able to help in some way. Perhaps you can offer something to make the work possible. Again, wait and see what you feel.

Assuming that permission is given to work, keep your awareness open to your feelings, thoughts and senses. Notice what you are, or are not, noticing.

The fourth step occurs when your awareness returns to normal, when the exercise is over or when your focus returns to your body. Say your "thank you's" in whatever seems an appropriate way and delicately withdraw all your energies back to your own boundaries. Spend some time centring and grounding yourself again.

The next, fifth stage, is to quickly go over in your mind what has occurred and to record what you remember in words, drawings, doodles, images and sensations. Note down memories as they come to mind. Very often your experiences can be very ephemeral, like dreams, and it can be quite easy to spend a lot of time describing a coherent narrative sequence of action that you remember easily, whilst missing that really significant image or phrase because it occurred out of context.

As soon as something new comes into your mind, make a note of it and then return to fill out the information when you have finished your current thread of thought. With vague or fast-fading experiences, going through each of your senses in turn may help to retrieve lost memories: how you felt, what you heard, what you saw, what you tasted (a variation on 'felt'), what you smelled, what you thought.

The sixth, and final, stage can be done at any time but should not really play any part in the previous stage. This final stage is analysis and interpretation of the material. This can be in context of your own personal interpretations, what a series of scenarios might 'mean', or in a broader context of comparison with other similar experiences.

Don't try to hunt for significance. Let it float to the surface of your mind when and if it is ready. Don't be too eager to accept as final any interpretation that seems to fit well enough. It is often easier to see a meaning that agrees with your current structure of beliefs than one that might make you question what you believe is true. The same vigilance and honesty is needed in the original recording of experiences. Do not censor your memories because they might seem politically, morally or intellectually incorrect. Each and every experience is the closest your mind can come to interpreting non-physical energy interactions in a way that you can register. "Mistakes" don't happen. A label or name that may be 'wrong' or 'inaccurate' at this level of reality is probably pointing you towards an interpretation that combines the qualities you associate with the 'wrong' label and the object or event that was so labelled.

To recapitulate, a useful protocol for tree spirit work will follow the main sequence of:

1. Initial Orientation. Balancing, grounding, centring. (That is, establishing a ground state.)

2. External Orientation. Aligning the self to surroundings. (Elements, directions, dimensions).

3. Focus On Your Intent. Greet and ask permission, then wait (Say 'Please').

4. Keep Your Awareness Open. (Throughout the contact time)

5. Withdraw Your Energies. (After completion say your 'thank you's' and gently return to yourself, centring and grounding).

6. Record Experiences. (As completely, vigilantly and honestly as possible using all means available).

7. Revisit Your Records. At some time look for possible interpretations and analysis. (Any conclusions or confusions can lead on to further explorations to clarify or expand understanding.)

The whole process can be seen as an alternating shift of focus. First, internal to the self, then external to relationship with the greater world, then internal once more for silent focus. This is followed by the external focus of greeting the tree spirit and opening up to experience, then once more moving internally to gather back your energies and to recapitulation. Finally, there is an external 'objectification' of experiences in analysis and interpretation.

49

As the work progresses the seer moves easily between the world within, the microcosm, and the world without, that is the macrocosm. One reflecting the other, each revealing aspects of a single reality to which the person experiencing belongs.

Chapter 3

Protection and Support

Preliminary exercises go a long way to getting you to work effectively with tree spirit energies. However, sometimes there may be factors of which we are unaware that can hinder our chances of success.

External influences may be interfering with 'reception', and for this some protection may be needed. If internal influences are a factor modifying our normal equilibrium, then support may be needed to return us to a working balance. In practice, protection and support come down to the same sort of solution: finding something that will return us to balance.

There is a common attitude amongst those interested in spiritual matters that regards as heresy the suggestion that protection of any kind might be a good idea. The feeling seems to be that even acknowledging a vulnerability is, in some way, encouraging it. This is little more than a philosophy of 'ignore it and it will go away'. The most oft- used reason for avoiding the issue of protection and support is another head-in-the-sand tactic: simply that one works 'from the highest good', or 'from the Light' or some similar phrase, is always going to be sufficient to counter all dubious influences. Nice idea, but really nothing more than wishful thinking, naive at best, arrogant, ignorant, self-deceiving and downright dangerous at worst.

We are human beings. Self-deceit is one of our species' most characteristic qualities. It is the price we pay for having incredible imaginative skills and the ability to re-invent the past as well as structure possible futures for ourselves. Anyone who believes they can escape this ego-based lens on reality is simply falling for an ego-based construction of reality. The only way to free oneself from this insidious loop is to acknowledge that all actions, opinions, thoughts, conclusions are going to be of limited applicability and only partially correct at the very best. Taking yourself too seriously and believing your own thoughts are the clearest and surest signs that you have lost the plot. In this state, the need for clarity is at its greatest, and so is the danger of becoming energetically hijacked.

The need for protection and support is not brought about by any personal fault or moral lapse. A good, honest, hardworking and virtuous ant scurrying across a city street is as vulnerable to being squashed as any other in his colony. There are forces, beings and entities in this universe of which we have no knowledge and who, equally, may have no knowledge or concern for us. Equally, there are beings who may find our collective or personal behaviour as annoying as we might find a bluebottle ricocheting off a windowpane.

The most helpful strategy is to routinely check if there is a need for protection and support before beginning any tree seer work. Self-testing using kinesiology or dowsing is the simplest method of checking. In the absence of these skills indications of the need for protection might be: confusion, problems arising from an exercise, the inability to break links after an experience even when the protocols have been followed exactly. The need for support might manifest as: difficulty achieving a clear experience or the inability to successfully ground and centre oneself sufficiently.

54

Malignant or conscious harmful intent is the rarest of causes that require protection. Though even this is really more common than most people would like to acknowledge – the 'evil eye' didn't vanish at the advent of scientific rationality, only the belief in it did. Protection can be required from a strong beneficent force as much as from a strong damaging force. The key is entirely personal to each individual, and it will be whatever outside force disrupts our energetic equilibrium in such a way that we lose track of our own personal 'resonant frequency'.

In scientific terminology, protection is needed whenever we become subject to 'entrainment'. Entrainment occurs when a stronger energy field influences a weaker field so that the weaker field begins to vibrate at the same frequency as the stronger. Sometimes this may be advantageous if there is an increase in orderliness and balance. Energy is neither good nor bad – but it can be inappropriate and untimely – the wrong thing at the wrong time. When this is the case, steps need to be taken to protect and reinforce the personal energy field, and this is where support techniques come in.

Although it is not necessary to be aware of the source of the problem to correct for it, knowledge of the type of energy can be helpful, if only to be aware of it in the future.

The Varieties of Stress Factors

Geopathic stress refers to the natural energies within the landscape and the planet that can sometimes create imbalance in individuals where they are exposed over long periods of time or have become sensitised. Geopathic stress is of two sorts: natural and man-made.

Natural geopathic stresses often occur where different patterns of energy overlap and interfere with one another amplifying their effect on the human body. We can become more aware of these energy tides around us simply by paying attention to how a place 'feels'. These energies can be a product of the interactions of gravity and rotation that tend to set up rhythms of standing (stationary and stable) energy waves across the surface of the planet. They can also be produced by the flow of molecule-thin water sheets altering electrical potential as they rise or fall through levels of soil and rock.

Man-made geopathic stresses are usually these natural flows or accumulations of energy that have been modified at some time by human intervention. The system of leys ('ley-lines') is an example of this type of manipulation. Such modifications might be intentional, but can also be accidental, like those created by arrangements of buildings or power lines and pipes disturbing the local flow of earth energy.

By far the commonest stressor is electromagnetic fields of industrial origin. These are inescapable anywhere on the planet's surface nowadays. Radio, television, microwave, satellite and military communications flood every inch of space. Electrical wiring, phone lines, metal pipes and metal surfaces distort, amplify and sustain strong entrainment fields that can quickly disrupt many aspects of the human energy field, even when they are not connected to any power supply.

Other environmental stressors commonly encountered are chemicals. Of these the most pervasive are plastics and other petrochemicals, formaldehyde (present in foams and furniture), pesticides (in nearly everything), perfumes (which very often contain some or all of the aforementioned substances), and so on. Chemical sensitivities are usually created or exacerbated where there is already strong electromagnetic pollution that has over-sensitised the immune system.

Noise, particularly very high and very low frequencies can be significant stress factors simply because they are not apparent as audible frequencies and have peculiar and sometimes distressing effects on the body, emotions and functioning of the brain. It is becoming apparent that locations can be given a particular 'vibe' by the way that infrasound is created by the natural materials and shapes modifying sound waves from other sources – the wind, the sea or the nearby hum of traffic or factory noise.

In places with a naturally peculiar resonance the effect can be overlaid in complex ways by human emotional energy – the 'ghoul' effect. Intense emotion seems to imprint the crystalline structure of rock or water and, over time, this can become a permanent energetic signature with each visitor's reaction to the existing 'vibe' augmenting and confirming it. Thus, a battlefield will have a pretty difficult energy to begin with, which will only be amplified by every visitor who mulls over the horror of the past.

With very strong emotional impressions a sensitive or sensitised individual can become a trigger so that a replay of some part of the original event occurs within the minds of those present – this is not a sentient spirit but a 'ghoul' – a memory of what an original participant experienced or witnessed.

Other Spirit Presences

As the air we breathe is composed of many different molecules of which we have little or no awareness, the space around us is full of other beings getting on with their own sentient existence. Paying attention in different ways, as we do when we begin to attune to trees and their spirits, can make us more visible at these other dimensional levels. Mostly we are ignored as 'only a human being', but sometimes, curious entities will hang around to see what is going on. Depending on their own interest and energy these onlookers may be helpful or may be a hindrance. Very occasionally they may have nothing better to do than follow you around or attach to some tasty energy centre left unguarded. Over the years we have met several people who have unwittingly picked up such 'etheric hitchhikers' just by visiting natural power spots. All were naturally sensitive individuals characterised by poor personal boundaries and very ungrounded 'spiritual' or 'imaginative' personalities. Unfortunately, many of this type have never really been properly grounded in their lives and are unwilling to 'get real' because it is seen by them as boring. This glamour of psychic sensitivity, of being special, can lead to being sectioned in psychological wards under a regime of mind-crushing pharmaceutical preparations. Because current sciences do not recognise the reality of any subtle life forms, experience of them is automatically a sign of aberrant mental activity.

Ignorance of other life forms and suppression of experiences does not make the encounters go away, it simply removes any meaningful context within which the individual can make sense of their own experiences. It is possible that you are mad if you are seeing weird things, you will almost certainly be driven mad if you are seeing weird things and no-one believes your experiences are real. Quite a high proportion of the instances that we see have been contacted by benign or even benevolent beings. The fear engendered by the experience turns out to be the main problem. Fear arises through lack of sufficient knowledge. In such circumstances fear further destabilises personal energy integrity, throwing the person's energies completely off-centre and losing groundedness. This further opens the psyche and subtle bodies to other, more damaging, influences. Following sensible protocols and ensuring you are fully grounded and centred is simply the single most important thing you can do.

In tree spirit work, non-physical beings are obviously going to be encountered on a regular basis and you will soon establish a useable frame of reference for those interactions. Human beings, either with or without physical bodies, can sometimes be an energy factor, usually as a mismatch of vibrations. Friction is always the key where human beings are concerned. It is easy to blame the other person for the disruption you feel, but essentially it is your own inability, at one level or another, to accept and integrate the difference of energies that creates the upset.

Cosmic Influence

The final category of factors is cosmic influences and these, though perhaps the least obvious, are always going to play a significant role in personal energy integrity. Not only do the planets of the solar system affect the energy status of all life forms on Earth as they form different spatial relationships with each other, they also enhance or interfere with each person's individual skills (as indicated by the natal astrological chart), whenever the planets move close to sensitive places on that chart.

Other, more distant, cosmic events, either physically apparent or on subtle levels, can also create changes in massive tides of energy that sweep the planet. Adjusting for these circumstances can make a huge difference to the 'reception' one is getting. This is the rationale for the 'hours' used in magical workings, where hours of daylight and darkness are equally divided into planetary rulerships beginning with the planetary ruler of the day. Thus the first 'hour' of Monday will be set aside for the operations falling under the influence of the Moon. The magical time was traditionally used for the gathering of plants or the preparation of medicines. Waiting for the right energetic tide before launching into the sea of reality saves time and energy.

In a way then, no matter what the source of possible interference, support procedures 'fine-tune' the personal energy field to get the best possible 'reception' in any circumstances. This helps to prevent any errant surge of energy from 'blowing a fuse'.

Inserting a simple question into your preliminary procedures such as :'Is this system [your body/mind/spirit] in need of protection or support?', will help to clarify your experiences. If the answer is 'Yes' then you will need to find out what support procedures are going to bring you back to a working equilibrium.

Because the sources of disruption can be very broad or extremely specific, there is a multitude of ways to bring support into an energy system. Very often, though, each person will have a relatively narrow range of circumstances that will habitually cause energy imbalances. As a solution, three or four support techniques will be found to be effective in most cases.

Dividing the support techniques into broad categories can help to narrow down the best options.

Support Using Grounding

The first obvious category is to check whether extra grounding techniques are required. Any technique may be sufficient or perhaps a very specific method will be needed.

1. Breath (such as axial breathing, breathing through the soles of the feet, slow deep breaths etc.)

2. Meridian Massage

3. Tapping in

4. Visualisation (such as a tree roots meditation)

5. Nutrition. (Usually energy-giving or grounding foods like sugars or carbohydrate. Meat is a 'noisy' food and will be unlikely to arise unless energy levels are so low that you really shouldn't be considering subtle work in those conditions)

6. Water. (Drinking a little, even just a sip, of good quality water can make a really significant difference to effective working. A sip of cool water is grounding to the body and will help to maximise brain-body co-ordination and mental focus. Dehydration is a common side-effect of modern living conditions and other drinks like tea, coffee or soft drinks are in no way equivalent to intake of just clean water as they are treated by the body as foods and not directly absorbed as water is.)

7. Water. (Can also be used as an energy tool in support work. A few drops are placed directly on the skin, such as at the forehead, navel areas or pulse points).

8. Physical activity. (This may be as simple as changing position, facing a specific direction, or sitting in a different way. Grounding movements like brisk walking, jumping up and down, stamping feet or clapping hands). Sometimes it is necessary to finish some completely separate activity because at one level or another it is dividing the attention. Doing the washing up, going to the toilet, taking the 'phone off the hook, feeding the dog, and so on).

Grounding techniques naturally divide into two types – active and passive. Passive grounding methods are those that require little or no thought to accomplish. They are best used when body and mind are so fuddled that clear mental focusing isn't possible. Active methods like visualisations can require a lot of energy focus to accomplish successfully.

Support Using the Sense of Sound

Sound is a powerful medium that moulds and directs matter. Using a specific type of sound can tune the energy bodies if part of the system has become 'off key'. The sound may be internal or imagined, or it may be actual.

A mantra, tone or affirmation may need to be vocalised out loud or imagined mentally.

Vocalisation, singing or chant all vibrate every aspect of the body and the intellectual or meaningful content can be unimportant when compared to that energy effect. Likewise the aesthetic content of a sound or piece of music will not necessarily play a significant part. Sounds that are displeasing to us are simply those whose energy effects we find uncomfortable at that time and place.

Support Using the Sense of Smell

Like sound, the sense of smell can create immediate energy changes and emotional climates without any apparent associative memory processes being involved.

Essential oils, being the purest and most intense of natural scents, are often indicated in support situations where the sense of smell is the key to rebalancing the individual. Simply smelling the essential oil is often sufficient, though it may be that the oil has to be worn on the body or diffused into the environment.

Other support may be incense smoke or smudge. Hydrosols, the water-based fractions produced in the making of concentrated essential oils, are becoming more available these days. Floral waters, such as rose water and lavender water are the same sort of thing and in some parts of the world, particularly Meso-America and Africa, floral water by itself is a potent tool in healing rituals.

Support Using the Sense of Sight

The sense of sight not only affects the visual cortex of the brain but also directly passes to and influences the hypothalamus and pituitary gland complex situated deep within the centre of the brain. Stimulation of these areas creates profound changes in nearly every system and organ of the body. These effects are known to be constant and free of any cultural or personal associations because they reflect the energy status inherent in shape and colour.

Support can come from these unconscious effects of shape and colour and also from the conscious symbolic forms created throughout history and in all cultures. They may be required to be actually seen by the eyes, or they may work equally well when seen by the 'mind's eye' of the imaginative brain. For those not used to the visualisation of fields of colour a useful tip is to imagine or remember a real object of the colour you need to use, and then either multiply the image until it fills your imaginative mind, or zoom in closer and closer until the colour is all that there is or, finally, try colouring the field with exactly the same colour or colours.

When attempting to identify the necessary support always remember to begin with large categories and then work downward to details. So when using colour, for example, begin by determining whether it is to be visualised or seen with the eye (from an external source). Is it a single colour, more than one colour, or a complex image such as a yantra, mandala or symbol. If the latter, from which culture does it derive, and so on. If a single colour or sequence of colours, does it belong to the simple rainbow spectrum? Is the first colour warm (reds, oranges, yellows), or cool (greens, blues, violets)? If it isn't a spectrum colour is it black, white, grey or a secondary or tertiary colour: browns, pinks, turquoise and so on.

Other Support Processes

Objects such as stones, crystals, personal power objects, tree essences, samples of wood, can all be drawn on for support, as can the aid of non-physical or spiritual beings whether guides, allies, ancestors or teachers.

The category of 'something else' is always important to remember, but don't become bogged down or inhibited by this useful process. If a support comes up that is impractical to achieve, simply find the next best feasible one.

Finally, as was said at the beginning of this section, you will find that in practice, one or two items or procedures will be sufficient in most circumstances and, after all, this is the origin of the amulet and talisman: a focus to help maintain effective balance through all the varied experiences of living. Remember, though, that a support should not become a crutch. Superstition has no place in this process. Just because you don't have a lucky stone, medicine bundle or whatever does not prevent you from accomplishing very effective work with tree spirits.

Chapter 4

The Dendrochronology of a Land

One of the earliest insights to arise on beginning to work with tree spirits and the energy of trees is an appreciation that there are many different perceptions of time. Human time cannot be the same as tree time when we live for little more than eighty years and trees can live for many hundreds of years. Science has largely ignored the time factor, failing to take account of processes that may not appear to be happening simply because they are of such a long duration. Redundant systems and apparent evolutionary dead ends are often those that, for the time being, are just waiting for a change in conditions to begin to flourish and become climax species once again.

At the beginning of the last century researchers demonstrated that plants showed purposeful intent in their behaviour once the speed of their processes was adjusted to a comparable time frame that humans could see. Working with tree spirits the flow of time across a land is often experienced as tides of life in different forms ebbing and flowing down the centuries. Even though the long aeons of change have been revealed by geology and palaeontology, even though archaeology has shown the long tides and shifting currents of human civilisations, the legacy of Descartes and his mechanical universe, and Darwin with his nineteenth century ideal of the present being the pinnacle of progress, the 'survival of the fittest', has blinkered us into seeing a linear movement of time rather than a cyclical recapitulation.

Ecological studies of small isolated plant communities show that there is a complex web of interactions, often occurring with chemical transmitters in parts per billion, which make a complete mockery of the idea of distinct species struggling to overcome rival species in a fight for survival. The chaos of the 'Wild' is being shown to be, in reality, a complex dance, perfect in its maintenance of a symbiotic equilibrium between all the living beings that inhabit it.

These days many talk of climate change. As if climate change were a new thing! Even within recorded history there are clear signs, were they to be believed, that catastrophic change is really quite a common occurrence. Present human culture has a very poor memory, partially because it relies on written documentation rather than the oral traditions of the ordinary people, who have always tended to remember a different sort of event – a history of a people and its land rather than a history of the famous and their personal achievements.

Not much more than the lifetimes of two yew trees ago, most of this land that is now the British Isles was under an ice sheet miles thick. Twelve thousand years ago things were beginning to change. Ice started to melt, (some evidence suggests a very rapid thaw indeed), sea levels began to rise, old lands were sunk and new coastlines created.

In this post-glacial period trees moved northward through Europe re-inhabiting lands that had not seen plant life for long centuries. Those trees that colonised Britain before the English Channel formed from melting icecaps, separating the land from continental Europe, are considered to be native trees. For the last twelve thousand years it is these trees that have developed communities and called bacteria, fungi and

68

insects to them with complex molecular languages, created the soil and the atmosphere of these islands. Yet even longer ago palm trees flourished here, and redwoods, and more recently (13,500 years ago) Britain was forested by firs and spruces. What we now consider to be 'our' native trees will not remain so in the future. It is a somewhat pedantic differentiation, a snapshot in time that was valid when taken but is inevitably going to fade and become outdated. For, from the moment that the land bridge to Europe was lost by the rising waters, plants found another way to move where they wanted. As always they employed the movers, the insects, animals and people to transport and replant them in new soils.

Today we are, as ever, in a landscape of transition. The countryside, what remains at least, is largely populated by the post-glacial native trees. The towns and cities, meanwhile, are inhabited by new species of trees mostly brought from other lands by humans who found themselves attracted by this or that aspect of the plants. Given the relatively short time that has elapsed, many of these trees have become naturalised – they set seed and prosper, beginning to fit in with or to mould their habitats. A great many others are as yet dependent on their movers for survival. But given that change is a constant, how many of these exotic species will react like the redundant species of the ecologists' systems and one day begin to achieve their potential?

Hierarchies and classifications are a human attempt to organise existence into a steady, reliable, understandable pattern. Without constant vigilance this convenient organisation of life becomes a tyrannous burden that excludes and denigrates those things that do not neatly fit into a pre-existing file. Racism, genocide, species extinction and spiritual alienation all stem from this tendency to want to order and control. The recent popularity of Celtic (or Celtkitche?) tree lore, with its tree oghams and tree calendars, has the tendency to create a false hierarchy in the landscapes that we, ultimately, have created. Those trees favoured with attention are lavishly described and eulogised, those not included in the obscure listings – and this contains a majority of our natives – fail to get a look in. Likewise in the field of alternative health, until recently, those trees making it into the Bach Flower Remedies, (about a third of the total number of those essences), were considered as powerful energetic healers, whilst the majority of British trees were not being considered in this light at all.

This dendrochronology is an attempt to begin to redress the balance. It records the flow of tree life into these islands, no matter what means of transport was chosen by the trees, nor when they chose to make their move. There are obvious periods where colonisation has been fast and furious, and someone with a better grasp of events might make interesting correlations between the arrival of a new tree spirit energy and a change in human affairs. Think in terms of large chaotic ecosystems rather than neat finite individuals, think in terms of spirits gathering together rather than horticultural whims and fashions, and interesting new waves of possibilities may start lapping at the edges of our awareness.

This is by no means a complete listing of all the trees that have visited or have established a presence in this land. Some trees have snuck in without being noticed until much later, some have come several times as seeds or seedlings or been brought by different individuals a few years apart. Sources can differ quite significantly as to when a certain tree was introduced, but arguing over five or ten years is not particularly fruitful to this present overview.

Just because we are looking at the dendrochronology of the British Isles, it is important not to lose sight of the fact that this process has happened in different forms, and continues to happen, throughout the world. A visitor to the distant and remote hills of Nepal might be amazed to see trees and plants from all over the world at the centre of everyday life. Bananas grow on sunny slopes alongside vibrant lilies from South Africa and marigolds native to Mexico. Native shamans even use some species of Brugmansia that originate in the jungles of the Amazon, and which are themselves thought by many ethnobotanists to be ancient cultivars carefully selected over thousands of years for their medicinal and spiritual properties.

Likewise across the islands of the Pacific the pioneering, colonising journeys of the Polynesian peoples can be traced from the plants that they took along with them. Apart from the palm trees, whose seeds carry from island to island on the tropical tides, a great many of the now naturalised plants on these islands were planted by man many centuries ago.

We must begin to see ourselves as much a part of the ecology of the planet as the pollinating bee, bird or bat. Part of our natural function is the transportation and propagation of plants. Cajoled by scent, shape, colour or chemical, humans serve their progenitor whenever they have hearts that are open to the language of trees.

Dendrochronology
(Literally: the science of dating (*chronos*) using trees (*dendron*) here used poetically as "tree time")

During the last Interglacial Period before the last Ice Age, around 13,500 years ago, Britain was largely populated by species of fir (*Abies species*) and spruce (*Picea abies*), with some birch and juniper.

Glaciation travelled as far south as a line drawn between the Thames and Severn valleys. By about 12,000 years ago the ice sheets began to retreat northward again.

10,000 years BP (Before Present)

Traditionally, native trees are thought of as those that colonised the land before rising sea levels from melting ice created the English Channel and closed the land bridge to the rest of the European mainland. As the ice retreated northward pioneer species also moved north, though at different speeds and with different areas of distribution, depending on the local conditions and from what direction they first became established.

Evidence of the following trees has been found from this earliest period:

Silver birch (*Betula pendula*) and downy birch(*Betula pubescans*)

Rowan (*Sorbus auouparia*)

Juniper (*Juniperus communis*) One of the considerable number of native trees that seem to be omitted from the Celtic oghams and later Celtic tree calendars.

Aspen (*Populus tremula*)

Bird cherry (*Prunus padus*) Better suited and more widespread in its northerly habitats. (Also absent from Celtic oghams and calendars)

Gean (*Prunus avium*) Remaining more populous in the southern regions of Britain. (Also absent from oghams)

Alder (*Alnus glutinosa*) At this early period it can be found gradually spreading along river valleys with a sporadic distribution.

Dwarf willow (*Salix herbacea*) and sea buckthorn (*Hippophae rhamnoides*) would have taken advantage of the conditions as ice retreated. However, alternate periods of wetter then dryer conditions saw considerable fluctuations in vegetation over this time period.

9,500 years BP

Pine (*Pinus sylvestris*) spread north-west from continental Europe but with later damper and more waterlogged conditions it became restricted to the Highlands of Scotland.

Sessile Oak (*Quercus petraea*) established itself in the thinner soils and cooler upland climate, followed later by:

English Oak (*Quercus robor*)

Wych elm (*Ulmus glabra*)

Black poplar (*Populus nigra*). Another tree absent from ogham lore.

9,000 years BP

Yew (*Taxus baccata*)

Holly (*Ilex aquifolium*)

Hazel (*Corylus avellana*)

74

8,000 years BP

Alder and willow become dominant species along river valleys.

7,500 years BP

Small- leaved lime (*Tilia cordata*) spread widely in woodlands and was more common than oak before Saxon times. (Another glaring omission from ogham lore).

Large-leaved lime (*Tilia platyphyllos*). Less common than small-leaved lime.

7,000 years BP

Hawthorn (*Crataegus monogyna*)

Midland hawthorn (*Crataegus laevigata*)

Ash (*Fraxinus excelsior*)

Other native trees that colonised Britain before it became an island:

The willow family, as pioneers, would mostly have been present from early times:

Crack willow (*Salix fragilis*)

Common sallow (*Grey willow, Salix cinerea*)

Great sallow (*Goat willow, Salix caprea*)

Bay willow (*Salix pentandra*)

Osier (*Salix viminalis*)

Almond willow (*Salix trianda*)

Eared willow (*Salix aurita*)

Purple willow (*Salix purpurea*)

Dark-leaved willow (*Salix myrsinifolia*)

White willow (*Salix alba*) may be a native tree or a very early introduction, as it seems to be distributed close to human settlements.

Whitebeam (*Sorbus aria*) (No ogham references).

Swedish whitebeam, Finnish whitebeam and Fontainbleu service tree are all natural crosses between similar species. Swedish whitebeam (*Sorbus intermedia*) is a hybrid between rowan and whitebeam and is naturalised, likewise the Finnish whitebeam (*Sorbus x thuringia*). Fontainbleu service tree (*Sorbus latifolia*) is a hybrid between whitebeam and wild service tree. It was named from the town around which it was found when first identified, but similar hybrids occur naturally in Devon, Somerset and South Wales.

Wild service tree (*Sorbus torminalis*) (No ogham references)

Crab apple (*Malus sylvestris*)

Field maple (*Acer campestre*) (Absent from oghams)

Elder (*Sambucus nigra)*

Spindle (*Euonymus europaeus*) (Mentioned in some ogham tracts but absent from current lists)

Strawberry tree (*Arbutus unedo*) Strictly speaking only native to the far south and west of Ireland. (Despite apparent significance to the Irish Celts, also absent from oghams).

Wayfaring tree (*Viburnum lantana*) (Upon which the oghams are silent)

Gorse (*Ulex gallica* and *U. europeus*)

Box (*Buxus sempervirens*), may well have been the last tree species to colonise Britain before the Channel became so wide as to prevent further colonisation. (No ogham references)

From about 6,000 years ago the Channel became a barrier to all further plant and animal colonisation. The native trees established a dense woodland cover in all but the highest or most exposed and thin soils. It was only with the warming of the climate and the arrival of significant Neolithic farming peoples from about 4,500 years ago that this forest landscape began to be modified, both by cultivation practices and with new species brought by man.

Many of the earliest introduced trees have no certain dates, and even the peoples who brought them can only be guessed at. The effects of trade and migrations are likely to have been much more complex than is now apparent.

3,000 years BP

Two of the earliest trees to cross the Channel were certainly beech and hornbeam. These have a natural distribution only in the south-east corner of England, but from there were planted west and north until they became a major woodland feature over most of Britain.

2,000 years BP

From about 750 BC Celtic (Iron Age) culture becomes increasingly evident on mainland Britain. By this time the following trees, if not already natives, were probably well-established introductions:

Violet willow (*Salix daphnoides*)

Common Pear (*Pyrus communis*) This tree as it exists now may be a cross between native and introduced species.

Cornish elm (*Ulmus minor var.*) Probably linked to the westerly movements of certain Neolithic tribes as is the :

English elm (*Ulmus procera*). There are many sub-species of elm with regional distinctions making it a very complex tree to study origins and cross-breeding.

From 100BC (approx. 2000 years BP)

Connections to the increasingly powerful Roman world and a relatively mild climate meant that the opportunities to introduce useful tree species were more frequent.

Trees thought to have been introduced under Roman influence, if not directly by Roman administration after the Claudian invasion of AD 43 :

Medlar (*Mespilus germanicus*). An early introduction into Europe from western Asia, an important Mediterranean food tree.

Fig (*Ficus carica*) Although documented plantings are much later, it is thought to have been first introduced as a Roman food tree.

Walnut (*Juglans regia*)

Sweet Chestnut (*Castanea sativa*)

With the collapse of the Roman colonies from AD300 onwards, and also with a worsening weather pattern over the next few centuries, there is little evidence of any new tree introductions until written documentation of the 15th and 16th centuries. Certainly plants would have continued to have been introduced as medicines, particularly with the growth of monastic establishments during the 12th and 13th centuries.

16th century

1500 Sycamore (*Acer pseudoplanatus*) is native to central Europe. The introduction date is not known but it was certainly being planted by the beginning of the 16th century at the latest. It rapidly established itself as a fully naturalised tree, and is an important shelter belt tree in the North.

1500 Stone pine (*Pinus piooa*) is probably the earliest introduced pine into Britain. Originally from the Mediterranean, where it easily survives the dry summers. It does very well in western England and the Scottish Borders. Stone pine is the source of edible pine nuts. Once over ten years old, it takes on its characteristic umbrella- shaped, spreading crown.

1500 Holm oak (*Quercus ilex*) is a native to the western Mediterranean lands. It is common in the Iberian peninsula where forests of holm oak still stand. The exact date is not known but it is thought that the tree was introduced as an ornamental parkland tree.

1536 Northern white cedar (*Thuja occidentalis*). Probably the first North American tree to be widely planted in Europe. An important medicinal tree, though doesn't grow well in Britain.

1548 Norway spruce (*Picea abies*) May have been introduced at an earlier date but definitely planted by this date. It is the native upland and mountain tree of Europe, absent only from the North European Plain.

1549 Mulberry (*Morus nigra*) Black mulberry has a native range in western Asia. Although already present from this date, it was only in the early 17th century that James I encouraged the planting of mulberry to sustain a home-grown silk industry .

1576 Cherry laurel (*Prunus laurocerasus*) Native to the Black Sea and the southern Caspian Sea. Introduced into Britain as woodland cover for game birds.

1582 Tamarisk (*Tamarix gallica*) Introduced from the Middle East by Bishop of London, Dr Edmund Grindal, during the reign of Elizabeth I, as a medicinal tree.

1500 – 1600 Almond (*Prunus dulcis*) Originally from Western Asia, then into the Balkans and Mediterranean, it was brought into Britain sometime in the 16th century. It is the earliest large-flowered cherry to flower in Britain, often even before the cherry plum.

17th Century

1600 Common lime (*Tilia x europa*) This hybrid between small-leaved lime and large-leaved lime would have naturally occurred in Britain from time to time. However, around this time it was a popular tree for landscape gardening, brought from European nurseries.

1600 Norway maple (*Acer platanoides*) This tree is a common maple to all northern Europe (not especially Norway), and probably was spreading towards Britain when the opening of

82

the English Channel prevented it from becoming established as a native. It was possibly introduced early in the 17th century but the first recorded planting is in 1683.

1603 Silver fir (*Abies alba*) The commonest of European firs, re-introduced for the first time since the last Ice Age.

1605 Horse chestnut (*Aesculus hippocastanum*). This tree was completely unknown to European botanists until 1596 when it was found in a small, mountainous area of Greece and Albania. It was introduced into Britain between 1605 and 1617.

1621 Lilac (*Syringia vulgaris*). Native to Eastern Europe and Asia Minor, John Tradescant introduced lilac into Britain.

1625 European larch (*Larix x decidua*). Native to the Alps and other European mountain ranges. The Duke of Atholl planted it as a forestry tree in his Tay Valley estates.

1629 Black cherry (*Prunus serotina*). Found all across North America. In Britain this cherry flowers in May. Medicinally, it is the most often used cherry.

1629 Stags horn sumach (*Rhus typhina*). Brought from North America by John Parkinson, the apothecary of James I.

1638 Robinia (Locust tree) (*Robinia pseudoacacia*). Introduced by John Tradescant. A native of the Allegheny Mountains and Middle Mississippi Valley, now common throughout the United States.

1638 Swamp cypress (*Taxodium distichum*). Another tree introduced by John Tradescant. It was the first redwood to be taxonomically recognised.

1648   Portugal laurel (*Prunus lusitanica*). A native of Spain and Portugal. It has finer leaves and a more delicate spray of blossoms appearing after cherry laurel.

1656   Red maple (*Acer rubrum*). This was one of the earliest trees to have been brought to Europe from eastern North America by John Tradescant the Younger.

1656   Tulip tree (*Liriodendon tulipifera*). From the eastern woodlands of North America by the Tradescants.

1660   Scots pine (*Pinus sylvestris*). Although a native of Scotland, it was only re-introduced into England around this date. First planted in northern Hampshire, it soon spread into the scrublands of Berkshire.

1664   Pencil cedar (*Juniperus virginiana*). Introduced from the seaboard colonies of North America.

1675   Honey locust (a variety of robinia). Introduced by Henry Compton, Bishop of London from the Mississippi Basin, North America

1679   Cedar of Lebanon (*Cedrus libani*). It is native to the mountains of southern Turkey and the Lebanon. Probably introduced by John Evelyn, or perhaps ten or twenty years before this date.

1681   Sweetgum (*Liquidamber styracifolia*). Introduced from Mexico.

1688   Box elder (Ash-leaved maple) (*Acer negundo*). Brought from North America by Bishop Henry Compton. It has a similar form to the tree of heaven or the ash: a small tree with a popular variegated form. Native across America and into Mexico.

1690 London plane (*Platanus x acerifolia*). A hybrid between oriental plane and the American plane trees.

18th Century

1700 Black spruce (*Picea mariana*) Native across Canada. It has a very tall, spire-like form. A tree was sent to Bishop Compton at Fulham Palace. It can be recognised by its pale bluish foliage and rounded bushy top once it reaches about 30ft (12m)

1700 Manna ash (*Fraxinus ornus*). Introduced from Asia into southern Europe and from there into Britain.

1726 Catalpa (*Catalpa bignoides*). Also called 'Indian bean tree' and 'southern catalpa', this tree is native from Florida to Louisiana on the S E. coast of North America. It was introduced into Britain by John Catesby.

1731 Dwarf fan-palm (*Chamaerops humilis*). The only palm tree native to Europe, growing along the dry Mediterranean coastlines. Quite hardy to British climates, especially in the south.

1735 Turkey oak (*Quercus cerris*). This is the latest possible date for the introduction into Britain by Exeter nurserymen, Lucombe and Pince. The tree originates from southern Europe and the Balkans.

1750 Oriental sweetgum (*Liquidamber orientalis*). Introduced from Turkey, this is an important tree for medicine and perfumery.

1750 Paper birch (*Betula papyrifera*). One of the birches introduced from North America, easily recognised by its whitish, peeling outer bark.

1751   Tree of heaven (*Ailanthus altissima*). Brought from northern China.

1752   Chinese thuja (*Thuja orientalis*).

1735   Pagoda tree (*Sophora japonica*). A similar looking tree to the black locust tree. Introduced from China.

1758 Ginkgo (*Ginkgo biloba*). Also known as 'maidenhair tree'. It is native to China and grown in Japanese temple gardens. The first specimen of the tree came to Britain in this year.

1758   Lombardy poplar (*Populus nigra 'Italica'*). Brought to Britain by Lord Rochford from its native northern Italy. It is a natural variation of the European black poplar.

1759   Caucasus zelcova (*Zelcova carpinifolia*). A variety of elm native to the Caucasus Mountains, introduced to Britain by way of France.

1763   Lucombe oak (*Quercus x Hispania 'Lucombeana'*). This tree arose in this year as a cross between cork oak and turkey oaks in a nursery in Exeter, Devon. Its own acorns were growing by 1792.

1764   Yellow buckeye (*Aesculus flava*). Native to the Great Smoky Mountains of Tennessee, North America.

1770   Irish yew (*Taxus baccata 'fastigiata'*). Two small upright yews were discovered in Co. Fermanagh, Ireland, one of which became the source for most Irish yews after 1820.

1780   Willow-leaf pear (*Pyrus salicifolia*). This small tree is native to Russia, Turkey, Iran and western Asia. The natural weeping form is the most popular for plantings.

1780 Grey alder (*Alnus incana*). Native to northern Europe, this alder has been used extensively in reclamation of industrial sites and land stabilisation.

1795 Monkey puzzle (Chile pine – *Araucaria araucana*). The first seeds were grown in this year in Britain, though a second wave of seedlings were successfully grown from 1844. The tree is native to the mountainous border regions between Chile and Argentina.

19th Century

1800 American eastern cottonwood (*Populus deltoides*). One of the American poplars to hybridise freely with black European types to create hybrid black poplar (*Populus serotina*).

1802 Oriental plane (*Planatus orientalis*). This is the earliest definite date for the introduction of this species. It is characterised by a deeply indented three-pointed leaf and the tendency to grow large, down-sweeping branches.

1804 Chinese juniper (*Juniperus chinensis*). Native to China and Japan, this is now one of the most frequently planted junipers in Britain.

1805 Chinese fir (*Cunninghamia lanceolata*). A redwood from Chusan Island in the East China Sea.

1820 Red Chestnut (*Aesculus x carnea*). This tree probably arose in Germany as a hybrid between the common horse chestnut and the American red buckeye (*Aesculus pavia*), and was certainly on the market by this date.

1820 Smooth Japanese maple (*Acer palonatum*). Introduced from Japan.

1826 Exeter elm (*Ulmus glabra 'Exoniensis'*). This variety arose in a nursery in Exeter, Devon certainly before this date.

1827 Douglas fir (*Pseudotsuga menziesii*). Introduced by David Douglas from its native habitats along the North-West Pacific coasts of North America.

1828 Madrona (*Arbutus menzeisii*). Called madrone in Oregon. Native to the west coast from British Columbia to southern California. Another species brought to Britain by David Douglas.

1830 Noble fir (*Abies procera*). From Washington and Oregon in the North American West. David Douglas brought this tree to Britain, where major plantings were undertaken in Scotland during the next few decades.

1831 Deodar (*Cedrus deodara*). From the Punjab, India. It is a large cedar with down-swung branches.

1831 Sitka spruce (*Picea sitchensis*). This tree grows from Alaska to middle California as a coastal species. It is the world's largest spruce. David Douglas sent seed in this year, though more were sent in1851. It is the best tree for western hills, peat soil and high rainfall areas. Friendly to bird species when young and in thinned plantations.

1832 Grand fir (*Abies grandis*). From southern British Columbia and northern California. Another introduction by David Douglas.

1837 Hungarian oak (*Quercus frainetto*). Native to southern Italy and the Balkans. It has a characteristic oak leaf, but it broadens out considerably towards the tip.

1838 Paulownia (*Paulownia tomentosa*). A native of China, though introduced to Britain from those growing in Japan.

1838 Highclere holly (*Ilex x altaclerensis*). This variety arose in Hampshire when holly crossed with Madeira holly (*Ilex perudo*), a common conservatory plant in stately houses, put outdoors in summer to increase flowering. The 'Highclere' types do not have the buckled appearance of the native holly's leaves, being more flat.

1839 Oriental Spruce (*Picea orientalis*). Grows in the Caucasus and N.E. Turkey. This was a favourite tree in the period between 1850 –1880, when it was the fashion to plant pinetums. This spruce has the shortest needle, dark green with a bevelled tip that remains green for many years.

1840 Austrian pine (*Pinus nigra var. nigra*). This is the black pine native to central Europe. It is commonly planted as a shelterbelt tree. It has a very black, scaly bark with short, stiff needles.

1842 Japanese red cedar (*Cryptomeria japonica*). Native to China and Japan where each country has different forms of the tree. It was first brought here from southern China.

1843 Aleppo pine (*Pinus halepensis*). Native to the hot Mediterranean, it grows well on hot, rocky sites. Easily identified by its bright green umbrella crown.

1843 Chusan palm (*Trachycarpus fortunei*). From South China, this tree was brought to Britain by Robert Fortune. The first plant was in 1839 but was kept indoors. This date is that of the first tree to grow outdoors in this country.

1844 Atlas cedar (*Cedrus atlantica*). Growing in the Atlas Mountains of Algeria and Morocco, the popular natural variation with blue- green leaves that grows amongst the more common green variety, was introduced the following year.

1845 Cider gum (*Eucalyptus gunnii*). Originally from Tasmania, this variety is probably the most frequently planted in Britain.

1846 Monterey Cypress (*Cupressus macrocarpa*). This cypress is native to a very small range of Californian headlands where it forms a low, scrubby tree. In Britain it was mainly planted in Devon and Cornwall where it grows into a tall, upward reaching tree with pale greyish bark, clearly visible amongst the dark green foliage.

1846 Coast redwood (*Sequoia sempervirens*). Found inland from the West Coast of North America, mainly in the easterly valleys of the Rocky Mountains. It was first collected from the Russian colony at Fort Ross, north of San Francisco.

1850 Blue gum (*Eucalyptus globulus*). Native to Tasmania. In Britain, it is subject to frost cutback but it quickly establishes itself and will shoot from the base even when killed right back.

1850 Caucasian fir (*Abies nordmanniana*). This is a common variety of silver fir found in gardens. It originates from the Caucasus Mountains of Eastern Europe.

1851 Red fir (*Abies magnifica*). Introduced to Britain from the Cascade Mountains of Oregon and the Sierra Nevada of California.

1851 Western hemlock (*Tsuga heterophylla*). This is the largest of the hemlocks. It was introduced by John Jeffrey, as a fast-growing evergreen – more than 1m a year. The tree is related to the spruces and is native to both sides of America, the Himalayas, China and Japan. So named because the smell of the crushed leaves are reminiscent of the poisonous herb (*Conium maculatum*).

1853 Hiba (*Thujopsis dolobrata*). A native of Japan.

1853 Giant redwood (*Sequioadendron giganteum*). Named 'Wellingtonia' in honour of the Duke of Wellington, it was first identified in 1833, categorised by botanists in1852, and first brought to Britain to be planted near Perth in Scotland.

1854 Mountain hemlock (*Tsuga mertensiana*). Native to the western Rocky Mountains and found by John Jeffrey.

1854 Lawson cypress (*Chamaecyparis lawsoniana*). Discovered in this year living in a couple of valleys between Oregon and California and in the Upper Sacramento River Valley. Seeds were sent to Lawson's Nurseries in Edinburgh. The first variant form arose at Knaphill in Surrey in 1855 and was named 'erecta viridis'.

1854 Western red cedar (*Thuja plicata*). Brought from the American west coast.

1854 Incense cedar (*Calocedrus decurrens*). Introduced from Oregon and California

1855 Nootka cypress (*Chamaecyparis nootkatensis*). Native to Alaska and Oregon in western North America. A very hardy tree growing near the snow line.

1858 Midland hawthorn var. 'Paul's Scarlet' (*Crataegus laevigata*). A red-flowered branch of Midland hawthorn was propagated in this year.

1861 Temple juniper (*Juniperus rigida*). Introduced from Korea and Japan.

1861 Hinoki cypress (*Chamaecyparis obtusa*). Introduced from Japan.

1861 Japanese larch (*Larix haempferi L. leptolepis*). Native to central Honshu and Mount Fuji. By 1940 it had become widely planted especially in central Wales. It has a faster growth rate than the European larch.

1862   Keaki (*Zelkova serrata*). Introduced into Devon from Japan.

1865   Katsura tree (*Cercidiphyllum japonicum*). The largest deciduous tree growing in China and Japan, this is an ancient species with no known relatives.

1888   Leyland cypress (*Cupressocyparis leylandii*). This tree arose at Leighton Hall near Welshpool as a natural cross between Nootka cypress and Monterey cypress. In 1911 it arose again, this time from different sexes of the same parent trees.

1891   Hybrid catalpa (*Catalpa x erubescens*). This tree arose in Indiana as a cross between southern catalpa (native to America) and yellow catalpa (native to China). It was introduced to Britain in this year.

1892   Balsam poplar (*Populus trichocarpa*). This is the commonest balsam poplar planted in Britain, originating from North America.

20th Century

1901   Sargent spruce (*Picea brachytyla*). Native to China, this is a popular tree for arboreta. It can be recognised by its regular down-sweeping branches and leaves with white undersides.

1901 Dove tree (*Davidia involucrata*). Also known as 'handkerchief tree', it was found in Sichuan Province, China, by Pere David. The tree is small with easily recognisable flower bracts that look like large white leaves.

1902 Roble (*Nothofagus obliqua*). A South American beech, native to a small area of Chile.

1904 Hybrid larch (*Larix x eurolepsis*). First seen at Dunkeld in this year. It is similar to Japanese larch but the seedlings are larger and paler in colour. It also has larger cones and a multitude of flowers and grows faster than its parents where conditions are difficult for them.

1910 Hupeh rowan (*Sorbus hupehensis*). Originates from Western China, easily identified by its pale pink or whitish berries.

1913 Rauli (*Nothofagus procera*). Another southern hemisphere beech from the same area of Chile as the Roble.

1948 Dawn Redwood (*Metasequoia glyptostroboides*). A few specimens of this rare relict tree were found in Hupeh Province, China, and seeds were sent from here around the world.

1950 Lodgepole Pine (*Pinus contorta*). This pine grows on the central and western mountain ranges of North America. From this date it has been a common planting for upland forestry in Britain.

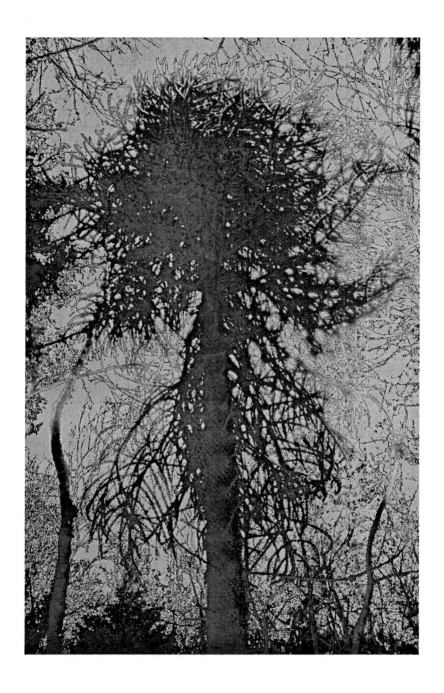

95

Chapter 5

Climbing the World Tree – Shamanic Technology

As it has developed over time, and as has been taught by the tree spirits themselves, the techniques and processes in the 'Tree Seer' books are naturally aligned to the shamanic traditions of the peoples of the world. Although these traditions are as varied as the cultures from which they have arisen, there is a core of belief and practice that can be recognised as emerging from the very nature of human experience and the human mind. In the same way that cars, trucks and tractors differ in appearance and specialist functions but have the same internal combustion engine, so the human being has the same structure of mind and nervous system. Certain things work well, certain practices change the way we see and feel, regardless of belief, system or culture.

There is an important distinction between using shamanic-based processes and actually being a shaman. A shaman is a specialist who seeks to heal rifts or alter the balance of relationship between the different worlds through directly interacting with spirits. In many traditional societies most members of the group will interact with spirits at some times in their lives – spontaneously, or in ritual and initiatory contexts. It is the degree of effective interaction with spirits, and the dedication to the maintenance of balance within the tribal group that sets the shaman aside. It is not a cosy job. Terence McKenna once described a shaman thus:

"Essentially, a shaman is someone deputised by a culture to go outside the culture. If you think of the culture as a spaceship, then the shamans are the people who do the EVA (extra–vehicular activities); they're sent outside to fix it because it can't be fixed from inside."

Sometimes the shaman is hereditary, more often a dramatic event initiates the training. The fully functioning shaman has become a person with energy pathways, perceptions and mind opened and stretched way beyond the norm for their culture. He or she is that scary person who knows more and sees more than ordinary people would really ever want to.

The most significant difference between true shamanism and many contemporary techniques that derive from shamanic models is the same thing that separates Western urban culture from traditional societies. The shamanic world-view is based on the acknowledgement of the existence of spirits and spirit worlds. There is no doubt. It is not possible to ignore this fact, and it is probably the main difficulty that arises when Westerners attempt to learn shamanic technologies. Is it 'all in the mind'? Is it 'just imagination'? Is it 'real'? As L. Lewis has pointed out:

"From a shamanic point of view, there is no distinction between 'real' and 'imaginary'. It's all part of the continuum of experience involving shifts of consciousness. From a Western psychological point of view, there is a distinction."

The keys to surmounting this hurdle are direct experience and patience. It is especially necessary to realise that, in contrast to the religious and scientific frameworks with which we are familiar that tend to be intellectual or emotional in energy, the processes adopted by shamanism are very much based in the body as sensory experience and sensory feeling.

Of what value are the shamanic traditions to us once we are successfully using tree-taught techniques? Firstly, they offer an established context of practice and a structured world-view, or cosmology, which can bring new insight and orderliness to experience. Whatever processes are learned and worked with there are clear benefits.

To begin with, there is a reaching outside of the personal confines of everyday reality in order to access different sources of power and points of view. We can learn how to open pathways to other, deeper energy sources that can be profoundly nourishing in a culture where the emotions and mental analysis divert a lot of attention away from what is happening around us. Perception can become freed from a rigidly human viewpoint as we experience points of view from the animal, plant and spirit kingdoms of consciousness. All this allows us to expand and construct new mental pathways so that creativity and flexibility increase.

The World Tree

In many cultures it is the tree that is used as the template to describe the relationship between other realms of spiritual beings and the everyday world of humans. The tree can be the map, as well as the means, to explore spirit worlds.

Like the three main parts of the tree, roots, trunk and branches, the universe of the shaman consists of three worlds that are interdependent aspects of the one whole reality. These three worlds can be understood as the most vital aspects of a shaman's consciousness (for in the ancient cosmologies there is infinite reflection: what is outside the person is also inside them, what is inside is the microcosm, what is outside is the macrocosm).

The Lower world is the foundation of everything. It is the source of energy and gives the shamans their power. The Middle world is the world as we know it, but seen through the eyes of spirits. It is the world of manifestation and brings awareness to the shaman. The Upper World is the place of knowledge and from here the shaman can receive clarity.

Power, awareness and clarity are the three essentials the shaman needs to work effectively. When the three worlds are working in harmony within the shaman, then the shaman can bring healing and harmony back to the world. Whatever method of working is undertaken, whether it as a healer, herbalist, spiritual advisor, guide of the dead and dying, interpreter of dreams, ceremonialist, storyteller, keeper of folk memory or arbitrator, the shaman restores balance through a powerful and intense relationship with spirits.

Entranced and Entrained

In the same way that we must shift our attention to different viewpoints if we wish to see the roots of the tree below our feet or the branches high above us in the sky, so the shaman must be able to guide awareness through the Three Worlds at will. The simplest way for a human being to shift awareness is through trance. The simplest way to enter trance is through entrainment. Entrainment is any activity that, by its steady repetition, sets up echoes in the way the brain functions thereby disrupting the normal way everyday reality is perceived. Slowing down, or managing to silence for a while, our learned responses to what we know and call 'reality', creates the opportunity for other equally 'real' but non-ordinary realities to sneak into our awareness. The use of sound and music, particularly rhythm, is an ideal medium for slipping into an entrained, trance state because right from the start music bypasses the intellect, aiming directly for the body and the emotions.

By means of song and drum the shaman enters non-ordinary reality and 'journeys' to the spirit worlds to seek the answers that are needed to restore harmony. These 'journeys', 'dreams', 'trips', 'flights', 'visions' take the practitioner into the non-physical worlds of the spirits, where with the aid of allies and guides, solutions are found. These spirit journeys are often seen by Western students as the 'best bit' of shamanic practice, yet it is the easiest part with which to become disillusioned.

One of the most important points when learning shamanic techniques is not to begin 'journeying' too soon. There is a tendency to want to rush into the 'full experience' and often too much is expected.

In the end it is more useful to be able to move into different states effortlessly and seamlessly – in the same way that breathing out naturally follows breathing in.

Begin with using the senses. Practice the exercises in these books and others so that you learn to pay attention in as many different ways as possible. Start by simply drumming, rattling and moving. If you involve yourself completely in the activity you will, before long, notice altered states as they come and go.

How much trance do you need? How altered do you need to feel to perceive altered states? Does it perhaps depend on how aware you are in the first place? If you consider that there is a big difference between the 'real' world, the 'physical' world, and the 'spirit' worlds perhaps you will need to feel that you have entered a completely 'other' reality, a parallel world completely different from this place now. If, on the other hand, you feel, sense or believe that there is an echoing of information from different levels of reality, if there is a reflection of all the other states in each state, or that this reality is as illusional or imaginal or mind-created, or mind-interpreted as any other, then maybe it is not so necessary to turn so far away from what is perceived as this reality 'here'. Anthropologists and the interested student both tend to be drawn to the overt, obvious and 'different' characteristics of shamanic awareness. To a fish air is a difficult concept and an almost impossible medium to conceive. To the human being, water is not an easy state to exist in. Yet the human hardly notices the air and the fish hardly notices the water. We have spent all our lives up until now learning to experience and react to our ordinary state of reality. It takes time and practice to learn another way. Working with the energy of trees and plants naturally helps us to loosen our concept of time, space, individuality and so on. Working with the energy of animals sets us free from cultural and learned patterns and allows our unique spirit and desires to flow guiltlessly and without judgement, in a space where these are not required.

The person who is an oracle can perceive spirit signs like tips of an iceberg in the seas. To the oracle what is noticed becomes significant. The required answer lies in extra-ordinary ordinariness, or in significant juxtapositions. Some shamans work with the oracular senses, hardly moving out of our ordinary worlds but understanding the extraordinary signs – sensing the patterns that flow from the bigger, non-physical, spiritual world. Other shamans leave behind all consciousness of this world. They travel to imaginal worlds, the non-physical sense realms, in order to find the answers to the questions they seek.

In the end, the drama of the shamanic ritual processes are only there to hasten the end result. The solution, the answer, the means to heal is all that matters. The shamans who cannot bring back harmony to the people are 'broken shamans'

How you step out of reality depends on your methods, your power, your internal needs, your culture, your predilections, your clarity, your trust, your spirit awareness, and the needs of your sponsors. Becoming familiar with the dynamics of basic shamanic journeying is like learning how to read a compass – whatever map you need to use, whatever you learn directly from the tree spirits – it will help you to orient your awareness in the spirit worlds.

Drumming Up Support

Using a 'sonic driver', an instrument that will create a steady, monotonous beat, is one of the easiest ways to begin to access the spirit worlds. Recently there have been discoveries that strongly indicate sacred sites, from caves to constructed monuments, were chosen because they enhanced, or were designed to create, particular sonic effects. Some amplify small sounds, some produce phenomenal echoes, some transmit or receive sounds made elsewhere. Sound is as much a part of our human psychic tradition as visual patterns are. The power of sound is a constant theme in the oral and magical stories of our ancestors.

A drum, preferably a single-headed frame drum, held in one hand and played by a stick held in the other hand, is the easiest type to use. An inexpensive bodhran, the shamanic drum of Ireland still used in folk music, is probably the easiest to acquire – though a longer drumstick would be needed to use it for steady shamanic beats. The advantage of this sort of drum is that it can be carried whilst moving around or dancing, can be played with a minimum of physical effort, and has a good resonant sound. Skin drums are always susceptible to changes in temperature and humidity, which alters the tension and thus the sound of the drum. In cold, damp conditions they can become dull and lifeless. It is possible to acquire single-headed drums that have man-made skins (or 'heads' as they are known). Made from a fibre-glass like material, they retain their tone in all conditions.

The volume that you beat your drum is not too important for attaining a trance state, but if you live in a situation where a drum is impractical, just experiment with other instruments. Trance music around the world is made on every sort of musical instrument, including the voice. However, to induce a trance effectively when working by yourself, it is much easier to use a method where the mind and thought processes can be relaxed. Beating a drum just requires a small hand and wrist action, playing a keyboard or other complex instrument, needs more focus of attention. The sound of rattles, having a higher pitch, carry shorter distances, and are often less intrusive than the loud resonance of drums. The jaw's harp, a shamanic instrument of Mongolian shamans, is excellent to use, though it can be tiring to the hand and mouth.

The regular and constant beat of the shamanic instrument is the driver that alters the brains functioning, but you will need to experiment with the number of beats per minute as some speeds will be more effective for you than others. Drumming for yourself, it is only necessary to maintain a beat that holds you in trance. If you are drumming for others it becomes more important to maintain an unchanging rhythm with which they can journey.

Most agree that certainly a speed of more than 120 beats per minute is needed to journey. This is approximately a beat of 'One and ....', that is, two beats a second. Practice for five, ten then fifteen minutes with this steady beat to see how it effects your awareness. Then repeat the process with a slightly faster beat, perhaps around 160 beats a minute. This speed is a more average speed for journey drumming. Increase the speed once more and repeat the process of watching your awareness whilst you maintain the beat. A drumbeat of 240 or more beats per minute is about the fastest that can be maintained without effort. This beat is about the equivalent of saying 'Mississippi', where each syllable is a beat of the drum.

The quality of the sound will vary considerably depending on the size of the drum, the thickness and tension of the skin, the speed of the drumming and the type of beater you are using. Choose a beater that feels comfortable in your hand. Add layers of cloth or leather if it is not thick enough to hold easily. Some beaters have a soft head whilst others are quite solid and this will change the loudness and resonant quality of the drum. The size of the beater will also produce different effects. Both with animal skin drumheads and with man-made varieties, there are variations of thickness across the drum's surface that change the tone or resonance. Experimenting with your drum will teach you the places where overtones build up, where the beats become higher or more resonant and so on.

Become proficient at maintaining a constant regular beat of equal loudness for twenty minutes or more. If you can record your practice it can be a very useful tool in tightening up your drumming. Very often, because we are slipping into altered states, the speed of the drum may seem to increase or slow down. Recording the session can show very clearly how our drumming would sound to other people! This change of speed may not be important to our own ability to journey, but it may be crucial if we are drumming for others.

Protocols for Drumming

Drumming itself can be a preparation for other types of work with tree spirits. It focuses mind and body energy on a simple task that has the effect of cleansing and empowering the space around us. The silence that is experienced after a session of drumming is more silent and more profound not just because of the contrast, but also because subtle resonances can still be felt in the atmosphere.

In many cultures the drum is the main vehicle, the tool, by which the shaman travels to the spirit worlds. The drum can also be the main tool for healing. In Siberia, contemporary shamans manipulate the sounds and rhythms of the drum to initiate the healing process in their patients. The drum, for them, is both the stethoscope and the scalpel. In this tradition the drum becomes a spirit entity in its own right, and with the death of the shaman the drum is also destroyed as it is so bound to the energy and power of that one individual.

The drum is a means to ensure two-way communication with the universe. It represents the awareness, the spirit, of the shaman, and also the resonant energy field of the universe itself as it responds to the movements and fluctuations of consciousness. Treating the drum with respect is a natural result of the awareness of its role. The best way to achieve a good working relationship with your drum is to work with it often. Take the time to journey to the spirit of your drum while you are drumming. Every drum has a spirit and a character of its own. Simply having the intention to meet the spirit of the drum will be sufficient. Your resulting experiences will be an expression of this relationship in some way. In time, you will get a feel for the way the drum works, what it is best at, how it can best be played, how it can best activate the healing processes, what spirits it is naturally attuned to, and so on.

However it has been made, of whatever substances, whatever its outward appearance, a drum, like everything else that has a manifest, physical form, has an awareness. Working consciously in this way with your drum will help to awaken its latent spirit energy.

Preliminaries – Clearing etc

There are many good reasons why it should become second nature before you begin any spirit work to clear and prepare the space. The methods you choose to use are less important than your understanding of the purpose of the process. In essence, you will be carrying out grounding, protection and support for yourself and those for whom you work, whether they are human beings or other spirits. Previous chapters in this book will have given you some ideas and methods. Choose those methods with which you are at ease. Make sure that you pay attention to these areas:

1) Define the space within which you work by energetically clearing it. Many cultures use a simple physical barrier such as a line of chalk or string, or a placement of incense or candles. The simplest way is to cleanse with incense the room you are to be working in.

2) Clarify your own intention and purpose and stabilise your mind. You have cleansed the external working space, now do the same to the internal working space of your mind. Grounding and centring exercises will create an uncluttered space within which you will be able to move much more easily between worlds. Any superfluous baggage, like emotional confusion or rigid mental expectations, will colour and perhaps distort your ability to have a clear experience. Go over the reasons why you are doing this work – it doesn't have to be momentous, life-changing stuff, just be clear about your intended purpose.

3) Link your internal world, the spirit worlds and the physical world. Whatever means you use should help to clear away limiting distinctions between here and there, now and then, ordinary and non-ordinary reality. Traditionally, this process often involves invoking the Directions and the Elements, thereby establishing the particular time and place within a universal context. This is like connecting your private telephone to the global network. All you need now are the right numbers and you will be able to access the information you need.

Signals - Call-back

Whenever there is more than one shamanic practitioner working together a system of signals is required that enables all the participants to know when to change the pace of the drumming, when to start a new song and so on. In core shamanism the main signal is the call-back signal. This is a change of pace and rhythm in the drumming that allows the journeyer to conclude his work with the spirits and to return to ordinary consciousness. The call-back signal is also useful for the solitary drummer too, as it creates a clear conclusion to the work. The exact nature of the signal can vary. One that is commonly employed is a short one or two second break in the drumming followed by four groups of seven beats. The drumming then resumes for several minutes, but at a faster pace than during the main journey. This period allows the journeyer to say farewell, return to the starting point and turn attention towards ordinary reality. Once returned, (and a predetermined signal can be agreed so that the drummer knows at what stage to conclude), the drummer gives a final call-back of four groups of seven beats.

Stopping the drum without any form of call-back can be extremely distressing to the journeyer. Even when the trance seems superficial, or the drum is no longer noticed in the awareness, the brain function has become entrained. A sudden cessation of the drum beat can be like throwing the journeyer straight from a deep sleep into ice-cold water!

Meeting Power Animals

Once you have become familiar and comfortable with the preliminary procedures and have a good feel for your drum, just spend time journeying with the sound, exploring how changes in the drum change your awareness, and meeting the spirit of the drum. This work establishes a firm basis for exploring the Three Worlds.

The next phase is to contact and to get to know spirits who will be your guides and guardians as you journey. In a great many traditional societies these personal guardians are animal spirits. To work safely and effectively in the shamanic spirit worlds it is necessary to accept that world -view as having an equal reality to our own ordinary reality. The problem with our usual view of reality is that it has become overburdened with human intellect and human values.

With the development of scientific rationalism in the 18th century, following the ideas of Descartes and his concept of a wholly mechanical universe, it became possible to see humans as separate from everything else – the only beings imbued with a rational mind and a perceptive soul. We still suffer from this limiting world-view today. Believing that humans are at the top of an evolutionary chain, we feel we are entitled to do anything we wish.

The shamanic world-view follows traditional patterns and sees human beings as simply another form of animal that relies on other plant and animal spirits to survive effectively on the planet. We are 'only human beings', with limited understanding and limited power. But we can learn to ask the appropriate spirits for help and advice. In order to work safely and effectively in the context of the Three Worlds it is necessary to adhere, accept and understand, this earlier cosmology.

To enter and work within non-ordinary realities it is helpful to feel 'non-ordinary' ourselves. Establishing a close relationship with an animal spirit blurs and shifts the normal human perspectives. The power animal is not just an ordinary animal, and the human being, who travels alongside it, is no longer just an ordinary human being.

The guardian animal, or power animal, is a distinct entity with awareness and personality of its own, yet it also shares energy, and is connected with, the archetypal animal of that species. It is one, but it also carries the energy and awareness of all. In a similar way there is a fluid but profound link between human being and power animal – a sharing of heart and a sharing of view, so that a merging of awareness can occur in and out of journey space.

Although plants are our progenitors and our healers, we share the world with animals in a much more visceral way. Looking into an animal's eyes reconnects us immediately with the presence of awareness of the World. It acknowledges and re-affirms our right to be alongside all other living creatures, sharing experience of life and the senses. Animals teach humans to stop living in the head and to begin to see with the heart. Animals cannot pretend what is happening is not really happening! Animals cannot disguise or excuse a desire, dressing it up as something else. The honesty, spontaneity, naturalness, transparency and clarity of animals is carried by the guardian animal spirit and imbues the practitioner with those traits that are essential for travelling in non-ordinary reality.

Each person has certain qualities of energy, certain ways of seeing, being and holding themselves. These tendencies are often emphasised and purified in the guardian animals that appear to us. However, what we learn to express in our lives, our survival tactics, are not necessarily anything other than a disguise to avoid problems and difficulties. A timid person may have learned timidity because a show of strength often seems to create more problems. In such a case the guardian animal is more likely to be a tiger than a mouse.

As part of the web of the world we cannot fail to be connected energetically to those other beings that resonate with the way we are as individuals, groups, families, tribes, nations. Becoming aware of guardian animal spirits is not so much a process of hunting and finding them as paying attention, being open and receptive and recognising their presence. It is not, for example, like a line-up for a school sports team: there is no need to worry about whose side you will be on or whether you will be selected at all!

Much of the available popular information on the subject of power animals derives from Native American Indian traditions, particularly the Plains tribal groups. The animals familiar to these peoples became woven into their cosmology. Cosmology, though, is not a science. It is an effective means to integrate the individual and the tribe with the Land where they dwell. It is therefore often inappropriate to transplant one cosmology to another place. For people who don't know the smell of a buffalo, the fear that the sound of a rattlesnake induces, whose only knowledge of the hummingbird or the dolphin is from natural history programmes on the television, it becomes a little bizarre that such exotic, foreign beasties should pop up in their journeys. The mind will supply the closest approximation to the spirit energies that it encounters and if the vocabulary available is meagre, then the imagery may also be limited or borrowed.

Many of us would be hard-pressed to name, or recognise the signs of, more than five or six plants, insects, animals and birds that live in the area where we live. Proper relationship requires recognition. Why working within the Three Worlds is so valuable is that it ties us more fully into the energy of the physical universe around us. Shamanic work is wholly practical. It is fuelled and driven by practical needs. It fails only when it fails to produce change at the level of ordinary, physical reality. Initial experience of guardian spirits and power animals in journeying may reflect a lack of local awareness. However, if the practitioner continues to work at this general, mythic level, there could be the possibility that there is not as much meat in the sandwich as supposed. Engaged shamanism is running headlong into reality, not running away into an idealised past.

Although the methods described here follow the processes used in core shamanism, it would be equally helpful to examine the possibility of other techniques. Kaledon Naddair and other British-based teachers within the druidic tradition suggest that the process takes as long as is needed. By exploring the native animals and birds, learning to identify them, studying habits and behaviour, looking at images, remembering encounters with animals that appear special or significant in some way, a truly personal 'feel' for some species emerges that reflects energetic links and an affinity that can become a relationship of guardianship and guidance.

Solo Calling of the Animals

1) Darken the room you are working in so that it is only lit by the natural light of a fire or candle flame.

2) Burn some incense or herbs and recognise, by offering the smoke or by rattling or drumming, the Elements and the Directions. This begins the process of entering a receptive trance state and lets the spirits know that you are working.

3) Sit on the floor, relax and begin to drum or rattle with a steady, mesmerising beat. Keep your eyes closed or slightly parted as you gaze at the fire or candle flame.

4) Let yourself be open to images and sounds of animals. Just let the images come and go through your mind as you drum or rattle.

5) After some while one animal will seem to be more persistent in its appearances. Ask if it is your power animal or guardian animal spirit and see how it responds. By a sign, behaviour or message it will become clear to you.

6) When your animal has appeared continue to drum or rattle while you maintain your attention on its presence. Feel the

nature of its power and energy. If you want, you can get up and begin to move with the energy of the animal as it moves through you.

7) Continue until you feel a strong solid connection with the animal. As you stop ask the animal to leave some of its spirit energy with you in your body.

Group Calling the Animals

1) Darken the room and light candles or a fire. Call up the Directions and Elements.

2) A drummer will establish a steady trance beat.

3) Stand with your eyes closed or half-closed so that you are focused within yourself. Use a rattle, or have a rattle in each hand and begin to follow the rhythm of the drum.

4) Simply rattle and move on the spot in whatever way you feel. Allow the energy to build up, and then simply move within that energy.

5) Don't get stuck in anticipating an animal spirit or even trying to identify a presence that you feel.

6) As you dance and rattle you will loosen up. You may feel a change of emotional state and a need to release sounds. If you are in a situation that allows it, go ahead and make noise. If not, noise can be quiet and just as effective – whistling, mumbling, grunting, whispering. Allow your body the space to know what it's doing.

7) Very often this sort of work gives the body energy and an opportunity to release deep stresses. This may release as sound or yawning, crying, jerking or shaking. Simply continue rattling and dancing and feel the energy of your helping

animal spirit.

8) If you are in a group it is important to keep the process internal – your eyes shut or downcast – and be aware that your presence and actions don't unduly interfere with those of your neighbours. You will also be more aware of the room becoming very busy with animals moving through and around your dance circle.

9) At the end, lie down and relax. Ask your animal to integrate with your energy and to keep in contact. Don't forget your pleases and thank you's.

Journeying to Find a Power Animal

To do this process you will need to have already established your entrances to the Three Worlds (see later exercises).

1) Follow all preliminary protocols and proceed along your Lower World tunnel.

2) An animal or animals may join you as you travel along the tunnel, or there may be one waiting upon your exit from the tunnel. In these cases ask if it is your power animal and look for a clear sign. Spend the rest of the journey getting to know it. Ask the animal to show you its skills and powers.

3) If no animals show themselves immediately, just start looking around and paying attention. Make clear your intention to find your power animal and send out a call for it. It is quite common to see brief glimpses before a clear identification is possible.

4) As many different animal spirits may be present, a common verification of power animals is that they are seen four distinct times, and that when asked they will display a clear sign of their connection to you.

The Nature of Power Animals

Guardian animal spirits and power animals are not simply a non-physical member of that animal species. They exhibit abilities that clearly show their special natures. They will be able to move through any element with equal ease. They can change size and they can change form whenever necessary, often appearing as a human being or a part human, part animal. Communication may be by behaviour, by telepathy or by voice.

Guardian animals may be of any species, though cultural preferences often favour some over others. Without elaborating very much, Michael Harner in 'The Way of the Shaman' suggests that aggressive insects and fish with teeth are best avoided in journeys as they may represent hostile energies. Domestic animals are also considered inappropriate, though many of these animals have been clearly significant in the past. For example cattle were sacred from Egypt, to India, to Scandinavia, to Ireland and were clear representations of specific aspects of power. Dogs and cats likewise have huge mythic history. Horses seem to be acceptable as power animals, even though few exist as truly wild animals. In the end any animal spirit that will be able to guide and protect you in the Three Worlds will be a power animal for you.

Mythical animals may also present themselves to you as a guardian spirit. In this case they are already dwelling within the flexible boundaries of the non-ordinary realms, often sharing the qualities of different Elements or an amalgamation of animals. In some cultures such animal guides are considered to be signs of special powers or aptitudes in the human with whom they are connected.

As the shamanic practitioner develops, the requirements of skills and power also change. This can lead to a changing of the primary guardian spirit or the addition of other animal spirits. At least to begin with, there may be some flexibility as

114

to the nature of the power animal until stability and clarity is established in the practice. The teacher of beginners is not necessarily the teacher most useful later on in one's studies. A change of power animal often indicates a new phase of working in the spirit worlds.

There is often a distinction made between guardian animal spirits and allies. Guardian spirits maintain the energy integrity and safety of their charge as they move through the spirit worlds. Allies are those spirits that may be of use for very specific purposes, such as healing a particular disease state or bringing knowledge of techniques or ritual. Allies are called by the journeyer when necessary, or turn up spontaneously where they are needed. Guardian spirits are constantly present, even though they may be simply keeping a watchful eye from a distance.

The behaviour of animal spirits may often seem peculiar or inappropriate from a limited human perspective. Remember that what we experience in trance states is the translation of subtle energy exchanges into mental picture stories that we can perceive with the inner senses. The animal guardian is wholly beneficial to the person they guard. Aggressive displays and any other interactions are simply the expressions of power and the transferral of energies that you need at that moment. If you see all your interactions with spirits as a continuous exchange of energy and information it will be easier for you to understand what is really going on during your trance journeys.

Using Discretion

The power animal is your most intimate associate in your work within the Three Worlds. As a source of your power and confidence it is not advisable to tell everyone the nature of your power animal. It is especially unwise to tell its name, if you have been told it – unless you have been specifically asked by your guardian to do so. On the most mundane level this avoids the tedious one-upmanship that occurs between individuals: the 'I've got better / bigger / more / power animals than you....etc.' Choosing to wear or display the attributes of your spirit animals should also be considered carefully. The same consideration should be given to any personal spirit names that you have acquired. These reflect fundamental energy qualities that you possess, and they are a means to track your unique signature wherever you may be.

A major oversight in the modern Western view of shamanic practices is the underestimation of the potential problems caused by what has been called the 'evil eye', 'sorcery' or 'witchcraft'. Within the traditional contexts of shamanic work the majority of cases requiring healing, soul retrieval and the like, are seen as being initially caused by the malevolent influence of spirits or other human beings. This rather dark view is often glossed over by commentators as though it were a superstitious cultural element in an otherwise spiritually uplifting technology. In fact, it is more likely that it is highlighting our own naivety and lack of willingness to recognise the subtle disruptive influences that our human emotions and strong desires have on the environment around us.

In the *Taittiriya Upanishad* there is a verse that begins:

> "Oh, wonderful! Oh, wonderful! Oh, wonderful!
> I am food! I am food! I am food!
> I am the food-eater! I am the food-eater! I am the food-eater!
> I am the singer! [literally: 'verse spinner'] I am the singer! I am the singer!
> I am the first-born of Truth........"

If a shamanic practitioner hasn't grasped this reality for themselves within the first few months of beginning work

116

they will be constantly fighting against the stream and will find it difficult to achieve any lasting benefits. For we must understand that all the worlds rely on constant exchange of energy and power. When we are not consuming energy or power, we are being consumed for our energy or power. This is the nature of existence. Some cultures present this flow as a violent fight, others will describe it using gentler analogies. The shaman understands the process and aims to manipulate the balance slightly to favour a positive equilibrium. The wise shaman will keep a low profile and will only manifest power as and when it is needed. To do otherwise would be to invite any hungry spirit, human or otherwise, to come and sup on the abundant energy radiating out for all to see. Those who lack power will seek power, those who lack food will seek food. There need be no moral judgements involved here, there is no right or wrong at this level. Every being has an equal right to survive. The system is well illustrated in the interactions of myth and fairy tale. In traditional cultures these oral teachings told everyone of the ground rules to follow in physical and non-physical reality. Reading these stories as if they were records of actual shamanic journeys can teach us a lot about how to survive on many different levels of awareness.

Beginning to journey to the Lower World

The Lower World is the foundation of all levels of existence. Hence it is often the first place the shaman will go for evaluating the power problems of the client and for seeking solutions by finding a more appropriate power. It is the roots of the World Tree, sustaining and upholding what is apparent in the world above, where we live our everyday lives. The Lower World is not the Underworld nor is it the Unconscious nor is it simply underground, though it can share aspects of all these concepts. As the source of energy and power for all things that exist, the Lower World contains within it all

117

possible expressions of time and place. The Lower World, like all of the Three Worlds, is not far away. It is right here. All that is needed is a sure method of turning our attention towards it, an entrance to the spirit worlds. Because it is within and beneath common perception, the doorway to the Lower World is conceived as a downward leading path or tunnel into the Earth. In some cultures the shaman does actually travel downward beneath the surface – into caves or ravines or into ritual buildings built into the ground, reinforcing the process of turning away from the normal world of light and noise. What is certainly required to enter the Lower World is the memory, if not the actual presence, of some kind of entrance into the ground. The nature and the size of the hole is less important than the automatic attraction it holds for the mind. A cave mouth, a well, a crack or crevice in a rock, an animal's burrow, a hollow tree or a space between tree roots, a spring - as long as the mind moves downward and is enveloped by the entrance it will work well. The entrance must exist in this world because it is this world that is our starting point. An imaginary entrance is much more likely to lead only into the world of the personal imagination.

First Journey into the Lower World

Take about ten minutes to make this initial journey and repeat it as necessary to refresh your experience and gain confidence in the process of journeying.

1) Follow your preliminary protocols and darken the room. Lie comfortably on the floor. Use a pillow or blankets to prop up your head or knees if you need to. Use a scarf to put over your eyes – this will help to cut out light a little more.

2) Relax and get yourself comfortable. A light blanket over you might keep away draughts and cocoon you from your ordinary world. Take a couple of deep, slow breaths and begin

to imagine the entrance to the Lower World that you have chosen. Use the memory of all your senses to bring that place to life. See all the surroundings as clearly as you can, as if you are really there.

3) As the drumming starts maintain your attention on the entrance and begin to move towards it. As you pass the threshold imagine strongly that you are entering into a downward moving passage or tunnel of some kind. Stand there for a while and let it form around you. If your attention wanders, just return to your starting point outside the mouth of the tunnel and repeat the process again. At this stage of the journey it is essential that you actively engage your imagination.

4) Move along the tunnel. Make yourself see with your imagination and travel down the tunnel. The speed you move will vary. If there seem to be obstacles, easily move round or through them. If you come across an insurmountable obstacle or the way is blocked somehow, return up the tunnel and begin again.

5) As you progress down the tunnel you will begin to see a lighted exit. As you reach the end of the tunnel you will find yourself in a landscape. Look around. Take time to stand there at the end of the tunnel and look out onto the Lower World. Take time for your subtle mind and senses to engage themselves and make sense of what they perceive.

6) If your guardian animal spirit hasn't already joined you, call it to you now so that it can show you around this part of the Lower World.

7) When you become aware of the call-back drum, say to your animal spirit that it is now time to return. It will accompany you back to the tunnel mouth and may well follow you as you move up towards the original entrance in this world.

Remember to thank your power animal before you leave.

8) Allow some time to review your experiences and to get fully aware of your body before opening your eyes or moving around.

Use these first few journeys to become better acquainted with your animal spirit. Learn its abilities, its favourite places and power spots and also places where you can access power or healing for yourself.

Journeys to the Lower World

For succeeding journeys to the Lower World remember to follow these steps.

1) Lie on the floor, eyes closed.

2) Repeat to yourself the intention of the journey three times.

3) The drum begins.

4) See the entry to the Lower World. Look around, engage your senses.

5) Pass through the entrance and down the tunnel, emerging into the Lower World.

6) If your power animal is not already there, call it to join you.

7) Tell your power animal of the purpose for your journeying.

8) Follow the guidance of your guardian animal.

9) When you hear the call back signal, or when the journey has been successfully concluded, ask to be led back to the tunnel. Say your thanks.

10) Travel back up the tunnel, come out of the entrance, and look around. Slowly let the scene fade and become aware of your physical surroundings once more.

Hollow trees are the access points to the Lower World in several cultures of America and Australia. Michael Harner was taught by the Conibo Indians of the Peruvian Amazon to follow the roots of a giant catahua tree down into the ground so as to reach the Lower World. Following this example might prove useful in order to explore a tree's subtle energy connections to its location and to understand the energy forms of the land where it dwells. There are several root-following techniques described in the Tree Seer work that have been found very effective at revealing hidden information.

Journeying to the Upper World

As the Lower World is equated with a downward journey into the earth, so the Upper World is an ascent into the sky. But in the same way as the tunnel leads to a different reality, rather than ending in dirt and rocks, the ascent passes beyond the sky, beyond the stars, beyond space into another dimension. To access the Upper World it is necessary to pass through an opening or hole in the sky. This can be seen as equivalent to being able to 'see through' ordinary reality, to 'reach new heights' of perception and understanding.

To journey to the Upper World it is necessary to have a place or a means of ascent that is anchored in this ordinary reality. Sometimes it is convenient to have an Upper World pathway located right next to your Lower World entrance. Again the actual means that is used is not as important as the fact that it must lead upwards into the sky. Stars and the red light of sunset have been traditional ways to get beyond the sky. Climbing up a tree or a pole, a vine, beanstalk, cord, ladder or rope are all well-known methods. Using smoke from incense or a fire, climbing through the smokehole in a lodge or up a chimney is also effective. Rising on thermals, slipping up rainbows, riding slanting rays of sunlight and climbing up steep hills or mountains all help to reach that place where the sky thins and the traveller can push through to the 'other side of the sky'.

The Upper World is a place to gain clarity and understanding. As you begin to journey here it is a good idea to ask your guardian animal to lead you to a spirit teacher or celestial guide and take the time to become familiar with the feel of the energy and the different types of landscapes that can be encountered here.

First Journey to the Upper World

1) Prepare yourself as usual, following the preliminary procedures. Lie on the floor and cover the eyes.

2) Focus on the intent of the journey, to visit the Upper World, and repeat the intention clearly three times.

3) Next, begin to call up into your mind the memory of the place and method by which you have chosen to ascend. Take a moment to fully engage all your senses on this process.

4) As the drum begins, begin to ascend, and continue until you pass through an opening in the sky of some kind. This may be easy or there may be a sensation of pushing against an elastic membrane. If your power animal is not already with you, call it to help you find an opening that you can pass through into the Upper World landscapes.

5) Repeat to your power animal the purpose of the journey and follow the animal as it guides you in your exploration.

6) When the call-back is heard, or when the purpose has been achieved, ask your guardian animal to lead you back to the

opening in the sky.

7) Return down your ascent path and find yourself back in the natural place where you began. Take time to feel back on the ground, look around again, and slowly let the imagery fade as you return to awareness of the body and the room around you.

Miððle Worlð Journeys

The Middle World is not the same as our ordinary reality, but it is that ordinary reality viewed through the lenses of spiritual perception. The Middle World journey allows a vision of the spirit reality that resides behind and within the tangibility of the physical world. Middle World journeys always have reference points that are recognisable to us as real places, even though they may appear very different through the non-ordinary perceptions of trance awareness. The Middle World journey re-connects us to the sentience of all beings and things because we are able to look beyond the outer, symbolic form to the functioning reality of the world. These journeys can be useful in teaching us about the nature and properties of the beings around us, and really help us to establish a relationship with the world.

The Middle World journey begins by travelling, not up nor down, but along. It is possible to begin a Middle World journey from the same starting point as the other worlds – simply meet your guardian animal and move off in some direction across the surface of the earth. Alternatively, and perhaps more logically, begin from wherever you are and return to your physical location at the end of the process.

1) After completing your preparatory practices, lie on the floor and cover your eyes to reduce the light.

2) Repeat your intention or the purpose of the journey three times.

3) As the drum begins, see yourself lying on the floor. Call your animal spirit to join you and tell it your intended destination.

4) Then see yourself and your animal leave the room through the door, window, wall or whatever.

5) Reach your destination and fulfil your intention.

6) On hearing the call back signal, ask your power animal to return you to where you are lying.

7) Say goodbye and let your consciousness return to the room.

Remember that in Middle World journeys, like those to the other worlds, your intention is the guide. Whatever you experience will hold the answers or information you need, even though it may be in no way like 'normal' reality. If we journey to see particular people it will only usually be to a spiritual fragment relevant to our needs – so it may or may not seem to look like the physical form we know. The same goes for places with which we are familiar.

Middle World journeys enable us to visit times and places that are important to us. Remember that time and space are properties of the physical universe. In non-ordinary reality all times and all places are accessible in an instant.

The Three Worlds are very generalised categories of awareness. It is not necessary to   adhere rigidly to their apparent structure in all your journey work. They are, like all other descriptions of reality, a model or an analogy made simple so that it can be easily understood. A single journey may take you through many of the different levels in turn, regardless of where you thought you needed to go or what entrance you used.

Other types of journey can be helpful in broadening out your map of non-ordinary reality, and if you have established a good working relationship with one or more tree spirits you will probably be led to places not described in any of the literature. Making journeys to the spirits of the Directions, the Elements, the Planets, the Seasons, as well as to different animal, plant and mineral species will all help to root you deeper into the spirit reality of the planet and clarify your perspective and understanding.

Tom Cowan has suggested some interesting processes to explore new perceptions of the world.

Allies From The Four Directions

1. Take a separate journey to each of the four Directions.

2. Ask your animal spirit to introduce you to a helping spirit in each direction.

3. Learn the name of the spirit, or what name it would prefer to be called by you.

4. Ask what power or assistance you can access from that direction. Don't be swayed by general cultural attributes – this is a personal ally for your unique energy and needs.

The same process can be used to investigate all kinds of energies in order to understand their functions.

Journeying Between the Elements

Tom Cowan (in "*Shamanism as a spiritual practice for daily life*"), describes some interesting techniques that help to clarify the continual interactions, the flow of energy, between different beings and states. This is an important concept to explore because it helps to bypass the human tendency to define a thing too closely, limiting its definition and state to a false set of boundaries. The language of shamanism, the language of the spirits, is very often intentionally oblique, reflecting the fluidity of the non-physical worlds. This liminal world, where the boundaries between things are blurred and perceptions are difficult to interpret, is a common motif in Celtic mythology and always presages contact with spiritual beings or the Otherworld. Dawn and dusk, riverbanks, shorelines, crossroads all reflect places of flux where the normal sureness of the conscious mind is suspended, allowing new possibilities and choices to be made.

Going between the seams of things, between the wave and the beach, between the root and the soil, between the flame and the log, between the bud and the stem, between the hill and the valley, takes us away from the limitation of definitions into directly experiencing the interaction and transformation of the elemental forces of the world. Instead of looking in from the outside it becomes possible "to know the spirits of those elements in ways they know themselves. We understand the intelligent nature of non-human beings in ways that we cannot fathom from the perspective of ordinary awareness."

1. Light a candle. Place a fist-sized rock in a bowl of water. Place them on the floor and sit about eight to ten feet away from them.

2. Take deep, slow breaths and notice the stillpoints between when you are breathing in and out. Don't change the quality of your breathing at all – just be aware of those small points of stillness.

3. Begin to experience these points as places outside of time and space. A condition where there is neither inhaling, nor pausing, nor exhaling.

4. Now send your awareness out to the space between the rock and the water or to between the wick and the fire.

5. Hold your attention there for as long as possible.

6. At the end of the process consciously withdraw your energy and attention back into yourself.

7. Focus on the movement of the breath, and then open your eyes.

Using a gentle journey drumming can help to extend your length of focus. Because our minds are used to having a defined focus, this exploration of Void (not emptiness, but lack of form), can, until it is more familiar to us, feel very disorienting and even threatening. The very lack of hard and fast certainties softens our own boundaries and our sense of being a discrete, unique personality. Sitting with the fear or confusion that arises will allow it to subside as we learn that this experience of Void is not the same as annihilation.

Working at a Place

The same process can be used to explore the energies of places.

1. Use a small drum or rattle to call the spirits and to focus your own awareness.

2. Whilst sitting at the spot, select a 'twilight' space, a 'gap', that involves the land feature whose spirit you want to meet. For example, if it features an oak tree, focus on the space between root and soil. If it is a stream, select a place between rock and water.

3. Prepare yourself by watching the places between your breathing for a few moments.

4. When you feel ready, send your consciousness into the place in nature with the request that the element or feature that is the spirit of the place respond to you in a way that begins a dialogue or a merging so that you can learn from it.

5. When finished, say your thank you's, then carefully and completely withdraw back into yourself.

With larger landscapes Tom Cowan suggests that two features are selected between which you are sitting, such as a hilltop and a wood. Watch the space between breaths for a while and then, rather than sending your focus out, expand your awareness and call the spirits of those selected features to join you where you are. Once you have settled with the energy, then ask to meet the spirit of the whole area.

One of the major advantages of working in this way is that it becomes a more respectful method of approaching the spirits, allowing the possibility of polite refusal, rather than jumping in and demanding communication!

Tips for Trips - Advice for Making Journeys More Effective

The right energy state with the right intention, the old 'set and setting', are prerequisites to successful journeying. Stumbling blocks thereafter tend to be due to misunderstandings, misinterpretation or poor technique.

Before the journey begins relax your body as fully as possible (one of the advantages of dance or movement before settling down to trance). Take several deep, full breaths and really feel that you are inside your body. Putting attention on the body helps it to relax tension and also prevents the mind from anticipating the experience too much.

All your points of departure, your entrances to the Three Worlds, should really give you a powerful sense of their own presence. They should evoke strong, though not necessarily clearly defined, feelings. If you are unsure try out several different locations – it can make a huge difference to your experience of the non-ordinary realities.

Repeat your clear intent several times, then let it go. The more focused the intent, the easier it may be to interpret the experience in that light. A woolly intent is more likely to give a woolly experience. Likewise with the emotional charge: if the purpose of the journey is of burning importance to you, the experience will be fuelled by your passion.

It is your mind that opens the door to non-ordinary reality. There needs to be an initial phase where you tune into the spirit worlds by strongly imagining the tunnel, the climb, the arrival of your animal spirit. The second phase begins when the unexpected takes over and you turn into the observer of events rather than the creator of imagery.

One of the most difficult parts of non-ordinary travel is the tendency for the rational mind to analyse all that is going on and to give a running commentary. This cannot really be avoided, except by a fuller immersion in the experience. Learn to turn your attention to your senses instead of the thoughts. A good way to bring together mind and experience is to narrate out loud as you journey. Record the journey on tape or make a running report of it to your audience. In many shamanic rituals the shaman sings the journey so that all can participate. Think of this as live poetry or tuneless song, rather than a football commentary. Continuity and cause and effect are less important than the numinous feel of power and wonder that can be built up.

If you are not primarily visual, and only a third of people naturally are, don't waste time and energy trying to see.

'Seeing' is as much about feeling and understanding. In a situation where you can't follow what is happening, take time to explore each of your senses in turn to identify what they are receiving. Your thoughts and your emotional reactions should be observed in the same way as the other five senses. All give a clue to what is going on.

It is common to phase out, to drop attention, to drift away from the thread of the journey. This often happens when there is a sudden change of pace or energy input. Because this is non-ordinary reality, time and space do not follow the same rules, so you can simply intend to return to the last point you remember and continue again from there. If things get very hazy check with your animal spirit and repeat the intention of the journey again.

Some very helpful advice is to learn how to wait with attention. This is not a scheduled broadcast – there are often pauses and the need to remain in silence. Don't panic, don't rush. Allow the experience to unfold at its own pace instead of trying to control it. See if you can find a waiting song, a tune or chant, which will keep the mind calm and attentive rather than letting it sink into a critical internal dialogue.

Always trust the experience. Don't be tempted to re-invent it or re-interpret it. Don't judge it for being wrong, and don't make comparisons to the experience of others. Some people make better narrators than others – it doesn't mean the experience was any clearer or better than your own.

The effectiveness of the journey is measured by the usefulness of the information received, not by how long, how detailed or how spectacular the experience. If the name of a remedy is all that is required for you to hear, so be it.

What we experience in journeys are beings of power. Making judgements about the appearance of a spirit is best avoided.

131

Good and bad are human distinctions that should be put aside as soon as the journey begins. In non-ordinary reality there are only helpful or unhelpful energies, depending on our needs at the time. A monster that appears, a demon or ferocious animal that threatens us, is always an interpretation of that energy by the mind. Everything has more than one state of energy, everything can contain its opposite. Treated appropriately, a monster can shapeshift into a beautiful spirit. Treated inappropriately, a benevolent spirit can become its opposite. Be guided by your power animal and other allies. Don't take the rules of ordinary reality with you when you journey – you will be travelling through different lands with different languages and customs.

Chapter 6

Healing Techniques

Wooden Pendulums as Healing Tools

Most people are familiar with the concept, if not with the practice, of using a pendulum as a dowsing tool. A dowsing pendulum can be anything. It is a weight suspended so that it can swing freely on a string or chain. Any balanced weight will be adequate to dowse answers to questions because the pendulum is simply amplifying the body's own subtle responses to the queries the mind asks. Pendulum dowsing, like dowsing with rods or a hazel stick, requires considerable training and control. Vigilance is especially necessary to ensure that accuracy and relevance are maintained. Most people can be taught to dowse, but few learn the skills necessary to maintain their accuracy and questioning protocols.

Healing with pendulums, however, is a different matter altogether. Here, there is no need to follow any system of questioning. The movement of the pendulum is not interpreted in any way – except that when it is moving then work of some kind is being done, and when the pendulum stops moving, that work is complete. When healing with a pendulum, it appears that the only function of the healer is to hold the end of the string. In actual fact, of course, the pendulum is still reacting to the energy fields of the healer and the patient, but there is no interpretation going on. The advantage with pendulum healing is that it 'does itself'. It can be taught easily and can allow significant degrees of healing to occur. With a few simple guidelines it can be self-regulating, reducing the risk of unnecessary or inappropriate energy work being done. The technique is so simple and flexible that it can be adapted to a whole variety of situations equally effectively.

The material with which the pendulum is made is one of the most important factors. Every type of wood carries its own particular qualities. As a healer you might have a favourite wooden pendulum, but how do you know if its energy will be the most appropriate to the work needing to be done? If you have a selection of different woods made into pendulums how can you be sure that the best for the job has been chosen? There is a very useful technique that can help you to establish which will be the best pendulum for the job you have in mind.

Pendulum Over Palm Techniques

a) As with all pendulum healing work, first establish your working parameters.

b) Intend or clearly state: "That this pendulum will only move away from stationary (or from a neutral, back and forth swing), if it can safely, effectively and quickly remove energy imbalances from this person." Using the pendulum-over-palm method it will be slightly better to start from a stationary, non-moving pendulum, but if you prefer a neutral swing, that is also OK.

c) By holding the pendulum over the open left palm of the patient's hand you are in a way asking the question "Is there a need for this energy?", although there is no need to think or say this at all. Once this is understood by the healer, the question doesn't need to be thought or verbalised.

d) A stationary pendulum of whatever wood, held over an open left palm will move in some way away from stationary

(or neutral swing) whenever its energy is required. If movement does occur, two things can be done.

e) First, simply leave it there until it stops moving – then you know that the body has taken enough of that wood's qualities as it requires at that time.

f) Second, if it indicates by movement that it can be of use, simply use that pendulum in whatever other healing techniques you plan to use.

Different types of wood can be quickly tested to see if they are appropriate for the work by using small samples placed inside a silver spiral on a short string or chain. These metal spirals can be found where tumbled crystals are on sale. Alternatively, but not so conveniently, a piece of flexible wire or thread can be used. This makes it easy to construct a good range of pendulums without having to have a large number of different pendulums. Small bottles of tree essences can also be used in exactly the same way, tying thread around the dropper cap or using very small sample vials in a metal spiral.

Simply remember that any motion of the pendulum indicates that the energy is needed, and that the degree of motion gives you a good gauge of scale from 'not much' to 'gimme more'.

The left hand of the person requiring healing is used because it is this side of the body that tends to be absorbing and receiving. You may find in some cases that the right palm is better. If no response is found in one hand, try the other.

A more elaborate technique, again very flexible to use, is derived from a short suggestion in Gurudas' *"Gem Elixirs and Vibrational Healing Vol. 1"*

136

Five-Line Clearing

Using a wooden healing pendulum, (one that has already been found to be the best for this particular person at this time using the above technique), the whole of the patient's body and auric field is systematically scanned. The pendulum, given parameters by the healer's intent, identifies and clears imbalances as it comes across them.

1) Imagine the patient's body is divided along its length by five lines. The central line passes up the mid-line of the body from just below the feet to just above the head. The second and third lines are parallel to this but pass up the body further out – say approximately up the legs, nipples, shoulders, to the space between the shoulders and neck. Again, these lines begin just below the level of the feet and extend to above the head. The two outermost lines, four and five, are imagined as being just outside the physical edge of the body and so encompass the non-physical energies only. Moving a rotating or swinging pendulum up these lines you can see that every part of the body will be covered on one line or another.

2) First you have established that this pendulum is appropriate to use.

3) Clearly intend that only those imbalances that can be removed "quickly, safely and appropriately" will be recognised and dealt with. There is no place here for over-riding the patient body's knowledge of what is best for it. The healer in every instance simply gives space and encouragement to the patient's own healing. Anything more is in danger of becoming ego-based manipulation ('sorcery' etc.). As another safeguard, it is as well to check that you as healer are "ready, willing and able" to do the work, and that the patient is "ready, willing and able" to have the work done. There are limitless imbalances in any one individual. Even if you were

to completely balance every aspect, remove every trauma, dissolve every stress, repair every anomaly, there would still be a universe of healing to do. We do not exist in a vacuum but are infinitely and eternally linked to all other aspects of creation – which each have their stresses, imbalances etc. Once our own balance is achieved then we start to be able to process our macrocosmic stresses. Here is the reality of the enlightened state of bodhicitta and bodhisattva-hood. No one individual, (because none really exists), can become fully enlightened (free from imbalance at every level of body, mind, spirit), until all other parts of the universe have achieved the same state of purity. So don't think about grandiose healing – just do the job in front of you.

4) With five-line clearing the order you proceed in is not that important. But we usually begin with the midline, then move out to the second and third lines, and finally the fourth and fifth lines. Begin below the feet and move upwards. The speed you work depends on you and the parameters of the work. (see later for the options you might choose.)

5) Set the pendulum in an easy neutral swing, back and forth at right angles to your body (following the line of your lower arm as it holds the pendulum. (It is better with this technique to start with a neutral swing as it takes less time for the swing to change to a indicating/healing movement.)

6) Smoothly move up the body holding the pendulum centrally over the line you are working on. Whenever the pendulum moves away from a neutral swing (in whatever way) simply hold it there until the neutral swing returns. This indicates that a block that is able to be removed safely has been worked on, and that it has been cleared as much as is possible at that time. When the neutral swing returns simply carry on up the line. Do this with each line in turn.

Just because an imbalance appears related to a physical part of the patient does not in any way mean that location is the cause of an imbalance. It may or may not be. The beauty and great virtue of this technique is that speculation is unnecessary and irrelevant. We cannot know the pathways of stress and healing because they are completely individual and unique.

The healer's mind tends to run in neutral during this process. This can make coherent communication a little difficult, but this neutrality may also give space for feelings and intuitions to arise that relate to the patient or the healing work being done. It is up to the healer to decide if it is appropriate to speak or to remain silent, but sometimes it can be useful to mention when particular ideas emerge, as the patient can often relate these to a problem or to a stress factor in the past. As all subtle bodies interact and overlay one another, working the lines on the physical body will also be working on the emotional, mental and finer spiritual aspects of the patient. Working on the two outermost lines tends to show more of the subtle stresses involved.

Sometimes the pendulum will keep spinning over a place for a long time with no apparent reduction in momentum. If there is not time to dwell there or if the healer is beginning to tire there are two options:

a) If you have woods, tree essences or other healing items, choose one by intuition or dowsing and place it on that area of imbalance. You will know that you have the right item, because once in place, the healing pendulum held above it will return to a neutral swing. Leave the item there whilst you continue the rest of the line. When done, remove the item and hold the pendulum over the area again. If the work is completed the pendulum will stay in a neutral swing. If more work needs doing (indicated by the resumption of a spin), test the item on the spot again and leave it to continue its work.

Another item may be needed if the pendulum doesn't return to neutral when the first item is put back in place.

b) If you don't have any other healing items, allow your mind to focus more sharply on that area and will the body to place its attention there to balance the stress. If in doubt, just carry on the line. Sometimes stresses need to be released in a particular order and a stubborn stress will easily balance itself once another area has been cleared.

6) When finished, intend clearly that the patient's energy field is grounded, balanced and brought back to a normal level of functioning. Remember to cleanse energetically your healing pendulum and any other items you have used before they are put to work again.

Options For Five-Line Clearing

1) Simply use the wooden pendulum as an assessment tool to show where imbalances are. Instead of keeping the pendulum in place until it returns to neutral, simply move on and record on a diagram etc. which areas show energy imbalance. This is a good technique to give you an overall view of what areas may need close attention.

2) Five-line clearing can be tailored to deal only with particular issues. This is created by the intention of the healer before working. For example:

- to clear stresses related to a particular set of symptoms (i.e. easing pain, improving function etc.)

- to release imbalances from specific levels of the patient (i.e. only the emotional, mental, spiritual bodies, or each subtle body in turn from physical, etheric, emotional, mental, astral, causal, soul, spiritual – this of course would take quite a session to achieve, but remember that only those appropriate stressors will show up in the work).

- To balance the patient in order to achieve a goal or outcome that is desired. This will then help to get rid of those blocks that are preventing success.

This will give you some idea how versatile a technique five-line clearing can be.

Five-line clearing can be done on yourself by drawing an outline person on a sheet of paper that then represents you. A witness, like a signature or piece of hair can help strengthen the link. Then simply dowse the lines as you would with a patient present. This can also be used as an absent healing technique, remembering that absent healing work needs energy permission to be ethical and requires impeccable personal energy management by the healer in order to avoid energetic problems arising.

Breath Spirit Healing

This method of tree spirit healing specifically derives from traditional Tibetan methods, though similar processes can be found in many traditional societies. Breath spirit healing potentises a material, in this case herbs, tree materials or incense, with the power of breath, sound and mind. It can be used to bring a certain tree energy into a person's life, to help with creating a closer personal and energy tie to that tree or to bring in an energy that is lacking so that healing can be more effective.

For those who want to immerse themselves in the wisdom energy of a particular tree this technique is invaluable. The process itself brings a closer attunement, and by using the empowered material that is created, the effect can be further enhanced.

1) Some vessel is required to hold the original material. In Tibet this is usually an animal horn fitted with a removable stopper and a small dispensing spatula, or a wooden replica of a horn. A deep wooden bowl could be used, though it is more practical to use a box or container with a lid, drilled with a small hole. (This allows the breath to be forcefully infused into the material without it blowing back into your face and all around the room!) Without such a method it would be possible only with a heavier, denser carrying medium, such as bark, roots or twigs. A turned, wooden pill-box makes a good container: it has a removable lid to place the material inside and usually has a good seal so that the empowered material can be stored in it. By drilling a small hole through the top and by making a wooden plug for that hole, a really efficient vessel can be made. Using a container that is made of the same, or another harmonious, type of wood to the energy you are infusing will naturally amplify the end product.

2) Once you have a good container the next consideration is the material that you will be infusing with tree spirit energy. The first choice would be material from the tree itself: leaf, flowers, fruit, bark and so on. However, whatever the material, it should be appropriate for how it is going to be used and above all, safe to use. Unless there is certainty about the safety of a tree material, it is better to use a neutral carrier. If the empowered carrier is going to be used as a medicine tea, for example, something like peppermint leaves, elderflowers, rose petals, linden flowers or any appropriate herb tea can be used. Neutral sugar or sac-lac tablets, as used by homoeopaths, are an easy way to take the spirit energy internally. If the material is going to be used as an incense a pleasant scented, slow-burning herb like cypress, pine, lavender, woodruff or mugwort can be used.

3) Place the carrier material within the container and reseal the lid. Hold it in your hands or place it close to you whilst you build up the spirit energy inside of you. Sit comfortably

and turn your attention to the tree spirit that you wish to infuse. The easiest way is to repeat quietly to yourself the tree mantra, feeling the tree's energy fill your body. Continue for as long as you can maintain attention without losing focus – begin with periods of not more than two minutes. At the end of each period, take the stopper from the hole you have made in the top of the container, and forcefully blow all the accumulated tree spirit energy into the herbal material. Replace the stopper and sit quietly for a moment before repeating the build-up of energy inside you. Depending on the circumstances the whole empowerment can be completed in one session, or spend a little time each day for a week charging the material.

4) Alternatively, combine the mind with the breath, and as you gaze at the tree itself, its visual symbol, its leaf, its form or even just its name, imagine that with each inbreath you are drawing in the spirit energy of the tree whilst every outbreath concentrates that energy at your heart, solar plexus or hara from where it can be blown out into the material carrier. (If you are using a tree itself as a focus make sure that full agreement has been established between you and leave a suitable offering).

5) At the end of the empowerment, or between sessions, make sure that the herbal material is well-aired and dry, otherwise mould might form. Label the material both with what it is and with what energy it has been empowered.

Elemental Balancing

Trees by their very nature have learned to remain in balance with all the elements that surround them. Without such balance they would be unable to survive in one place. In this way, trees express a holistic balance through their own unique and particular balance of Elemental forces. Because each tree species has evolved to take advantage of different conditions, each demonstrates a particular Elemental picture that can be helpful to the healing of an individual. Identifying the trees required for a healing situation can thus help to reveal a person's unique state of Elemental balance or imbalance. Such an assessment of tree energies, when placed with keywords and descriptions, can help to show strengths, weaknesses and patterns that the individual is working through at that time. This diagnostic approach can be helpful in clarifying the understanding, but it is not necessary for effective healing – which can rely solely on the inherent energy of the trees themselves. Simply placing the tree energies in an appropriate energetic relationship on or around the patient can open the correct healing pathways and bring about an Elemental re-balancing at quite deep levels.

"Two Wheels" Elemental Balance

In all cultures the Elements are associated with the cardinal directions of the compass. However, every tribal grouping, religious tradition or philosophy, places the Elements at different positions with a great variety of different associations of colour, emotion and meaning. The human need is for local order. Things have to make sense on the ground, in the landscape, throughout the life of the tribe, and because local geographies and climates are so various, so are the correspondences that emerge.

In this type of healing, then, there is no need to know and use a formal relationship between Directions and Elements – unless it is the wish of the healer and the patient to adhere to a certain cultural pattern. What is important is to establish the correct relationship between the patient and the environment, an appropriate orientation between the inner, personal microcosmic Elements and the outer, macrocosmic Elements of the world at large. The macrocosmic energies, after all, are the resources that our inner energies draw on for nutrition and balance. Any incorrect relationship of these two

144

is likely to develop into an inability to heal effectively.

Once the correct relationship has been established between the individual and the world at large (the first cog or wheel of this healing procedure), then the specific tree energies can be introduced that will ease the effective flow of energy between the outer and inner Elements and bring an internal balance (the second cog or wheel that integrates the relationship of the Elements in the body).

Procedure:

1) Assess which is the optimal direction to which the person should be facing. (or, if lying down, which way the head should be directed). This is easily achieved by getting the patient to take a moment or two to settle and become aware of how they are feeling and sensing, and then asking them to turn slowly in a circle a couple of times and simply stop and face the direction that feels most comfortable. Whether they stand or sit, they remain facing this way throughout the healing.

2) If a fixed cosmological system is not going to be used, the next step is simply to find which tree energy (in the form of a wood sample, tree essence etc.) is to be placed in relation to the patient. Which wood is to be placed at the front, at the back, to the left, to the right, and at the centre (held in the hands, for example).

3) (If a fixed system is going to be used then there is usually a natural correlation between which Element is seen as being in front, to the left and so on. How these theoretical dimensions relate to the actual physical position chosen by the patient may offer an added level of explanation. For example, the South might be seen as where we naturally face, with the North to our backs, and so on. If the patient has intuitively chosen to face West, this might, within the system being used,

indicate a certain type of Elemental imbalance. A generally applicable example of how the Directions might relate to behavioural tendencies and qualities of awareness could be: FRONT: to where one looks, the future, goals, hopes and aspirations, vision, motivation. BACK: causes of current states, originating factors, stimulus, reasons, motivating forces, the past. LEFT: emotional patterns, needs, support, gestalt (intuitive wholes). RIGHT: mental patterning, belief systems, strategies, conceptions and misconceptions. CENTRE: core balancing traits, equilibrium factors, judgement, focus of awareness, personal balancing trend.).

4) Once all the tree energies are in place there will be an interaction between all the forces involved. The patient should be asked to maintain an awareness of the presence of the different wood energies around them and to be open to any movements or shifts of energy at the level of feeling, emotion or thought processes.

5) The process is complete when the patient no longer feels movements of energy and when there is a feeling of centred balance, or a feeling of 'return'.

6) Remove all the tree energies and take a little time to relax before resuming normal activity.

Using a simple journey drumming throughout the process can help to integrate the process more rapidly and relax the patient. Using the spirit imagery or the mantra of the tree whilst placing the balancing materials can also increase the energy flow.

"Three Tree Healing"

This is another pattern of tree energies that can be helpful to achieve balance, stability and security. It can help to release creative potential by shifting blocks and changing how circumstances are viewed.

The idea for this healing technique arose whilst working with the energies of juniper and spruce. An understanding arose that certain types of tree in an environment form a triplicity of energy that maintains and upholds the spirit of a place. For the land in Sweden this balance of polarity seems to be held by juniper, spruce and pine. Perhaps in Britain the tree energies that balance polarities may be the traditional triplicity of oak, ash and thorn.

In the healing of an individual's spiritual space 'Three Trees' can be used whenever there is a loss of centre, an instability where there is a questioning of identity and purpose. It will also help to resolve problems in the acceptance of the reality of opposites – where there is a denial of the validity of polarity, the full pendulum swing of human existence from one extreme of experience to the other.

All triple concepts can be brought to a new resolution: left –right – centre (this might be present in physical coordination problems and mental confusion); male – female – neutral (in sexual identity and roles); mother – father – child (in nearly all relationships with other people and with the world); contraction – expansion – equilibrium (the nature of all states of matter and activity); body – mind – emotion (or other triplicities that define the human energy systems); past – present – future (the traps of cause and effect, habit patterns and fears).

In the Vedic philosophy of India the archetypal triplicity is defined as sattva, rajas and tamas, called the three 'gunas' that manifest all creation from the three primal deities, Vishnu, Brahma and Siva, down to the creation of the Elements that combine to form time and space.

Sattva is the cohesive tendency, represented by the deity Vishnu, the Preserver. All the universe tends to gravitate towards the centre, towards more concentration, more cohesion, more existence, more reality, light, truth and so on.

Tamas is the tendency towards disintegration, represented by the deity Siva, the Destroyer. Everything that is, must come to an end. Tamas is centrifugal energy that leads to inertia, the movement towards dispersal, disintegration and annihilation. It is the desire to be still, to be the boundless Void, to sink into the substratum of existence, to become indestructible.

Rajas is the tendency to resolve and balance, represented by the deity Brahma, the Creator. All manifestation depends on the correct balance of cohesion and dissolution, Vishnu and Siva, sattva and tamas. Rajas manifests as a revolving energy, space- creating and time-creating.

With these three fundamental triple energies brought to a balance it is potentially possible to remove all problems to do with outcomes and resolutions. 'Three Trees' will help manifestation and solidity because it balances all three fundamental tendencies of creation.

Procedure:

1) In every case, as the imbalances are unique to each person and situation, it will be necessary to find out the most appropriate three tree energies to use. This can be done by dowsing (or, for example, using the wooden pendulum over the hands as previously described), by intuition or by divinatory journeying or dream.

2) The next stage is to determine how the trees are going to be placed in relation to the body or the space. These three trees

will form a triangular relationship upon, around or within the body of the individual or environment being treated. For example, if the person is seated on the ground, one tree's energy might be placed to the front and the others to either side. Alternatively, the trees might need to be placed in a triangular relationship upon the body, such as in either hand and at the heart. One or more trees may need to be outside of the person's energy field. Begin by finding the place of one tree and then move on to the others. The orientation in space will be unique to each case, but it will always be triangular.

3) The final assessment will determine what is the best form for the tree energies   to take. There can be many alternatives: samples of the wood ; tree essences, either in their bottles or as drops; the tree spirits can be placed or invited to inhabit the space and balance the person; the mantra, colours, visual patterns and other attunement methods can be used.

4) As with Elemental Balancing ask the patient to remain open and aware of the energy relationships. As the process comes to a close the attention will naturally return to a focused awareness calmly resting within the body. Any feelings of tension or discomfort, physical or emotional, can be eased by attention to the movement of breath in and out of the body.

5) Carefully remove the tree energies or ask the spirits to return to their places and allow time for the patient to settle into the new balance before asking them to move or return to normal activity.

6) Check whether any support is needed to maintain the new state. This might be a process of bringing to mind those trees used, or to take the tree essences, or to repeat the mantras, or simply to recall the triangular relationship of all energies. The process may need to be repeated several times if old

patterns re-assert themselves after a little time. If this is the case begin the process from scratch – the trees needed may have changed.

Tree Essences and the Nature of Flower Essences

Putting aside vague references from some ancient and traditional sources that are open to interpretation, flower essences were developed in Britain by Dr. Edward Bach in the 1920s and 1930's as a way for ordinary people to reduce the emotional roots of their illness patterns. Although a GP and a homoeopathic doctor, Bach saw his Remedies essentially as a soul medicine. He discerned types of behaviour, corresponding to, but not overtly related to the twelve zodiac signs, and found those flowers that would help to balance the negative states each type tended to demonstrate when under the pressure of stress and illness. These original 'Twelve Healers' were termed 'soul healers'. Later, Bach added remedies that were to address temporary states brought on, not by the soul's own patterning, but by the circumstances of life.

Flower essences have a very specific preparation. Made by placing flowers from the same species on the surface of pure water held in an unmarked glass bowl in full sunlight. The water, after several hours at least, is potentised by the process and bottled with alcohol as a preservative. (See the previous Tree Seer volumes for more details)

In those days the herbal roots of medicine were still apparent and obvious. Medicine was a guild rather than an industrial complex. Flower remedies were a fringe development from out of homeopathy and herbal traditions. Today the situation is very different. There are many thousands of flower essences worldwide, and although the majority are small and locally active in their own communities, the alternative systems of healing are increasingly seen as a threat to established medical monopolies. It is no longer possible to call anything except the original Bach preparations 'remedies', because this implies medicinal properties and therefore medicine, which requires a medical license and industrial processes to comply with governmental regulation (under advice from the experts who work for the multinational petrochemical-pharmaceutical corporations). It is no longer possible to define or describe flower essences in terms of their potential for healing physical symptoms or conditions of a medical nature, despite the wish of many practitioners and journalists to offer 'fixes' for this or that complaint. At the roots of this tangled state is an inability to change perceptions about the nature of wellness and illness. Even the most ardent complementary therapist has a tendency to fall into mainstream, orthodox thinking, tainted by the two-hundred year old model of a mechanistic universe that colours all education and 'expert' opinion. The head rules the heart, the intellect rules the mind, the expert rules the masses, science rules nature.

Science has developed so that we can analyse and define. It relies upon scientific method, which itself is totally dependant on repeatability. If an experiment cannot be verified by repetition, it cannot be held to be scientifically valid. Because of this peculiarity, one-off events are invisible to science.

Unfortunately, life itself is a non-repeating process. Life that is pinned down simply ceases to be alive. Similar patterns do re-occur, but variables are the only stable factor. Nothing in life is repeatable. Time and space are simply not compatible with repetition. Science thus finds that it can only be truly certain in areas devoid of life processes, with frozen states. Everything else is elaborate guesswork, (the arts of probabilities and statistics).

In contrast, poetry deals with fluidity. It deals with similarities and analogy. Poetry talks about something by talking about something else. It sees by looking out of the

151

corner of the eyes. Looking at the space an object or feeling leaves in the space around itself. Defining by the relationship of similars and dissimilars .

Spirit worlds and the subtle worlds are non-physical. They are difficult to see because they are so full of unpredictable life. Peripheral vision catches them. Metaphor and simile describe them. Define spirit and it vanishes. Like sub-atomic particles (the fundamentals of all matter), it is not possible to know all qualities simultaneously. Ironically, things that are classified and defined are no longer the things that were to be classified and defined. At best, the defined object has become an echo, a trace of something that has moved onwards into the rest of life.

This is the situation, as well, with flower essences. Defining them in terms of classification and purpose is like grasping a wriggling eel too hard: it simply slips through the fingers and what remains is not the essence, but only a hint or a trace of its presence.

In tho ond, dofinition and oatogorioation io not holiotic — it io reductionist science. Its aim is to reduce variables, to limit the sphere of a thing until it becomes small enough to be understood easily by the maximum number of people. If flower essence therapy desires to become a holistic system then it must learn to communicate in its own language – the language of life, which is spirit language – poetry. Poetry is not verse, it is not doggerel. Poetry is the science of spirit. Poetry does not create definition, it doesn't work with intellectual understanding. Poetry works when it hits the heart, when there is a global feeling of empathy – an inhalation of recognition. If we only work within a pseudo-scientific, mock-intellectual model, what flower essences are will escape us. We will be left with another dead medicine administered by experts. Another jargon for another elite tribe.

152

A flower essence is the root of life. It sustains by being inextricably connected to its source. It begins healing by transferring the life from that source to the hole, the rigidity or the emptiness within the individual. An essence reconnects.

The essence of something is the most fundamental, therefore the most universal of energies. It is the smallest thing possible and having no mass, no size, it can be everywhere simultaneously. Like the spirit worlds and those angels dancing on pin-heads, time and space become irrelevant.

Flower essences are almost exclusively used for what would be called healing purposes. These healing effects, though real, may only be a side-effect. Essences work because they allow us to integrate a new view of reality. The view of reality belonging to a tree or plant or whatever, is free from the accumulations of human culture, beliefs, doubt, fear, expectation, and memories that ultimately separate us from a real, immediate and vivid experience of being.

A real sense of separation is what prevents us from being in perfect, seamless unity with the web of wholeness. This apparent sense of separation limits our beliefs in the possible, the potential for fullness, and it diverts our core energy away from the ability to perceive, and then re-establish, harmony where 'mistaken intellect' has taken hold.

Illness manifests where fractures occur in Reality. When there is, on whatever level, a denial of the continual, abundant flow of universal energies that pervade every particle of space and time.

When we take an essence we re-enter the world a little more. We move inside Reality and turn away from our illusory selves. This is the way in which we can work with tree essences. We use the essences as a key to enter into the

Reality of the Trees, to understand and work with the trees. In this way it is possible to enter into a new harmony with the trees, rather than simply taking the tree essence only to give ourselves more harmony.

Using essences as a primary way to attune to trees has led directly to the development of the techniques in this series of books – using the mental and sensory processes to deepen the experience of the spirit reality of trees.

It is important that essences are not thought of as medicines, or as medicinal products, though they are healers. Current governmental bodies have stated that anything that changes physiology, or that purports to change physiology, can be classified as medicine if the body of evidence points in that direction. Perversely excluded from such considerations are non-nutritious foods such as sugar, chocolate, tea, coffee and so on, that currently are not popularly thought of as medicinal in any way, but that obviously change physiological function - indeed were introduced as cultural drug stimulants because of their effects rather than for their taste.

There are other things though, that have a healing effect that cannot reasonably be called medicines, although they can be used in a healing or medicinal context. Positive emotions like happiness and love are known to have strong beneficial effects on the physiology, and even to have effected 'miracle' remissions from terminal diseases. Emotions cannot easily be marketed as a standardised product, but there is another thing that has a powerful healing effect that can be closely compared to the nature, function and effect of flower essences, and that is music.

Music itself cannot become a product. Each live performance is unique and unrepeatable. Like a flowering plant, a piece of music may have a very detailed, prescribed form, but each individual performance will never be identical.

154

When music is recorded, it is that record of the performance that becomes a product. Yet the tape or CD is not the music itself – it is simply a bit of moulded plastic. Likewise, the essence is nothing other than a recording of the plant (or other) energy. It is not the plant itself. Chemical analysis of a CD will not reveal the music. Chemical analysis of an essence will not reveal the plant energy. A CD is a vehicle for a specific performance in time and space, free of the limits of time and space. An essence is the vehicle for a plant's energy collected at a specific time and space, free of the limits of that time and space.

Recorded music is not music until it is put through a compatible system. Without a CD player a CD is just a pretty coloured disc of plastic. Likewise, an essence is simply a bottle of water and preservative until it is 'played' by the compatible system of the individual living being. A CD that is incompatible with the machine will not produce music, and an essence that is incompatible with a living system will not produce a healing effect. This is the so-called 'self-regulating' property of essences.

Flower essences do not travel along physiological pathways. They do not directly or indirectly affect organs or systems within the physical body. Molecules of essence do not attach to cell receptor sites, they do not mimic hormone secretions, they do not activate or suppress any nerve responses.

It is not possible to produce the music held on a CD from an old-fashioned needle record player. The systems are incompatible. CDs work with the non-physical energy of light (the laser reader) to produce the music. Essences do not work with the physical body. They are 'read' by the light vibrations of the subtle bodies, chakras, nadis and meridian systems – the minidisc magic of the human being.

The fact that the end product is music does not mean that the CD is materially the same as the Berlin Philharmonic Orchestra. The fact that the result of using an essence has a healing effect does not mean that the drops are the same as, or equivalent to, medicine.

A piece of music is defined by its structure, yet the same music can be recorded in different ways whilst still remaining true to the internal architecture of sound. Essences can be made from the same sources (plant, flower, or other), by different people and the interpretation, the emphasis, may be different. In the same way that some people might like the interpretations of the conductor Herbert von Karajan, others might prefer the interpretations of Simon Rattle. The different styles of interpretation create different degrees of harmony and disharmony, pleasure or discomfort, calm or agitation within the energy field, nervous system and emotions of the listener. The essence of the same flower from different makers ('conductor' would be an appropriate term here as well), will emphasise some qualities and play down others. This will also create personal preferences for one make of essence over another.

Music can be easily shown to initiate profound changes in emotions, nervous system, brain activity, thought processes and hormone levels yet music is not regarded as medicine. A GP is unlikely to prescribe ten minutes of a Bach partita three times a day. There is a common acknowledgement that some experiences, music among them, can be healing. Looking at flowers, being given a bunch of flowers, standing under trees, walking in nature, are often experienced as healing. Surely essences are simply a way of recording these energy experiences in a convenient form. They are as ephemeral as canned air or a bottled view, as powerful as a panorama of the Himalayas or a Handel oratorio.

" 'Fetch me a fruit of the banyan tree.'
'Here is one, sir.'
' Break it.'
'I have broken it, sir.'
' What do you see?'
'Very tiny seeds, sir.'
'Break one.'
'I have broken it, sir.'
'What do you see now?'
'Nothing, sir.'
'My son', the father said, 'What you do not perceive
is   the essence,
and in that essence the mighty banyan tree exists.
Believe me, my son, in that essence is the self of
all that is.
That is the True.
(*Chandogya Upanishad VI* , 13)

Using Essences in Sequence

Illness and disease develop like a tangle begins in a length of
thread. At first there is just a kink or a loop but very soon
other parts of the thread get caught up, and before you know
it there's an impenetrable nest of knots. The only way to
prevent the situation from becoming worse is to carefully
begin teasing out a little bit at a time and see which knots are
preventing other parts from unravelling.

To use another analogy, the wellness of a person is at the very
centre of a maze made from the stresses and fractures of that
life. In order to bring effective healing it is usually necessary
to proceed in a specific and unique pattern. First this knot has
to be released, then we need to turn away from the apparent
goal for a little while in order to pick up the right path again,
and so on. This technique allows a deep and significant, rapid
healing to occur by applying essences in a sequence especially
suited to each person. Each essence applied to a wrist pulse or

taken by mouth points the healing forces of the body in the direction it needs to go to unravel the knots of the problem, to find the balance point at the centre of the maze. The procedure is easy but care needs to be taken in maintaining an open and safe space as stress release can be unexpected and sometimes dramatic.

1) With such powerful processes as this it is always advisable to make sure that the work proposed is safe and appropriate for the individual at this time. It is detrimental to force the release of imbalances that the body is not willing or able to release as they will simply re-occur in the same or a different form. The more precise the target is, the more likely will be success.

2) Sequences of essences are easy to do with tree essences, but bringing the energies of a tree using wood or any other attunement method like visual form or mantra into the person's energy field will also work well.

3) Find which tree energies are needed and in which order they need to be introduced.

4) Allow the patient to settle and calm themselves for a moment. Suggest that they turn their attention lightly on the area being addressed by the healing. Ask them to remain attentive but open to changes that may be felt through the body.

5) Introduce the first tree energy into the energy field. If it is an essence, place on a wrist pulse, chakra point, or a few drops in the mouth. If a sample of wood, place it in their hands. If a visual key, ask them to gaze at the design. If a mantra, have it repeated for a little while, maybe between thirty seconds and a minute.

6) Remove the energy from the patient's aura and let them rest for a minute or two to absorb and process the energy.

7) Repeat the sequence with each tree's energy until all have been brought in turn into the patient's aura.

8) Allow a good period of time to relax and return to a state of equilibrium before resuming normal activity. The process can be supported by preparing a bottle with all the essences in. This can then be taken over the next few weeks. The combination will effectively continue the same healing in a more gentle way. Samples of wood can be used together in the same way.

The Tao of Trees

Of all the major philosophies in the world, the Taoism of China is the most aware of, and sympathetic to, the natural world. Indeed Taoism could not exist without constant reference to the natural universe around it. It is therefore quite natural to find many techniques and practices that use the inherent energy of trees for healing and spiritual development. There are many parallels between the energy techniques of Taoism and those of Tibetan Buddhism and Dzogchen. It is as if the Taoists simply were able to take advantage of the more abundant landscapes of China to expand their cosmology into the world, escaping the almost inevitable trap that all other major religions fall into of distancing the spiritual from the mundane, ultimately leading to the rejection and alienation of humanity from creation.

In "*Opening the Dragon Gate: The making of a modern Taoist wizard*" by Chen Kaiguo and Zheng Shunchao, there are several references to tree energy work. Whist travelling through forests the three sages and their pupil come across a particularly useful arrangement of trees, where a different species is growing in each cardinal direction and a fifth is growing centrally. What makes this grove so useful is not only the exact alignment to the directions but the fact that each tree characterises one of the five Elements that relates to that direction. In the east is a pine, in the south a paulownia (foxglove tree), in the west an aspen, to the north a cedar and in the centre, a willow. The apprentice, Liping, is taught how to walk along a particular route between the trees so that the interaction of the external Elements with his internal elemental makeup is brought into a better balance to enable him to get rid of illness and to prolong his life. Using breathing techniques, posture and breathing techniques it was possible for the sages to activate latent abilities in their student.

Throughout the book are examples of seemingly ordinary things becoming the source of great transformation. It is the awareness of the sages that can discriminate the powerful from the ordinary, rather than formulae and recipes handed down from predecessors. Their goal is to train Liping to perceive the relationship of humans and other beings as part of a single universal system so that he will avoid disrupting the equilibrium whilst at the same time using those energy relationships as a way to nourish life, strengthen the body and increase longevity. The systems of feng shui have the same goals but often slide from genuine perception of unique circumstances to become first, a less effective, and dogmatic, magical prescription and then, finally, simple superstition. There are, for example, references in some texts to the energy qualities of certain species of trees, their Elemental makeup and the imbalances that they can correct in humans. It is interesting to see these correlations, but it is always important to remember that every situation is unique. A tree of a certain age, with a certain form, growing at a particular place within an environment, may have an entirely different energy from another tree of the same species somewhere else. One may be appropriate as a healing tree whilst the other may not.

During their wanderings in the forests of China the three sages and Liping come across a very large, old pine tree. Liping is taught to exchange energy with the tree, 'radiating and absorbing auras of ethereal force.' The purpose is to create an equilibrium of all polarities and the five Elements within the body. The technique involved standing close to the tree with arms extended and palms facing the tree. The tree is visualised as a column of energy of the appropriate colour for its Elemental qualities, and gazing ahead with eyes nearly closed, the legs are slowly bent and straightened with torso remaining upright, so that the hands sweep slowly up and down the tree trunk. Moving upwards on the in-breath and moving downward on the out-breath, Liping was taught to imagine his palms radiating energy of the same colour as the tree so that an equal energy exchange was taking place between him and the tree. At dawn and dusk he would practice with different species of trees and learn different postures.

Similar techniques are found in "Chi Nei Tsang: Internal Organs Chi Massage" by Mantak and Manaween Chia. It is worth looking in some detail at the structure of these methods, not least because of their clarity, precision and the fact that this is a living tradition working with tree energies that has been in existence for countless generations.

One of the key reasons for working with trees in the Taoist tradition is that the two fundamental polarities, Heaven and Earth, or yang and yin principles, are seen as being held in a dynamic equilibrium within the tree. Because trees dwell in a state of constant meditation, sharing their energy fields can help humans to achieve a greater clarity and awareness, whilst at the same time there can be a mutual healing of energy blockages in devitalised areas.

Different species of trees have a natural tendency to help balance certain ailments, due to their Elemental makeup. It is suggested that trees around human habitations are often easier to work with because they are familiar with human beings, though individual trees might be more willing to work with you than others. (The Chinese Taoist has none of the existential guilt that seems to pervade Western awareness. A tradition of looking to live in active harmony with the universe sees humanity as a part of the Pattern, rather than as an unfortunate blot on the landscape.) Large, but not awesomely huge trees, are better to work with than small or young trees – there must be some sense of power without feeling overwhelmed in the tree's presence. However, if there is a real need for healing energy it is better to seek out a big tree. Small and medium trees are best for 'playful interaction'.

These Taoist practices follow a recognisable pattern, with each one bringing in different mind-guided energy flows to activate or clear specific energy channels. Advise for beginning the contact with the tree and for withdrawing back into normal activity are precise and elegant, and can be adopted whether or not the actual Taoist energy exercises are used.

Establishing Communion

1) Work with all sorts of trees, but focus on one at a time. Visit it regularly. There should be some feeling of empathy and tenderness, but you do not always need to feel in control.

2) Take time to just relax in the presence of the tree without adopting any emotional or mental stance – just be yourself.

3) When you want to begin, relax and centre yourself. Feel that your boundaries are softening, allowing yourself to become more receptive and vulnerable. Feel your energy open like a flower, neither emitting nor absorbing energy – simply just becoming open and available.

162

4) Extend your energy towards the tree with a friendly, open, offering attitude. When the tree responds by extending its own energy towards you, accept it and breathe it into your body with a welcoming feeling.

5) Remain centred within your own awareness, neither approaching nor retreating. Just observe the subtle relationship between you and the tree. Take your focus to your connection with the tree without trying to change or analyse what is happening. Do not deepen the communion or lessen it. You control your energy and watch the tree as the tree controls its energy and observes you. This is a neutral state called 'parallel tracking' and it can occur several times during a session.

6) Allow the energy field between you and the tree to intensify, thicken and contract so that there is an increase in the feeling of closeness – though this may not involve any physical movement.

7) There is now a sense of both of you being enfolded in an energy cocoon while more and more of your inner cores are exposed to each other. This can often occur spontaneously as energies begin to be shared.

8) At this point a directed flow of energy between you and the tree can be established. Use your mind to define the direction of flow. Imagine energy flowing in a continuous stream through both your own and the tree's energy systems. As this happens 'taste' the tree's energy as it enters your body and notice how your energy feels when it returns to you from the tree, enhanced with a cool, healing quality. (See later for suggestions of energy flows).

9) Extending the energy exchange to a deeper level can be achieved by placing a particular part of your body in contact with the tree. Then breathe the energy back and forth. Allow

the energy flow to find its own circuit or direct the flow as it moves between you and the tree.

Withdrawing and Closing.

10) The entire process is brought to a close very gradually and clearly so that the energy harmony is not disturbed, and both you and the tree retain your own energies intact without any drain or leaking into each other or the environment.

11) Begin to withdraw your attention from the contact by becoming more aware of yourself. At this point the tree's energy will often also be drawn into your body, so just gently push back at the stream of energy to prevent most of it from entering you at the same time as allowing your human energy to return.

12) Allow the tree energy to flow back into the tree, but keep your own conscious energy within your body. In a while, the tree will see what is happening and will also begin to sort out its own energies. You will begin to feel fully back in your body. (When there has been a deep sharing of energy, focus attention on the navel area and allow excess energy to flow back into the tree. Push back any other energy the tree feeds to you. Return to your own energies in steps, withdrawing to a shallower level of communion each time so that your energies become safely untangled.)

13) Eventually the flows of energy exchange come to a standstill and you have returned to a state resembling parallel tracking. Now it is possible to finally sort out if there is any energy that needs returning.

14) Now it is time to close the process. This is achieved with a precise gesture that breaks the connections, locks in place any healing that may have occurred, and acts as a thanks. The closing can be a movement, a sound, or just a change in the

subtle energy field, such as a handclap, a bow or a nod of the head.

Patterns of Energy Flow

There are many different pathways by which energy can be visualised as moving through the body and between body and tree. In the traditions of Taoism each has a particular usefulness to the practitioner. Here, though, we simply offer some suggestions for you to try out.

1) Absorb the tree energy with the palms of the hands. Draw it up into the arms and to the shoulders and then to the top of the head. From here let it move downward through the chakras to the base of the spine, to the soles of the feet and about ten feet into the ground. From here it moves into the roots of the tree and up the trunk to where it can circuit again into your palms.

2) See the tree energy enter through your left hand, up the inside of the left arm to the left shoulder and the left ear to the crown of the head. From here it moves along the same pathways down the right side of the body to the right palm where it circles back into the tree and out again into the left hand.

3) See the energy flow similar to 2) but have it move along the outsides of the arms.

4) Send your energy through the tree's trunk from your right palm to the tree, from the tree to your left palm, and then back again. Make sure that your energy penetrates that of the tree.

5) Practice with different parts of the tree. Begin with the upper trunk; kneel and practice with the lower trunk; then practice with the roots of the tree. Feel the tree's energy and

exchange the force with it.

6) Absorb the tree's energy into your crown and let it flow down to the feet. Allow it to move beyond the soles of the feet into the ground. Here it is absorbed by the roots of the tree, where it passes up the trunk and the cycle continues.

7) Gently touch a tree with one palm or fingertips. Allow time to establish an energy contact. Just breathe energy back and forth between the hand and the tree. Gradually extend the movement along the whole arm to the heart centre. Continue this for some time. Now contact the tree with your other hand as well. Draw in the tree energy along the same hand to the heart centre and let it flow out through the other arm. Reverse the flow of energy every so often.

8) (Same as 7), but let the energy flow down to the navel centre and back from there. Follow the direction of the energy as it moves back into the tree.

9) From a distance gather energy at your navel centre and bring it up to the crown. Project it out into the top of the tree's trunk. Let the energy flow down the trunk to the roots and the earth. The Earth energy purifies any imbalances in your own energy. Bring up the energy through the soles of the feet and up the spine to the crown. From here project it outward again to the tree.

Chapter 7

Tree Teas

The 'vegetalistas' of South America get to know the plants and plant spirits they are to use by drinking heroic amounts of often toxic and even life-threatening plant extracts. This would be a pointless exercise were it not to confer considerable knowledge unavailable by more moderate means. What can the actual ingestion of plant matter bring to the healer? Despite appearances, life differs very little at its most fundamental levels. The DNA of one species often only has one or two major differences from another species. The DNA of plant cells can have more than half its complete structure identical to animal cells. The interesting thing about DNA and cells is that it has been recently discovered that communication between cells is largely carried out by light. Bioluminescence at subcellular levels, particularly from the complex proteins like DNA, is a major factor in balancing the complex workings of a multi-celled organism.

How can a tree spirit come to know a human spirit except by sharing its qualities? Without learning the language of a plant how can the healer ask for its help? Without learning the language of the healer's heart how can the plant spirit interpret the flows of energy from the human being? When we ingest a plant, the language of its light, its DNA, its pattern, becomes a part of our own patterning. It doesn't remain whole at a physical level but energetically the tree remains a tree and its language or its essence can be thought of as integrating with the knowledge of the body in some way, adding to our library of information. Plant becomes person, person becomes plant. A plant person, a 'vegetalista', a tree seer, has become familiar with the spirit of plants – enough to shift awareness away from the human to bring in the healing qualities of those plants that are the healer's allies.

Anyone who works with plants makes special connections with some species. The healer and seer simply take this relationship and builds upon it to a very high degree. Outside of an established and well-controlled traditional training it is unwise to throw oneself into the plant kingdoms without knowledge. On the other hand it is worthwhile to explore as many of the qualities of the trees we work with as possible. We can take the regime of 'drinking plants' and transform it into a much safer learning process using the traditions and techniques of herbal medicine. There are three main ways of preparing plants for medicine. The simplest is using fresh herbal material or drying it, the second is making a water-based preparation, and the third is to make an alcohol-based preparation. With tree teas what we are making is an infusion, a tisane or a decoction.

An infusion is made thus:

1) A teaspoonful of dried plant is placed in a teapot or similar vessel.

2) Fill the pot with boiling water, a cup for each teaspoon of herb used.

3) Leave to steep for ten to fifteen minutes.

4) Drink hot.

Tisanes make a weaker infusion and should be used where the plant material is unfamiliar or of uncertain effect.

1) Use a tea-strainer or small muslin bag. Place the plant material in the strainer.

2) Steep the herbs in a cup of boiling water for a minute or two.

3) Drink when the temperature is right.

To make a stronger water-based mix a decoction can be prepared. Decoctions tend to be used with the more woody parts of a plant.

1) One cup of water is added to a saucepan for each teaspoon of herbal material. Add enough material and water to allow for reduction.

2) Bring to the boil and simmer for at least ten to fifteen minutes.

3) Strain and drink the tea whilst hot.

With decoctions the same material can often be reheated several times, though the strength of the decoction will diminish each time.

With tree teas we are less interested in the medicinal effect and more focused on the quality of imbibing the spirit energy of the tree. Some trees can be used quite frequently and have well-known beneficial effects. Others, however, have little information available on them and these should be treated with great care. Always treat a new tree with caution – individual responses can differ widely. Remember, that for our purposes we are not using therapeutically active doses, so unless you really know what you are doing, stick to the tisane or infusion with a minimum of plant material.

The basis of herbal knowledge – the folk healer and the oral tradition – is rapidly disappearing. Medical herbalism is being fast subsumed by pseudo-industrial protocols, and many traditional herbal medicines are quietly disappearing off the shelves. Keep good records of your experiences. Be careful and thorough. Your knowledge may be very valuable soon enough – but remember the main focus of this work is bringing the tree spirits to your awareness so that they can heal. Don't fall back into the trap of believing in the medicine. Medicine only helps to heal a body whose spirit has already decided to turn towards health. A change of spirit is what heals.

Protocol for Taking Tree Teas

1) The effects of tree teas are best felt on empty stomachs and at a time or place when you can focus on the energy of the tea, rather than getting distracted by everyday matters.

2) If you do not know how you feel physically, mentally and emotionally before you drink a tree tea, you will not know what effects are the result of the tree's energy. Follow the protocols for grounding, protecting and preparation as in any other tree seer work.

3) It is generally considered unwise to continue taking any herbal preparation for more than two weeks without a break. With tree teas, use them regularly for a week, then leave it for a week or two without taking any others. With strongly medicinal or unknown tree teas use half of what you would consider a minimum amount and only ingest a sip or two.

ALDER (*Alnus glutinosa*)

Leaves or twigs can be made into a tea. They have slightly different actions. The bark is tonic, containing a high proportion of tannins. It can be effective for sore throats and mouth ulcers.

The leaves have a tradition of use as an anti-inflammatory and they are also astringent. Bruises and swellings, water retention and the kidneys are helped. There are no contraindications.

APPLE (*Malus domestica*, *Malus sylvestris*)

The fruit, fruit pulp, juice, bark and leaves can be used. The leaves make a pleasant tea by themselves. Apple is a general tonic, aiding digestive processes and supplying useful nutrients. The apple juice, pulp and peel are a gentle sedative (which combined with lemon balm makes a useful nightcap). The juice cools fevers and the pulp can be used externally for sprains, cramp, inflammations and flesh wounds.

High in iron and vitamins, apple is a powerful anti-oxidant and cleanser.

Only excessive ingestion of fruit, or eating crab apples raw, is indicated as causing abdominal pain and indigestion.

ASH (*Fraxinus excelsior*)

Leaves, fruit and bark can be used safely. Ash is mildly purgative and astringent. The bark has been used as a tonic for the liver and spleen and as it induces perspiration (i.e. it is diaphoretic), ash is used to break fevers.

The ash seeds within the keys contain an edible oil.
Ash leaves steeped in water helps reduce water retention, rheumatism and arthritic conditions. No contraindications.

ASPEN (*Populus tremula*)

Aspen is similar in its constituents to all other poplars. It contains phenolic glycosides including silicin, an anti-inflammatory related to aspirin. The bark is the most often used part.

Internally aspen is used for fevers, pain, cystitis, rheumatism and arthritis.

Externally it can be used for muscle and joint pain, colds and flu.

There are no contraindications unless you are sensitive to aspirin-type medicines.

ATLAS CEDAR (*Cedrus atlantica*)

It is only the volatile oil extracted from the wood that is used medicinally as an antiseptic and for chest and circulatory problems.

Externally the oil is used to alleviate muscle aches and pains. Leaves and simple tisanes are generally safe but best avoided during pregnancy as in active doses it is an abortifactent.

BAY (BAY LAUREL (*Laurus nobilis*)

Bay has long been used for the high concentration of volatile oils in its wood and especially its leaves and berries. It is warming and an aid to digestion in small doses. Large doses can induce vomiting.

Bay is antiseptic and antispasmodic so useful for colds and coughs. Externally bruises, muscle stiffness and 'damp' conditions like chest infections can be alleviated. The leaves have been used as a tea, which is mildly excitant and narcotic. Berries in large doses should not be used when pregnant as they have been known to induce abortion.

BEECH (*Fagus sylvaticus*)
Medicinally the bark is the most important, producing by dry distillation a tar (known as creosote, but not to be confused with creosote oil, made from coal tar), This concentrated extract is unsafe to use, especially by arthritics and those with kidney complaints. Formerly it was used as an expectorant to relieve chronic bronchitis, as a remedy for toothache and as a relief from itching caused by psoriasis and other skin diseases.

The nut has a high proportion of nutritious oil (a substitute for olive oil) and roasted they can be a substitute for coffee. The leaves in a tea can be mildly stimulating and antiseptic.

BLACK POPLAR (*Populus nigra*)
Same as aspen.

BLACKTHORN (*Prunus spinosa*)
Similar in medicinal properties to all the Prunus Family, blackthorn has an astringent bark that reduces diarrhoea and can help lower high temperatures and fevers. The berries (sloe) are very astringent and are used in skin toners.

Leaves, flowers, bark and berries can be used as a tree tea.

Blackthorn is purifying to the body and helps to eliminate toxicity. As in other prunus species, bark and seeds contain substances that convert to hydrocyanic acid (cyanide). This is safe in small doses and is the active principal in alleviating coughs and respiratory complaints. Other members of the cherry family have much higher proportions than blackthorn, especially in green tissues.

Only over-indulgence in raw fruit will produce stomach-ache or diarrhoea.

BIRD CHERRY (*Prunus padus*)
See Blackthorn. Also, cherry stalks have long been used as an astringent and tonic for chest complaints, upset digestive systems and anaemia (primarily the high levels of iron in the fruits).

Cherry is slightly sedative and calming in its action.
Avoid the use of kernels – they have a dangerously high level of hydrocyanic acid.

BOX (*Buxus sempervirens*)
Bark and leaves were formerly used as a violent purgative and for life-threatening fevers such as malaria. The bark was used to eliminate intestinal parasites.

However, box is highly toxic, inducing abdominal pain and vomiting. It may prove fatal.

This is unwise to use as a tree tea unless one leaf only is placed in the water for a very short time. It would be much safer just to use the tree essence.

CATALPA (*Catalpa x erubescens*)
The bark and fruit of catalpa have been used to break fevers and to quieten asthmatic coughing. It is slightly narcotic and this, along with its sedative properties, has made it useful for childhood ailments.

The roots are poisonous and not to be used.

Hybrid catalpas may have slightly differing properties, so use with caution as a tree tea.

CEDAR OF LEBANON (*Cedrus libani*)
See Atlas Cedar.
Branches are chipped for oil distillation or dried for use in decoctions. Cedar is a useful antiseptic and fungicide. It can be calming to the nerves and works with circulatory and respiratory systems.

Do not use in excess if pregnant, and avoid the essential oil.

CHERRY LAUREL (LAUREL - *Prunus laurocerasus*)
Cherry laurel contains high concentrations of prulaurasin, especially in the leaves and fruit. This becomes hydrocyanic acid (cyanide) and so should be treated with caution. Young leaves and the seeds are the most toxic.

The pulp of the fruit has been used to give almond flavour to alcoholic drinks but generally only water infusions are used. Laurel is sedative and narcotic. Externally it has been used for itching skin and as a local analgesic. The water has been used internally as a soother for coughs, whooping cough and asthma. It also acts as a digestive tonic.

Cherry laurel is incompatible with cocaine, Peruvian bark, caffeine and casein.

Use with extreme caution: fruit pulp or old leaves are the safest to use, but only in very low concentration.

CHERRY PLUM (*Prunus cerasifera*)
See both cherry and plum for family characteristics.
Cyanide producing compounds tend to be highest in the green

parts of the plant and the fruit kernel. Bark of twigs, fruit stalks and stem bark are the lowest. Picking and ingesting leaves activates cyanide compounds, but drying the leaves tends to destroy or inactivate them.

Caution: use dried leaves or bark only, and in small amounts.

COAST REDWOOD (SEQUOIA – *Sequoia sempervirens*)

Among the Kashaya Pomo Indians of California, a poultice is made of the warmed fresh leaves as a remedy for earache. The sap, which is gummy and resinous, is also infused in water and taken as a stimulant tonic when the individual is rundown. These uses suggest that sequoia would be fine as a tree tea.

COPPER BEECH (*Fagus sylvatica var. purpurea*)

See beech.

CRACK WILLOW (*Salix fragilis*)

All willows contain high levels of acetylsalicylic acid (aspirin), especially in their bark. Unlike the commercial preparation, willow salicin does not cause thinning of the blood nor bleeding in the stomach lining. Crack willow has amongst the highest levels of salicin, though white willow is favoured by herbalists.

Willow can ease muscular and joint pain, control fevers and act as a mild sedative. It is a useful anti-inflammatory, astringent and pain reliever.

DOUGLAS FIR (*Pseudotsuga menziesii*)

Some of the chemical compounds isolated from this tree are known to be anti-bacteriological and insecticidal. There is evidence that Douglas fir has been made into teas and as a coffee substitute. Amongst the Kwakiutl peoples of British Columbia the burned and pulverised bark is infused to combat diarrhoea. The green bark has been used, infused to regulate excessive menstruation, for intestinal bleeding and for stomach problems. The pitch from the tree has been used to relieve sore throats and coughs. Traditionally it has been used in sweat lodges and steam baths, presumably for its antiseptic, cleansing and warming properties. Moderate use as a tree tea should present few problems.

ELDER (*Sambucus niger*)
Elder provides a wealth of medicinal remedies. Leaves, bark and raw berries have toxic cyanogenic glucosides so need to be treated with caution. Drying may reduce toxicity. Flowers and dried or cooked berries are much safer for everyday use. Leaves and bark are diuretic, laxative or purgative, depending on the amount used.

Externally the leaves are useful for controlling bleeding, healing burns and chilblains and as an antiseptic. Leaves boiled in water make an effective insect repellent.

Flowers are a stimulant to the immune system, induce perspiration, relieve coughing and increase the flow of breast milk. Berries are laxative, soothing to the nervous system, pain relieving and detoxifying.

Caution: For tree teas use only small amounts of leaves or bark, preferably well dried, or they will cause nausea or worse.

ENGLISH ELM (*Ulmus procera*)
In herbalism, the main elm species used is the American slippery elm, which has the highest mucilaginous inner bark of any tree. English elm bark has been used similarly as a

178

relief for skin disorders, wound healing and for soothing inflammation.

FIELD MAPLE (*Acer campestre*)
Like all maples, field maple has a sugary sap, though nowhere near as abundant as in the American species. The bark of the field maple is used medicinally as an astringent and has been seen to slightly reduce abnormal cholesterol in the blood.

There are no contraindications as a tree tea.

FIG (*Ficus carica*)
Fruits are used to soothe internal tissues, are mildly laxative and nutritious. Young branches are used to help respiratory conditions. The leaves lower blood sugar levels and the latex from cut leaves contains a digestive enzyme (chymase) which acts as a coagulant and has a fermenting action. It is also analgesic and helpful for insect stings and bites.

Caution: Skin contact can be a skin irritant in sunlight, and an allergen. The sap is a serious eye irritant. Diabetics should be wary of fig's effect on blood sugar levels – though it can help to augment treatments of some forms of diabetes.
The fruit is probably the safest part to use as a tree tea.

FOXGLOVE TREE (*Paulownia tormentosa*)
Leaves and fruit have been a famous tonic for longevity in China, where the tree originates. No contraindications are indicated for moderate use as a tree tea.

GEAN (WILD CHERRY – *Prunus avium)*

The cherry stalks are most often used as a diuretic and normaliser of uric acid levels in urine (helpful for gout).

The bark can lower fevers and if a small incision is made in the trunk, an aromatic resin collects that can be used as an inhalant for persistent coughs.

Cherry leaves macerated and fermented are an aromatic addition to pipe-smoking mixtures.

Caution: Seed kernels should never be used as they contain high levels of hydrocyanic acids. As tree teas, dried leaves are better than green leaves to use, as toxins have then been reduced.

GIANT REDWOOD (*Sequioadendron giganteum*)
No information.

GINKGO (*Ginkgo biloba)*
The leaves are mainly used together with the fruits and seeds. The list of medicinal properties for this tree is impressive: anti-inflammatory, anti-aging, anti-asthmatic, anti-oxidant, anti-allergenic. Ginkgo increases oxygen delivery to the brain, improves blood circulation and protects the heart. It results in better oxygenation of the body, thus making all systems more efficient and less prone to the damage of oxidants and toxins.

Ginkgo is safe to use long term but caution is needed as it may interact with any anti-coagulant being prescribed such as aspirin or warfarin. The seeds can also cause skin irritation.

GLASTONBURY THORN (*Crataegus monogyna biflora*)
See hawthorn.

GORSE (*Ulex europeus, Ulex gallica*)

Gorse has no recorded major use as a herbal medicine, but is well known as a nutritious food for cattle and horses. Young branches are the most tender, but gorse is usually crushed to soften the spiny leaves for foraging animals.

Caution : Do not use the seeds in tree teas as they contain a toxin, cytosine.

GREAT SALLOW (GOAT WILLOW, PUSSY WILLOW – *Salix caprea*)

Like other willows, great sallow bark is high in tannin and also salicin, the natural analgesic and sedative.

No contraindications for use as a tree tea.

HAWTHORN (*Crataegus monogyna*)

Hawthorn is one of the most important herbs for the health of the heart. It regulates the heart function, reduces high blood pressure, restores elasticity to the blood vessels. It also reduces palpitations and giddiness.

The flowers have been used as a soother of sore throats and the bark is effective against fevers and malaria. It has a mild tranquillising effect. Flowers, leaves and bark can be used.

Caution: If blood pressure-lowering drugs are being taken or if blood pressure is already low, hawthorn is contraindicated in medicinal doses.

HAZEL (*Corylus avellana*)

Hazel leaves are astringent and promote wound repair. They have been used for diarrhoea, bruising and varicose veins.

Hazel leaves have been recently found to contain taxol, the compound in yew leaves that has been used as a cancer controlling medicine.

The nuts are highly nutritious, whilst the oil has been successful as a gentle means of eliminating parasitic intestinal worms from children.
No contraindications as a tree tea.

HOLLY (*Ilex aquifolium*)
The leaves are used herbally for fevers, influenza, catarrh, bronchial complaints and rheumatism. The juice of the fresh leaves have been prescribed for jaundice and smallpox. The dried, powdered berries stop the bleeding of wounds.

Caution: Berries should be avoided. They are violently emetic and purgative, causing extreme vomiting.

HOLM OAK (*Quercus ilex*)
See oak. The wood of holm oak is as useful as that of English oak. The bark is very bitter. It acts as an astringent and so is useful for diarrhoea, dysentery, sore throats and inflammations. It is antiseptic and slightly tonic. Bruised leaves can be used as a poultice for healing wounds.

Caution: Oak bark is very astringent and will decrease the ability of the body to absorb nutrients. Only use internally for three or four days at a time.

HORNBEAM (*Carpinus betula*)
The leaves of hornbeam have been used as a compress to heal minor wounds and to control bleeding. They are astringent. The leaves placed in water produce a soothing eye lotion.
No contraindications as a tree tea.

HORSE CHESTNUT (*Aesculus hippocastanum*)

Leaves, seeds ('conkers') and pericarp (conker-shell) are all used medicinally. The leaves have a clear narcotic effect – a cupful of infused leaves will induce a deep calm sleep.

The plant is rich in vitamin K and its astringent properties make it ideal for circulatory disorders, haemorrhoids, varicose veins, chilblains and bruising.

Recently horse chestnut has found a niche in the beauty industry because it improves skin tone and, as they say, 'reduces the signs of aging'.

Drowsiness caused by the leaves should be taken into account.

ITALIAN ALDER (*Alnus cordata*)

See alder. Alders are astringent and tonic, encouraging the healing of damaged tissues. No contraindications indicated.

IVY (*Hedera helix*)

Ivy leaves are bitter and aromatic, (though nauseating). They have anti-bacteriological properties and have been used for their antispasmodic action in whooping cough and as an expectorant in bronchitis. They lower fevers and have a quietening effect on the peripheral nerves, useful for rheumatic pain, gout and neuralgia.

Ivy can be used externally, but internal use must be treated with extreme caution as an excess destroys red blood cells, causes irritability, diarrhoea and vomiting. Ivy can also be a skin irritant and allergen.

Caution: As a tree tea use only mature leaves. Do not steep. Use no more than one or two leaves. Avoid young leaves and berries as they are the most toxic parts.

JUDAS TREE (*Cercis siliquastrum*)
There are records of the leaves of the American species of
judas tree having stimulating and astringent properties, and
of it being used in systemic infections as a tonic alterant.

No known toxicity. Use cautiously as a tree tea.

JUNIPER (*Juniperus communis*)
Leaves, ripe fruit and bark are anti-rheumatic, diuretic,
soothe inflammations, are antiseptic and stimulate digestion.
Juniper has been used for cystitis, urethritis and kidney
inflammation as well as aches and pains in the bones and
muscles. Externally juniper can reduce neuralgia, headaches
and rheumatic pain.

Caution: Juniper can be a skin irritant. It is unwise to use
juniper where there is kidney disease or during pregnancy
(because it stimulates the uterus and may induce abortion).
Do not confuse this species with its relative, cavin, which
should not be used internally at all.

LABURNUM (*Laburnum waterii Vossi*)
The sap of the tree makes a mild purgative with a sweet,
honey-like flavour. However, all other parts are highly toxic,
especially the seeds that contain cytosine.

Caution: Not safe to use as a tree tea.

LARCH (*Larix decidua*)
The bark of larch is good for chest infections, coughs and
colds. Externally larch can help rheumatism, skin disorders

and the healing of wounds. It is antiseptic, astringent and expectorant.

The leaves are rich in vitamin C, so can be helpful in preventing colds and other infections.

Caution: Best avoided, especially in concentrated oil form, with kidney complaints.

LAWSON CYPRESS (*Chamaecyparis lawsonia*)
Many American cypresses have medicinal uses amongst native peoples. Poultices have been applied to the site of serious bacterial infection suggesting antiseptic properties. Decoctions of the stems of various cypresses are recorded as having been used to reduce the symptoms of coughs and colds, and to combat rheumatism. As no specific information has been found regarding this particular species, use carefully as a tree tea.

LEYLAND CYPRESS (*Cupressocyparis leylandii*)
No specific information found on these species, but all cypresses have high concentrations of aromatic essential oils, with each species having a particular character.

Wood, branches, leaves and fruit cones are all aromatic. Use sparingly as a tree tea.

LILAC (*Syringa vulgaris*)
The leaves and fruit of lilac have been used as a vermifuge – helping to clear the body of parasites. Lilac also helps to reduce fevers and has been used in the treatment of malaria. Its action is tonic. Use moderately as a tree tea.

LIME (LINDEN – *Tilea x europea*)

A well-known herbal remedy, it is the flowers and the flower bracts of the lime that are collected and used as a tea to calm the nerves. Lime induces perspiration, is diuretic, soothes irritated states and so is useful to aid peaceful sleep. Lime helps to soothe coughs and colds and is an immune stimulant. Its gentle stress-reducing properties and pleasant taste make it a safe remedy.

Lime flowers are best used fresh or within a year of collection as their active properties decline over time. Also, flowers are picked when freshly opened as their narcotic properties increase markedly with age.

Caution: As with all sedative herbs, caution should be used when already tired as drowsiness will increase.

LIQUIDAMBER (*Liquidamber styracifolia*)

Also known as sweet gum from the aromatic resin found in the trunk. The gum is antiseptic, anti-inflammatory, expectorant and anti-microbial. Liquidamber can be used for colds and coughs, asthma, sore throats, fungal infections, scabies and cystitis.

The resin is an irritant and burns unless diluted. Leaves and twigs will contain a lesser proportion of active principals, so will be less likely to cause problems as a tree tea.

LOMBARDY POPLAR (*Populus nigra 'Italica'*)

See black poplar.

LUCOMBE OAK (*Quercus hispanica 'Lucombeana'*)

See English oak.

MAGNOLIA (*Magnolia x soulangeana*)
The flowers and bark of various magnolia species are used for fevers and for lowering blood pressure, but use ranges widely depending on species. As with all major medicinal plants, the use as a tree tea needs to be moderate and cautious. Chinese texts caution against the use of magnolia during pregnancy.

MANNA ASH (*Fraxinus cornus*)
Manna ash is well known and popular in southern Europe as a nutritious and gentle tonic. The sap is used as a mild laxative and a soother of irritated tissues. Its sweet taste gave the tree its name – inaccurately associated with the Biblical manna of the desert, where this tree cannot grow.

Caution: Undiluted sap may cause allergic reactions.

MEDLAR (*Mespilus germanicus*)
The medlar has been used as a source of fruit and for jelly-making since Roman times at least. Like most fruits it has a laxative action. The leaves are astringent and the bark reduces fevers somewhat. The powdered nutlets or seeds have been used to eliminate small stones from the body, but as they contain a high proportion of hydrocyanic acid, these are the one part of the plant that should be avoided completely in tree teas.

MIDLAND HAWTHORN (*Crataegus laevigata*)
See hawthorn. A tonic to the heart and circulation, safe except when taking blood-pressure lowering medication where it might interfere with their effects.

MIMOSA (SILVER WATTLE) (*Acacia dealbata*)

There are many different species of acacia from semi-tropical, tropical and desert regions of the world used for medical purposes. Each species varies in its properties but generally bark, gum, seeds and leaves are used. The bark is especially astringent. Many species have high proportions of dimethyltryptamines (DMT) in the bark, making it one important part of ayahuasca analogues.

Caution: Do not use as a tree tea for more than two weeks at a time. Red blood cells are destroyed by high levels of catechins present in acacia.

MONKEY PUZZLE TREE (CHILE PINE) (*Araucaria araucana*)

The large nutritious seeds of the Chile pine have been the major source of food for the Araucana Indians, eaten raw or boiled. No information regarding other parts of the tree. No toxicity recorded.

MONTEREY PINE (*Pinus radiata*)

See Scots Pine. All pines are rich in resins, waxes and volatile oils that are antiseptic and stimulant in their actions. Bark, resin (collected from vertical cuts in bark), leaves and young shoots are used. Some possibility of skin irritation, especially from resins.

MULBERRY (*Morus nigra*)

Mulberry has been used as a medicinal and food plant for centuries. All parts are used. The twigs are a stimulant to the immune system, the root bark relieves toothache. The fruit is rich in vitamin C, is an immune stimulant and antioxidant. The leaves, fruit and bark are astringent, help to regulate blood sugar levels, and alleviate neuralgia and toothache.

No toxicity or extra caution with this tree tea.

NORWAY MAPLE (*Acer platanoides*)
Each species of maple has a slightly different chemical makeup. All have a sugary sap, but European species are not as productive as American species. The bark of maples tends to be astringent. All the maple species are fine as tree teas.

NORWAY SPRUCE (*Picea abies*)
Buds, leaves and resinous sap, rich in essential oils are used medicinally. Spruce is antiseptic and antibiotic. It soothes inflammation, is sedative and expectorant. Young leaves are rich in vitamin C and make a tasty tea. As with all concentrated extracts the resin may be allergenic to some.

OAK (*Quercus robur, Quercus petraea*)
Oak is very rich in tannins, which are the main principal in its astringent properties. Oak gall apples are a deformation of the bark caused by insect larvae. They are the most astringent of any part of the tree.

Bark and fruit (acorns) are most medicinally used as an astringent that controls bleeding, and as a decongestant. Internally oak has been used for diarrhoea and dysentery. Externally oak is useful for wounds, sore throats, mouth inflammations and haemorrhoids. Leaves are used as fodder for cattle.

Caution: Astringents reduce the ability of the digestive tract to absorb nutrients. Only use internally at any strength for three or four days at a time.

OSIER (*Salix viminalis*)

As with all other willows, osier is analgesic (pain reducing), anti-inflammatory, astringent and fever-reducing. Use only lightly for tree teas.

OLIVE (*Olea europea*)

The leaves of olive are diuretic and relaxing. Both leaves and fruit lower blood pressure and have been used for headaches and urinary infections.

There can be stomach irritation, so olive is best taken after meals.

PEAR (*Pyrus communis*)

For such a well known domestic fruit there is little medicinal information and no known toxicity.

PERSIAN IRONWOOD (*Parrotia persica*)

No information found on the uses of this tree. Treat with caution.

PITTOSPORA (*Pittospora tenuifolium*)

No information. Avoid or use with great caution.

PLANE TREE (*Platanus x acerifolia*)

No specific information.

PLUM (*Prunus domestica*)

The bark has been used as a cure for diarrhoea, whilst the fruit eases constipation, being laxative and vitamin rich. The bark also reduces fevers. Seeds (stones) are to be avoided as they contain a powerful glycoside, amygdalin. Tree teas can be made of all other parts.

PRIVET (*Ligustrum vulgare, Ligustrum ovalifolium*)
Internal use of privet is not recommended as it can produce allergic reactions. In the past the decoction of leaves was used as a gargle for swellings, abscesses and ulcers in the mouth and throat. Bark was used to stimulate the activity of the stomach. Externally, privet can be used to clean wounds and to promote their healing.

Chinese privet (glossy privet) has a longer medicinal usage but is not used internally either.

Avoid or treat with extreme caution as a tree tea.

RED CHESTNUT (*Aesculus x carnea*)
Treat red chestnut the same as horse chestnut. It is anti-inflammatory and restores elasticity to the veins. The fruit and fruit capsule are the most active chemically.

RED OAK (*Quercus rubra*)
Like English oak and the other oak species, red oak has a high tannin content, especially in the bark, acorns and galls. This gives the tree its astringent, tonic and antiseptic properties. As with other oaks do not use as a tree tea for extended periods as the tannins can prevent nutrient uptake.

ROBINIA (*Robinia pseudoacacia*)
The bark of the robinia is a strong emetic, inducing vomiting, and has some compounds that are quite toxic and so should be avoided.

The leaves too are an emetic and increase the flow of bile. The flowers have a laxative and antispasmodic effect and produce an aromatic oil that is used in perfumery.

Use cautiously and sparingly as a tree tea.

ROWAN (*Sorbus aucuparia*)

The leaves, bark and fruit of rowan are used medicinally. It is best, though, to avoid the actual seeds when possible as they contain hydrocyanic acid –though this would only present a problem in very large doses.

The bark of rowan is astringent, as are the fruits, which are also a remedy for diarrhoea. The leaves have been used for sore throats, heartburn and thrush. The fruits are high in vitamin C.

SCOTS PINE (*Pinus sylvestris*)

The bark and leaves (needles) of pine are rich in volatile oils of great value as they are antibacterial, antiseptic and anti-oxidant. Pine oils work particularly well with the lungs and sinuses, so are useful for coughs, chest infections and stuffed-up sinuses. There is an inhibition of staphylococcus bacteria. Aching muscles are also relieved.

Tolerance to pine oil is good, so as a tree tea twigs and needles should present no problem.

SILVER BIRCH (*Betula pendula*)

The bark of birch is a diuretic and laxative. The leaf buds, whilst also diuretic, are rich in potassium and so prevent a sodium-potassium imbalance that often occurs with other diuretics. Cystitis reacts well to birch buds.

The leaves and sap are also used as an anti-inflammatory for arthritis, gout and psoriasis. The sap can be tapped in early spring as it first rises, making a sweet, clean wine. All parts are good for tree teas.

SILVER FIR (*Abies alba*)
The buds of silver fir are antiseptic, anti-inflammatory and antibiotic. The needles are useful as an expectorant and a bronchial sedative, soothing coughs. The bark is astringent and antiseptic. The resin, richest in volatile oils, waxes and resins is anti-inflammatory, antiseptic and vasoconstrictive. It is useful for fevers, to tone circulation, to relieve muscle pains and improve digestion.

The concentrated oil and resin should be avoided internally as they are too strong, but tree teas from twigs and needles should present no problems.

SILVER MAPLE (*Acer saccharinum*)
The bark of silver maple can be used for coughs and cramping pains as it has the effect of breaking down muscle spasms. The sap is one of the sweetest of the maples growing in Europe. Fine as a tree tea.

SPINDLE (*Euonymus europeaus*)
All parts of spindle are useful medicinally, but dosage is very important: the incorrect level causes violent purging and vomiting. All parts, bark, roots and berries are a very bitter astringent that stimulates the gall bladder and liver as a digestive tonic (or irritant, depending on dose).

The roots have a laxative action. The berries have been used for skin disorders and to expel intestinal worms.

Extreme caution is required as all parts are harmful if eaten. Best avoided as a tree tea or use in very small amounts.

STAGS HORN SUMACH (*Rhus typhina*)

A root extract can be used to calm fevers. There is a high tannin content that makes this sumach astringent and a remedy for diarrhoea. The fruits are also cooling and diuretic. The actions are astringent, antiseptic and tonic.

Sumach is also very mucilaginous and can help soothe skin irritations. Use as a tree tea in small quantities.

STRAWBERRY TREE (*Arbutus unedo*)

The leaves are astringent, diuretic and can be useful in kidney infections as a renal antiseptic. The fruits contain twenty per cent sugars so they can be turned into jams and preserves.

A powerful alcoholic liqueur is made from the fermented fruit which has a narcotic action in large doses. Fine as a tree tea.

SWEET CHESTNUT (*Castanea sativa*)

The leaves of sweet chestnut are astringent and can relieve severe coughs, including whooping cough. They also reduce mucous, ease sore throats and can relieve the pain of rheumatism and heavy periods.

The seeds (nuts), unlike those of horse chestnut, are edible and nutritious.

No cautions are indicated for sweet chestnut as a tree tea.

SYCAMORE (*Acer pseudoplanatus*)
The great maple is not as medicinal as others of the maple family. Like them, sycamore is high in tannins and complex sugars. The sap can be made into a wine in spring and autumn. No level of toxicity or caution in use is known.

TAMARISK (*Tamarix gallica*)
The branchlets and leaves are astringent, diuretic and prevent diarrhoea. Compresses of tamarisk have been used to stop bleeding. The tree was originally imported into Britain as a medicinal plant.

TREE LICHEN (*Usnea spp.*)
The species of tree lichen known as usnea are particularly powerful immune system boosters. It consists of two intergrown plants (algae), the inner of which is an immune stimulant, the outer plant is antibiotic.

Usnea has shown itself effective against tuberculosis bacteria, staphylococcus, streptococcus and pneumonococcus strains. It helps with lung infections, abscesses, wounds, fungal infections and vaginal infections. It can be a mouth irritant if taken in strong concentrations.

Collect only from wind-blown or fallen wood to keep populations healthy where they are found.

Safe as a tree tea, tree lichen when used medicinally needs to be ground up thoroughly.

TREE OF HEAVEN (*Ailanthus altissima*)
This is an extremely astringent and bitter plant – particularly the inner bark and roots, which are used medicinally. High levels of quassinoids make it an effective anti-malarial and

anti-parasitic medicine. Tree of heaven is also anti-spasmodic and soothing at the correct doses, lowering fevers, relaxing spasms and slowing the heart rate. However, it can be purgative and cause vomiting quite easily. Leaves and flowers are probably safer to use than the bark or roots because they contain lower amounts of the active chemicals.

Use with caution – not dangerous, but there are unpleasant side effects with overdose.

TULIP TREE (*Liridendron tulipifera*)

The bark of tulip tree is a stimulant tonic that has been used to aid chronic intestinal diseases. Its effect is warming and calming, useful for rheumatism and for stabilising emotional turmoil. It can increase perspiration and may be diuretic.

VIBURNUM (*Viburnum tinus*)

No specific information on this species. However, two other viburnums are medicinally active. Guelder rose (*Viburnum opulus*) and black haw (*Viburnum prunifolium*), have a bitter, sedative bark that is antispasmodic and specific for regulating uterine function. Because of this, they should be avoided during pregnancy. The fruits of other species of viburnums are toxic when raw, but some are used in cooked form.

WALNUT (*Juglans regia*)

Walnut leaves are astringent and expectorant. As a liver stimulant they help detoxification, and they are also laxative, relieving constipation. These factors make walnut helpful for skin conditions.

The bark of walnut is antibacterial and astringent, whilst the unripe fruit expels intestinal worms. Walnut soothes irritation and increases the flow of milk in nursing mothers. No cautions for use as a tree tea.

196

WAYFARING TREE (*Viburnum lantana*)
Like other viburnums, wayfaring tree has bark that acts as a uterine relaxant, so it is helpful for period pains. It is calming, and relaxing, lowering blood pressure and reducing anxiety, irritability and insomnia.

Avoid the bark when pregnant and treat cautiously if you are being medicated for abnormal blood pressure.

WEEPING WILLOW (*Salix x chrysocoma*)
Like other willows, weeping willow contains high proportions of salicin in the bark, used as an analgesic, sedative and tonic. No cautions to use, except to those on prescribed aspirin-type medicines.

WESTERN HEMLOCK (*Tsuga heterophylla*)
This tree is no relation to the umbelliferous plants of this name that are very toxic and should be avoided (hemlock, water dropwort etc.)

The needles of the tree are effective for arthritis, rheumatism and colds. The bark, for colds, mouth and throat infections, wounds, diarrhoea and cystitis. Western hemlock is high in volatile oils that are warming, stimulating and antiseptic. It is useful as a circulatory stimulant, and also contains compounds that prevent damage to tissues by free radicals. As with all volatile oils, internal use in concentration is to be avoided.

As a tree tea western hemlock still contains a high proportion of resinous oils, so use cautiously.

WESTERN RED CEDAR (*Thuja plicata*)

The related tree, white cedar or 'arbor vitae' (*Thuja occidentalis*) is mainly used in herbal medicine but western red cedar has similar actions. The leaves are high in volatile oils containing a significant proportion of thujone, which in high doses can cause haemorrhaging and damage to the nervous system. However thuja is also antifungal, antiviral, destroys intestinal worms and is also anti-tumour in its actions.

Internally, western red cedar can help beat serious infections and cancers. Externally, it prevents viral and fungal infections and is effective on skin cancers. Internal use, even as a tree tea, should be with very small amounts and only for a few days at a time.

As it stimulates menstruation it should be avoided as a potential abortifactant during pregnancy.

WHITE POPLAR (*Populus alba*)

The poplars are similar to the willow family in chemical makeup. They, too, contain salicin that reduces inflammation and pain. The bark is used as an astringent and diuretic and has a cooling effect.

White poplar can also be used as a tonic bitter and alterative (alteratives improve the general functioning at every level of the body). All parts can be used as a tree tea.

WHITE WILLOW (*Salix alba*)

White willow is the most widely used willow in European herbal medicine. The salicin content of the bark makes it a useful anti-inflammatory, sedating and analgesic herb. Willow salicin does not thin the blood as aspirin does.

Tree teas can be made of all parts.

WHITEBEAM (*Sorbus aria*)
The bark of whitebeam has an astringency that makes it effective for treating sore throats and diarrhoea. The fruit is edible and can be used in the same way. Seeds are best avoided, as in all sorbus species, they contain small amounts of hydrocyanic acid.

WILD SERVICE TREE (*Sorbus torminalis*)
The berries and the bark of wild service tree are astringent and can be used to help with sore throats and colds. It can also prevent diarrhoea. The fruits are edible, and , when the tree was more common, were an important food source in autumn. No cautions have been found.

WYCH ELM (*Ulmus glabra*)
All the elms have a soothing mucilaginous inner bark that forms a protective barrier when rubbed on the skin, making it a soother of sores, ulcers and skin problems. It can be effective with sore throats, heartburn, coughs and irritated lungs. It also coats the lining of the digestive tract so it can calm upset stomachs, stomach ulcers and irritated intestines.

Elm is generally safe and tolerated. Fine for tree teas.

YELLOW BUCKEYE (*Aesculus flava*)
Buckeye is the name given to American chestnuts. Their actions are similar. Bark and seeds contain anti-inflammatory compounds that have been used to relieve toothaches, haemorrhoids and so on. No toxicity is indicated in the low doses used in tree teas.

YEW (Taxus baccata)

The bark and needles(leaves) have been used both in Europe and North America for various ailments. However, yew is primarily of importance today for its taxol, a compound found to be useful in destroying cancer cells. (Taxol has now been found in hazel leaves as well).

Yew is extremely, and unpredictably, poisonous. The leaves are the most poisonous part, but all parts except for the red fleshy arils surrounding the seed are to be avoided. Compounds in yew act with a paralysing action on the heart – you can be dead before you know it - and they also provoke abortion.

Only the arils of the fruit can be eaten or used as a tree tea, and then the seed inside must not be swallowed. Treat with extreme caution.

Chapter 8

Tree Initiations and Other deep Contact

Tree attunements help us to become familiar with the feel and energy of certain tree spirits. They can be likened to regular visits to people who may either become our close friends or just stay as acquaintances whowe see now and then. Beginning to make deeper contacts with tree spirits through initiations or other processes could be compared to having a friend to stay, not just for a few hours, but for several weeks. A whole new wealth of detail and character begins to emerge. Communication can occur at profound levels and a lasting bond may be forged.

Such deep links with a tree spirit can happen spontaneously. There can be an instant recognition that establishes a bond in which the spirit can offer different ways in which the individual can benefit from the relationship. The initiations and other processes suggested here are to allow seeds to be sown for future deep contact with those spirits. Noticeable changes may not always be seen right away, though sometimes the impact can be dramatic. Initiation should not be seen as a commitment. Choosing to continue a relationship is the commitment. We cannot promise that we will become lifelong friends with someone before we have even met them properly. Beginning the process of a deeper contact with tree spirits simply indicates that we are willing to open ourselves

202

more fully to their teachings should the right circumstances come about at some time in the future.

The nature of the tree initiations differs greatly from tree to tree. Some are elaborate, some are simple. At the right time and place for you they will all be equally profound. Many initiations can be adopted as an ongoing regular practice to come into the presence of the tree spirits. When a good contact has been established the spirit may suggest changes to the procedures to better suit the energies of the individual.

With some of the initiations the information we have been given is precise and clear. With others the information is more suggestive and sketchy. Taking time to sit with the more subtle instructions may reveal to you ways in which they can be carried out. Don't get unnecessarily hung up with the possibility of more than one interpretation. Your intention and the clarity of your energy will help you find the most appropriate expression. Be patient and be attentive. If it is useful for you to work with certain tree spirits then the right information will present itself.

The Yew Initiation

" The yew tree is the vertical axis,
the constant of existence,
the immutable substance of being
that nonetheless can be manipulated
or integrated by mankind as a life-taker
or a life-giver,
a tree of life or a tree of death,
a poison or a medicine,
darkness or light."

(from 'Tree: Essence, Spirit and Teacher')

The yew, as the oldest tree of Europe and perhaps of the whole world, is a powerful spirit to contact. Not everyone is comfortable with the intense grounding power, but we feel that everyone should be given a chance to experience the energy of yew for themselves. As it is a relatively simple initiation it also makes a good introduction to the process of meeting the tree spirits.

With all tree initiations it is usually best to spend time familiarising yourself with the relevant attunements and getting to know the qualities of the tree at as many different levels as possible.

What is needed:

A small piece of yew wood or the yew flower essence.

1) Lie down with your head towards the north.

2) When settled, place a small piece of yew wood, in the centre of the forehead.

3) Make a clear intention 'to receive yew initiation'.

No specific length of time is given, but it is useful to intersperse journey drumming with periods of silence. Twenty minutes in all should be sufficient.

If it is not possible to lie down, then sit facing north and use yew flower essence on the forehead or place the wood on the top of the head. It is helpful to have someone else present who can place the wood and do the periods of drumming.

The Elm Initiation

What is needed:
A bowl made from the wood of the elm; a thin stick of elmwood; a magnifying glass or a small nugget of natural gold ; water.

> " We offer to teach you –
> the invisible tribe of Elm."

(Elm spirit, from "*Tree: Essence, Spirit and Teacher*")

1) Begin with a few minutes of chanting the elm mantra (Tai ch' chay tay. Yow) and drumming to build up energy. Two variations of initiation were suggested.

2) Pour the water into the elm wood bowl

3) Drop the nugget of gold into the water and stir the water with the elm stick in a gentle, conscious manner as if mingling or weaving the energies of the gold with the energies of the wood and water.

(If there is no gold available, use a magnifying glass to focus the rays of the sun into the water and use the stick in the same way.)

4) After a minute or so lay the stick aside and dip your fingertips into the water.

5) With a few drops from the bowl symbolically wash the hands.

6) Take some more water on the fingertips and touch it to the forehead, then draw a line from the centre of the forehead up to the top of the head and back to the nape of the neck.

7) With a little more water touch the ears, eyes and tongue.

8) Sit back into a comfortable position and rest in silence.

9) If awareness slips or focus is lost, just repeat the process.

The Ivy Doorway

" Ivy is a tree that moves;
a vegetal snake;
a green sea of leaves;
it can become a gatekeeper and a useful guide."

"... unless you travel via the intermediary of Ivy or some other similar tree spirit, it is not easy to gain access to the deeper levels of Tree wisdom that is the Deep Forest."

" The serpent, the wise snake, is the ivy that lives in the duality of dark and light, summer and winter, intoxication and sobriety, life and death. Only a teacher who has travelled every possible path can know every step of the way and be for us a safe guide."

(from "*Tree: Essence, Spirit and Teacher*")

The process is a combination of chant and vision.

What is needed: a black and white image on card or thick paper.

1) Create an image of a doorway with a semicircular arch within which is silhouetted a large five-pointed ivy leaf. The archway is black and the leaf is white. Position the image so that it is slightly above your eye level, but that causes no strain to keep in easy view.

206

2) Make a clear intention " to open the Tree Doorways" and then gaze easily at the image whilst chanting or mentally repeating the Ivy mantra ("Ki jaa oh trri..").

3) When the eyes tire simply close them for a while and continue the process internally.

4) A time will naturally come when you feel a shift of awareness. Simply relax and allow the experience with the Ivy spirit to unfold.

Oak Initiation

"As the oaken cup holds the acorn,
  the seed of life,
  so the oak tree holds safe the world of form."

"The oak and oak spirits are a doorway, and a door is either a means of entrance or a means of obstruction; it is either open or shut. The Oak initiation can be like this also. The initiation process may hand the participants a key, but the door and its keyhole still need to be found before what is beyond the door can be revealed."

(from "*Tree: Essence, Spirit and Teacher*").

What is needed: twenty or thirty oak leaves, collected fresh or fallen.

1) Construct a circle of oak leaves on the floor, large enough to stand or sit in comfortably. Place all the leaves in a clockwise direction (stalks facing anti-clockwise).

2) Enter the circle and turn slowly round until you find the most comfortable direction to be facing. Sit down or remain standing.

3) Visualise a horizontal door or hatchway under you in the floor and intend clearly "to allow the door to open".

4) Repeat for about five minutes the following variation of the oak mantra: "Or. Tar. Bey. Pey. D'hay".

5) Then rest in silence for two minutes or so.

6) If other people are also participating at this point they slowly walk around the circle, once clockwise and then once anticlockwise. If no other people are present the initiate visualises those tree spirits that have gathered around performing these actions.

7) Leave the circle and sit alone in a quiet place to stabilise the energies.

Holly Initiation

"..... The entrance to the Holly spirit can only succeed by passing between, that is balancing, the energies of desire and wisdom, head and heart."

"Light and dark,
 life and death,
 fear and bliss,
 can all be encountered here,
 in the balance of the holly spirit"

(from "*Tree: Essence, Spirit and Teacher*")

208

What is needed: flower essences of hazel and hawthorn: a drink made from edible fruits and berries; natural incense; a high-pitched bell, bowl or gong.

1) Begin by spraying the essences of hazel and hawthorn within the room.

2) Close your eyes and visualise yourself standing in front of an oak doorway. On one side of the door is a hawthorn tree, and on the other side is a hazel tree. Take time to build up this picture. Are there any other images on or around the door? Allow time for the imagery to clarify.

3) Wait patiently in front of the doorway until it opens. As it does you will see a passageway, the left side in darkness, the right side in bright light.

4) Move down the passage until it becomes a dark tunnel where the only light is now coming from the far end.

5) As you emerge from the tunnel you will find yourself in a light space of some kind. Allow time to understand the sort of space you are within.

6) At this point, keeping eyes closed, a drink is brought up to the lips and a little is sipped. The drink represents blood, the blood of the earth, and can be made from an infusion of edible fruits and berries (sloe gin is a good base (containing blackthorn and juniper), rose hips, crab apples, cherries, strawberry tree fruit, blackberries etc.)

7) Once the drink has been tasted intend clearly to 'meet the Lord of the Forest'. Stay attentive and still for several minutes.

8) Now an incense is lit and breathed in. Use plants from your locality that you have gathered and blended, such as cypress,

cedar, pine, lavender, sage, dried mushroom, dried moss, lichen, thyme and so on.

9) Now you enter a light, warm, directionless cloud. The Holly tree spirit teacher will come to you here. Take as much time as you like to communicate with each other.

10) When it is time to leave you will see an ivy tendril somewhere close to you. Follow it until you come to a white archway through which only darkness can be seen. This is the Ivy Gateway. Take time now to clarify and remember your experience.

11) When ready, step through the Gateway.

12) Complete the process by striking or ringing a high-pitched bell or gong. Listen to the resonant sound until you feel centred within your body once more.

Maple Initiation

This process is the same for any member of the maple family that you may wish to work with. The only thing that is needed is a regular time over a couple of weeks to repeat the energy visualisations.

First Phase

1) Imagine a large globe of golden light above your head. It has a diameter much greater than the width of your body. Place an image of the particular maple that you are working with at the centre of the sphere – a silhouette of the leaf shape can be a good clear image to use.

2) See the golden light, as if it were like the consistency of honey, slowly drip downward onto the top of your head.

3) As it does see a small opening appear in the top of your head. It is the end of a very thin tube, like a thin bamboo cane or a drinking straw, that you extend downward the whole length of the spine to its base.

4) See the golden liquid slowly fill up the whole of the tube.

5) At the end of the session see the top end of the tube seal over as if it were drying on contact with the air. (Next session, the first new drops from the sphere will dissolve the solidified light so that you can absorb more).

6) Allow the globe to gently disperse as if in a gentle breeze, and allow all other images to fade.

7) Repeat this process for five or seven consecutive days.

Second Phase

1) For the next three days repeat the imagery of Phase One, but now, as the tube is filled with light, see it expand outward to a much greater diameter, until eventually the whole of your body can easily fit inside it.

2) At the end of each session allow the tube around your body and the sphere above it to gently dissipate as in a gentle breeze, or, re-absorb both sphere and tube into your body as if you were breathing it into yourself at each breath. Allow the energy to permeate your body systems.

Third Phase

1) Spend time over the next week or so repeating the process, but now you will be allowing the whole globe to gradually sink down into the tube, passing down its whole length.

2) When you can bring the sphere fully into the expanded tube, the next stage is to simultaneously imagine that your own body is becoming very much smaller at the same time as both tube and sphere rapidly expand into space.

3) In this vast new space allow communication between you and the maple spirit to take place.

4) At the end of this stage of the communication shrink down the globe and allow it to take up a position at one of the seven major chakra centres. It is most likely to be at the sacral or solar plexus, but it could be at one of the others.

5) Allow any excess energy to dissipate into the space around you or return it to its source.

6) Shrink down the tube to a small size and reduce its length from both ends until it disappears.

Access the Maple spirit energy from its chakra home whenever you need to use the energy or to contact the spirit. Alternatively, quickly repeat the whole process in one session to re-establish the communication links.

Birch Initiation

The actual Birch Initiation will be given to you directly by the Birch spirit. That initiation will be wrapped around, and depend upon, the unique personal beliefs and fears that lead to misunderstanding and the obscuring of the unity of your life.

What is needed: It is useful to have a high-pitched string of bells or a bell tree. A sistrum-type of instrument could also be easily made from thin discs of metal threaded onto wire.

Preparatory Procedures.

1) Repeat the birch mantra internally for at least three minutes. ('Koo. Show. Tie. Paa). Any other attunements can be done at this time also.

2) Make a good contact with the ground and begin imagining that a system of roots is forming. See the energy of the Earth as a deep magenta colour. Magenta energy flows back up and begin to fill your body. Each breath brings in more magenta energy.

3) As the magenta fills your body from the ground upwards, watch until it reaches the level of the solar plexus. Here the energy turns to a golden glow.

4) The energy continues to rise up the body and when it approaches the head it turns to a deep indigo blue energy.

5) When the energy reaches to the very top of the head it rises in a column of white light that spreads out and fountains down to the earth, to be re-absorbed by your roots.

6) As your attention is held by this circulation of white light, become aware that within it can be seen shimmers of blue light.

7) If you have a string of small bells or a bell tree, or a recording of small bells (like falconers use, or Indian dancers), listening to this high frequency resonant sound at this stage is useful. If you have your own bell-string or bell-tree, gently shake it whilst the visualisation is maintained.

8) Listening to the trance bells, feel the white and blue shimmering light expand outward from your central axis dissolving away any sense of physical and energetic separation from the spirit of the birch.

9) You will come to rest in a spacious, dimensionless state where a free flow of energy exists between you and the spirit of the birch.

10) When it feels time to return, bring your awareness back to your mid-line, the sense of your body, your breath, and when you feel ready, slowly open your eyes.

The Lime Initiation

1) In the centre of an open space, stay centred on the spot, standing. Repeat the mantra of lime to yourself a few times. (Daa gi hey, daa gi hey, daa gi hey)

2) Slowly walk outward a little way and then turn in a tight curve to your right to bring you back to the central spot.

3) Next walk out in the opposite direction. This time turn in a tight curve to your left and return to the central starting place.

4) Turn to face a new quarter and walk purposefully out, then turn again to the right and return.

5) Finally, walk outward facing the last quarter, turn to the left and return to the central point. In this way you would have described by your movements a four-lobed or four-petalled shape.

6) Next, walk out from this point in a straight line for as far as it is possible to go in the space you are in. At the maximum extent of the line, stop and turn to face the starting point.

7) Here, now, acknowledge the energies of the universe and the Elements. Firstly, bring your hands together near the base chakra at the base of the spine and sweep them down

and away to the Earth in an expansive arc.

8) Next, take your hands to your heart chakra at the centre of the chest and again sweep them down and away outward from the body.

9) Lastly, take your hands up to the top of the head and sweep them outward and upwards from here.

10) Walk back to the original starting place.

11) Finally, sit down and repeat the lime mantra for a short time before remaining quietly in a meditative state.

Cheяяy Initiation

What is needed: a bowl or some other small vessel made of copper; cherry wood sticks or staves; water.

1) Begin with a minute or so of attunements to cherry (using the tree essence, mantra, trance position, wood, and so on.)

2) Place the cherry staves across the top of the copper bowl covering as much as possible of the opening.

3) Take the water and drip it over the cherry wood so that it filters down into the bowl. Leave the bowl quietly until it is needed later.

4) For a few minutes repeat the cherry mantra quietly to yourself with eyes closed. Speak in a whisper and move your lips to the sounds. (Cho paa t. r. paa)

5) When you have settled into a comfortable rhythm add the colours of the cherry colour sequence to this mantra in the following way:

With "CHO" - see a turquoise light at the thymus gland (upper centre of chest).

With "PAA" - see a gold light at the solar plexus.

With "T. R." - see a turquoise light again at the thymus.

With "PAA" - see a pink light between the first and second chakra around the pubic bone, or the inner centre of the pelvis.

Repeat this process from about three to five minutes at least.

6) Now take a cherry wood piece and dip it into the water. Draw the visual symbol of cherry (like an upturned bowl or a circle with an opening downward), on the centre of the forehead. Place the cherry piece beside the bowl. If there are several participants everyone uses a new cherry stick to repeat the process.

7) Pour a little water into your hands from the copper bowl and drink it

8) Sit in quiet space for at least seven minutes.

Strawberry Tree Initiation

1) Become comfortable in the tree trance position. Lie on the right side. Knees are drawn up to the chest, into the foetal position. The right hand is placed over the eyes. The left hand is on the heart.

2) Begin gently whispering the mantra to yourself. (Kee ny re koo sha, kee ny re koo sha.......)

216

3) As the sound falls into its natural rhythm, imagine hearing the mantra flow with waves as they break on a seashore.

4) As the feeling of the shore clarifies and you sink into the experience, have a clear intention to meet the spirit of the strawberry tree.

Poplar Initiation

This initiation process is applicable for all members of the poplar family. Carry out attunements to the species that you want to link with before you begin this initiation.

Phase One

1) Stand in the centre of an open space. Begin to walk outward, slowly, in a tight anti-clockwise spiral.

2) When you have reached the extent of your space, reverse the direction and walk slowly inwards in a clockwise direction until you reach the original starting point.

3) Stop and sit at the centre. Begin to build an image of the poplar you are working with. Imagine that your own body is taking on the form of the tree. Stay with that image for as long as you can.

4) When you lose the focus of yourself as tree, repeat the outward and inward spiralling walk. Repeat this sequence of activity and visualisation until a point arises that, when you sit, you can feel yourself neither completely human nor wholly tree. Your awareness is present and relaxed but you have become ambivalent or unconcerned about your exact physical form.

Take as many sessions as you need, over several weeks if necessary, to build up the ability to link with the tree and then rest in formlessness. At the end of each session, make sure that you ground and centre your energies back into your body before resuming normal activity.

Phase Two

5) Repeat all the stages of Phase One and then sit in the centre. Imagine your body as a single drop of water that is suspended, ready to fall.

6) Allow yourself to fall as far as possible. Just let go and drop. Feel the speed and certainty of your descent.

7) At some point the fall will cease. It may be that it feels like a solid surface has been met with and the drop has been dispersed. Or it may be experienced as a change of awareness. This may be indicated by a loss of awareness for a moment, or a definite change in how you feel, or a sensation of being lost or having forgotten for an instant what is happening.

8) If at this point you judge that you are not fully engaged within the experience at a deep enough level, repeat the visualisation of the falling drop. Form another drop where you are and allow that drop to fall further until a definite energy shift is felt.

9) Where this shift occurs, remain alert, relaxed and open. It is here that the spirit of the Poplar will be met.

10) To bring the process to an end, take a deep inhalation and imagine bringing all the scattered elements together and return to your normal level of functioning. An effective alternative is to imagine a film playing in reverse in slow motion: the water reassembling itself into a drop and then flying upwards to rest at its starting place.

Other Deep Contacts

With some trees much less direct instruction has been received about the processes of initiation. Perhaps the activity of thinking about what could be meant by the words is a necessary part of building a closer relationship, perhaps it needs to be a more personal discovery, or maybe we just weren't tuned in enough to get the instructions in a clear enough manner. Here are a few clues. We have called them Tree Sutras, rather than Initiations. They may point the way to action.

Rowan Sutra

1) Establish silence.

2) Establish a point of attention in the silence.

3) Allow the flow of energy tides to move through you.

4) Shape the tides and read them.

Willow Sutra

1) Fire within water. The vessel that holds water is not made of water. From where does the fire arise?

2) The relationship of fire and water.

3) Spirit – breathing from the outside to the inside.

4) The relationship of joy and sadness, of coming and going, of moving and of motionlessness.

5) Is the vessel that contains nothing, a vessel?

6) Spiritus – moving breath. What is the breath that is not moving?

7) The relationship of breathing in and breathing out. The relationship of inside and that which is not inside. Fire within water.

8) Spiritus – movement of mind. Spiritus – moving breath.

9) What is the vessel that holds thought?

10) The relationship of sense and sensation. From where does fire arise?

11) The moment when one thing stops and another thing starts.

12) Bringing together fire from one side and water from the other side, slowly.

13) Watch the spaces between. Spiritus – neither this nor that. Extinguish what distinguishes, remaining with what remains.

14) Fire within water. Food within eater. Spiritus – that which fills the spaces between. Neither coming nor going.

15) Between thought and what is not thought. Between breath and what is not breath. Between meaning and what is not meaning. Between resting and what is not resting. Between movement and what is not movement.

16) Fire within water, and what is between them.

17) Extinguish what distinguishes, remaining with what remains. Spiritus, spiritus, spiritus.

18) Opening out, unfolding, relaxing. Each part floating away from each other part.

19) Allowing silence, and the absence of silence.

20) Flame inside a drop of water.

21) Allowing an inflowing of breath and an outflowing of breath.

22) Flame inside a drop of water. Burning and extinguishing. Losing and finding. Holding on and letting go.

23) Joy and the absence of joy. Pain and the absence of pain. Time and the absence of time. Remembrance and the absence of memory. Breath and the absence of breath.

24) Fire within water.

Pine Sutra

1) Complete darkness until all there is darkness.

2) Remain in darkness

3) Kindle with sparks

4) The scent of pine needles

5) Darkness with the memory of light.

6) Remain

7) Encompass that which extends beyond light and darkness.

8) Remain

9) Kindle understanding

10) The scent of pine needles

11) Remain

Chapter 9

New Tree Essences

ASPEN (*Populus tremula*)

Aspen is one of the white poplars. It is native to Britain and was one of the pioneer trees to colonise the land when the ice retreated. The aspen is a delicate, open, upright tree that tends to be found in clusters on the edge of woodland in damp soils. Except for the Scottish Highlands it is nowhere widespread, but can be found locally throughout Britain. The tree suckers freely from its shallow roots so many thickets are probably shoots from the same tree. One of the largest organisms on the planet is said to be an aspen in Colorado that covers thousands of acres with genetically identical suckered clones. Aspen has a smooth silvery bark, marked with dark horizontal pores, that darkens and furrows with age. The leaves are regular and oval in shape with an undulating margin held on large flat stalks that allow the leaves to tremble in the slightest of breezes. Catkins appear early in March, male and female on separate trees. The male flowers are brown and the female are green turning to white, woolly seeds in May or June. Although fast growing, the aspen is short-lived and only reaches a height of sixty feet (20m) in Britain. However, as Stephen Buhner points out, the roots of aspen are ancient and can live for thousands of years sending up new trees across the landscape. The seeds of aspen germinate overnight and grows very rapidly – this and the suckering of the roots makes it unpopular with farmers. The American species of aspen "Populus tremuloides" is a sturdier tree. Both yield salicin and populin in the bark, useful in fevers as a febrifuge and tonic.

The Essence:

Keywords: " Delight" Intuition and intellect; balances over-analysis; mind transcends the personal; fears calmed; broader perspective; clarity of humour; amusement; original humour; manifesting wisdom; enlightened laughter; communication of dreams; wise laughter.

The main energy of aspen is the protection of the soul's wisdom and the ability to manifest wisdom in practical ways.

There is an ability with aspen to communicate in novel and completely original ways in order to express your individual uniqueness. A sense of humour relies on a broad perspective and a vision of life with limitless possibility. This essence brings that ability to place oneself in context with others and to accept that fallibility is inevitable and inescapable. The letting go of personal foibles, the ability to accept with good humour our own imperfections and bizarre habits and beliefs, comes with the absorbing of the energy of aspen.

The Large Intestine meridian can be quite affected by the negative emotional qualities of stuffiness and constipated attitudes, as well as guilt and shame. Aspen brings a sense of humour and an appreciation of one's own failings, which is a great destroyer of fear. Any fear ultimately reduces down to fear of change, fear of letting go. Taking oneself too seriously encourages fear because it dampens down the ability to change, to flow and to modify one's behaviour.

Aspen has an opening and balancing effect on the mind so that fears are calmed and a space is created within which one can think and organise, reconsidering options for action. Ultimately this then leads to better decision-taking.

Aspen

The brow chakra is significantly affected. Firstly, there is a soothing and peaceful effect on the overactive imagination. This will take place both when the mind is dwelling on unlikely future scenarios and also when it is busy with inner visions of a more transpersonal nature. With this peace comes the ability to express ideas and concepts that are, by their very nature, difficult to categorise. Intuitive insights and imaginative creativity become a lot easier to share with others in language that can be understood by all.

At the finest spiritual levels aspen again works with the mind, opening and balancing the intellect so that it takes creative potential into its functions. This integrates intuitive insights within the intellect and prevents over-analysis of situations by the rational mind. This, in turn, greatly enhances the effectiveness of meditative states because there is a much greater coordination between different levels of the mind.

Ultimately, this can bridge the gap between abstract and particular, absolute and relative, form and void, intellect and transcendence.

Signature:
As with all the poplar family, the leaves of aspen are held on long, thin stems that allow them to vibrate in the slightest of breezes to aid cooling and water transportation. Those who are of an overly serious disposition often associate this with a trembling caused by fear or grief. Those who are amused by the beauty of constant change in life may, on the other hand, see the vibration as a continuous wide-eyed chuckling at the wonder of creation.

The real constancy of the aspen is held in the vibrant root system. Above ground the changes wrought by time and circumstance on the tree are able to be treated lightly – more suckers can replace lost trees, and a single tree can soon become a grove. When there is a deep peace and stability change can be welcomed and enjoyed for the new experiences it brings.

ATLAS CEDAR (*Cedrus atlantica*)

Atlas cedar comes from the Atlas Mountains of Algeria and Morocco in North Africa. It has been planted in Britain since 1844 but the largest number of trees are now blue Atlas cedar, a natural variation that is found growing amidst the more common dark green variety in the wild. The tree grows to 35m. (110 ft.) and has slightly ascending, sweeping branches. (The three main cedars planted in Britain can be identified thus : Atlas cedar has Ascending branches, cedar of Lebanon has Level branches, Deodar has Descending branches).

The bark of Atlas cedar is a smooth dark grey with fine fissures. Needles grow singly on new growth and in rosettes on mature stems. Like all cedars, the Atlas cedar flowers in autumn. Male flowers are upright, cone-like and pink, turning yellow when heavy with pollen. Small green female flowers become large pot-shaped cones with a sunken top that disintegrates after two years to leave the central spike.

Atlas cedar, also called African cedar or satinwood, gives a distilled oil that used to be known for helping bronchitis, catarrh, arthritis and skin eruptions like acne.

The Essence:

Keywords: "Resilience"; removal of out-of-date patterns; clearing the way to do what is needed; achieving a personal Path; resilience to cope with change and adversity; confidence and self-sufficiency for those feeling isolated and unsupported; cleansing of stresses and a smoothing of subtle energy to encourage the body to better use healing energy; determination to pursue personal fulfilment; understanding and flowing with the constant changing state of creation.

Atlas cedar essence is of great benefit for those who feel they lack a worthwhile direction in their life, or who face opposition to their chosen way of life. By giving the impetus to follow a personal path it allows the growth of personal power and clarity of awareness. Our lives are often a compromise between what we really want to do and what we feel we must do. Layers of conflict and resentment build up that drain away energy, enthusiasm and optimism. This turbulence can be reduced when all a person's energies start to move smoothly in the same direction.

Atlas cedar helps those who feel unsupported and who lack the encouragement of others. It provides the energy to take full advantage of every opportunity and the practical initiative to make something from nothing. Self-confidence increases so there is less need to seek the approval of others. The energy of this tree can be extremely supportive where there is isolation from others. Its energy allows acceptance of one's situation without denial. It can provide the means to escape the feelings of isolation, or it can offer new viewpoints where the benefits of the situation can be acknowledged. Self-sufficiency is encouraged.

All the chakra system is brought to a better state of equilibrium and this encourages a return of emotional stability. The overall balancing effect also helps the system to remain centred during times of change. It creates a calm receptivity that allows healing energy to move effortlessly through the whole of the body.

Atlas cedar helps to clear the etheric body of old, unwanted patterns of energy. These subtle scars can act as focus points for physical problems and reduce the flexibility of the body's systems to deal with new stresses.

There is a greater organisation and flow of information that calms and clarifies deep levels of personal energy patterns.

Atlas Cedar

Fears and anxieties are reduced and it becomes easier to see what needs to be done to get the best out of each situation in life.

Finally, Atlas cedar brings the ability to experience the underlying creative patterns of the universe. It becomes easier to see the constant flow and change in all things, the continuous re-patterning and re-capitulation of the infinite creative urge without repetition. Sensitivity to these flows makes it easier to deal with beginnings and endings and to plug oneself into a place where the maximum life energy can be accessed. Patterns from the past are also more readily available and can inspire new ways of using ancient technologies.

Signature:
The cones take two or three years to ripen and remain even when seeds have been dispersed (resilience).

DOUGLAS FIR (*Pseudotsuga menziesii*)
Douglas fir is a magnificent tree, one of the largest in the world. It is native to North America and makes up a significant proportion of the temperate rainforest of the Pacific North-West coast. It can grow to over 300ft (100m.) in America and to 180ft (55m.) in Britain, though as a commercial forestry tree it is rarely left to grow more that 100 ft (40m.) because of the sheer difficulty in moving the huge trunks.

Douglas fir is named after David Douglas who sent seed to the Horticultural Society in 1827. The Latin name remembers Archibald Menzies who first found the tree and sent a sample of foliage to Kew in 1793. The original site where seed was collected happened to be ideal for growth in Britain, especially around Perth in Scotland, from where Douglas originated. Many of the first trees are still growing well. Stands of

Douglas fir are often left in forests as shelter belt for less robust species.

Douglas fir has a corded, corky bark of dark grey or purple. Its foliage is held on large down-swept branches and is a dense covering of rich dark green that deeply shades the ground underneath. The leaves have a sweet, fruity scent. Cones of Douglas fir are easily identified by the papery forked tongue emerging from the base of each scale. Male flowers are small yellow buds along the end of branches, whilst female flowers can be found at the end of branches as red-orange tassels.

The Essence:
Keywords: "Standing alone"; relatedness; finding one's place; room to expand; need to be a part of, need to be apart from; parts of a whole; spontaneous energy; freedom to be oneself; living life to the full; balancing the flow; connectivity and relationship; energy to grow; for those who feel they stand out in a crowd, who feel a sense of difference that inhibits the way they wish to be.

The primary energy of Douglas fir concerns itself with finding space to be and to act as oneself. All aspects of this relationship with the world outside, and to finding one's place in the world, are brought into a better balance with this tree's help. It gives the dynamism for spontaneous activity, which is nonetheless appropriate and balanced. Energy to grow and space to act are easier to find.

The Triple Warmer meridian is concerned with the maintenance of the body's own internal systems, ensuring a correct working relationship between organs. When imbalance is found in this meridian Douglas fir will naturally help to restore calm equilibrium. This will be particularly pertinent when there is stress around issues to do with being alone or being with others. Where there is a need to feel part of a

Douglas Fir

group, of belonging and being valued, as serving a useful function in a group but where there is also a need to be apart from the pressures and commitments of complex relationships, this tree essence will help to resolve the opposing tensions.

Extra energy is given to the desire to live life fully and openly but not to become reckless, nor to retreat from fear of danger. This essence can bring a feeling of belonging that encourages the openness of the heart centre. The sense of supported freedom relies on a good connection to the energies of other people. Being too dependent on how others feel, relying on their obvious encouragement before any activity is even contemplated, is indicative of imbalance and a lack of life force. On the other hand, Douglas fir will bring a more appropriate perspective to those people who disregard totally the needs of others or who fail to reciprocate with the normal sharing of energy. In this way Douglas fir helps to maintain a correct flow of energy relationship between the self and others.

At the most refined level this can manifest as an open appreciation of all things, an understanding that every life and every object has its own inherent value in the context of the whole. Douglas fir brings us the clarity of awareness to recognise this connection between all individual selves. It helps to cleanse and purify those separating and limiting belief patterns that prevent the true expansion of self-awareness. Ultimately realising that the sense of self, of unique being-ness, is not just a property of the sentient, living individual, but is simply a reflection, at the finite level of perception of an unlimited all-encompassing nature, a characteristic of every aspect of existence. "I am" is no longer just a barrier that exists to prevent the victory of "I am not". "I am" simply becomes the uniting universal consciousness reflected in every aspect of that creation. "I am" is simply the "I am" with this particular viewpoint, from this body, at this

233

time. Everything else's "I am" has the same validity and the same significance – it is the same substratum of awareness, the same foundation of being. In this sense there are no individuals, only points of view.

Signature:
The size, mass and solidity of the tree. Its ability to protect its neighbours. Its great height reflects the breadth of perspective. Its deep green foliage, the Heart centre, focus on relationship with the world.

EUCALYPTUS (CIDER GUM) (*Eucalyptus gunnii*)

The Eucalyptus family is native to Australia and Tasmania. It contains over three hundred species, which are adapted to conditions of heat and dryness by having leaves that are thick and leathery and that turn their edges towards the sun to reduce evaporation.

The cider gum has become a popular ornamental tree because it is fast-growing and has juvenile leaves that are a striking blue-grey, and, unlike the mature willow-like leaves, are rounded and stalkless. Where it isn't subject to frost damage it grows up to 100ft. (30m) with an open, airy crown. Eucalyptus flowers have buds that are cup-shaped and covered with a membrane that is thrown off as the flower expands. The fruit also has a cupped shape containing many seeds.

Eucalyptus growing in high ravines have been measured at over 480ft – taller than the Californian sequoias. Because of the tree's phenomenal ability to draw groundwater into its roots, eucalyptus species have been planted in swamp zones in many parts of the world to effectively control malarial mosquito infestation by drying up the ground. The leaves of many species contain a pungent aromatic oil (though not much is present in the cider gum), and this contains a

powerful antiseptic and disinfectant. The lungs and airways are effectively cleared by the oil's vapours. In the trees the aromatic oil and resinous gums are produced to reduce water loss.

The Essence:
Keywords: "Sustenance": opportunity; restoration of energy; clarification and space; smooth integration of energy; correct relationship and flow; intuition; meditative practices.

Eucalyptus creates the space we need to be creative, and also brings the discipline needed to creatively organise our energies. It becomes easier to take advantage of the existing conditions in a way that benefits our lives.

Intuition, our grasp of larger patterns and underlying energy fluctuations, is brought into a better relationship with the feelings of the body. This means that we are more likely to notice the signals our body gives out as it recognises changes in the subtle energy fields around us. With this intuitive body wisdom, our awareness becomes more firmly rooted in the senses and the body, helping us feel more in control of our lives, calm and integrated.

A dynamic energy is set up in the Central meridian, balancing the life energy there. Eucalyptus will help to direct the individual to those types of practical activity that help to maintain the integrity of this important energy channel. It will encourage whatever is required to grow and become more powerful in oneself. Those who are in a chronic state of confusion and enervation, showing lack of motivation and energy, would find an ability to focus on activities appropriate to the restoration of their natural state of health.

All the chakras are helped by the energy of eucalyptus to have a more efficient, interactive functioning. It brings an increase in energy and a better distribution of resources, so that the whole body works more smoothly and is better able to cope with new stress and more effective at releasing existing stresses in the body.

A quality of space and freedom is also felt in the mind. It becomes easier to see things more clearly and in original ways. Eucalyptus brings a discipline to organise and to make the most of any situation because it can help to reveal the most important underlying truths.

At the subtlest levels of function eucalyptus takes the mind to the very finest levels of awareness where it becomes possible to discern the seeds of ideas and the beginning of thoughts as they emerge from the base of consciousness. This makes it a useful essence for mantra meditation and those types of contemplative practice that involve witnessing.

Coordination of the most fundamental levels of mind creates a deep silence with alert awareness.

Signature:
The ability to draw a phenomenal amount of water from the ground (drawing up energy into its life channels); movement of leaf surfaces to reduce evaporation from strong sunlight, (the ability to adapt to current circumstances, making the best of difficult surroundings).

FIG TREE   (*Ficus carica*)
The earliest record of figs in Britain is from the beginning of the 16th century, though there are references to much earlier plantings, and certainly the Romans may have established figs in their farm villas.

The fig is part of the large and important Ficus family that ranges across all the warm and tropical areas of the world. Some are large trees, some are climbers or vines. The fig tree

Fig Tree

that we are familiar with originates from Persia, Syria and Asia Minor and was a major food plant around the Mediterranean area. Warm, south–facing sites in Britain suit it well and the tree will fruit successfully. Fig will set seed and grow into mature trees only where there is very fertile ground or extra heat. Colonies have formed on the banks of the River Donn in Sheffield fed by the warm waters from local steelworks. Others have set seed down-river from sewage works and in cemeteries.

The fig tree is a low, widespread tree growing to 25ft (8m). Trees of over three hundred years have been recorded in England. The leaves are easily recognisable with thick, leathery, hairy surfaces with between three to five deep rounded lobes. The flower of the fig is completely inside the immature fruit and is pollinated only by a small gall wasp that burrows its way through the skin. Figs fruit twice a year: in May the fruits ripen in the warm weather but these are often destroyed by the cold of the autumn months. Edible figs tend to be those that bud later in the year and survive the winter to swell in the following spring and summer.

The fig tree was sacred to Bacchus and was thought to have been discovered by Saturn. Figs can be fermented when ripe and made into a wine or brandy. Fig trees are important sacred trees in India – the Bo Tree, under whose branches the Buddha gained enlightenment, is a species of fig. Sacred trees, found in every Indian town and village with their roots painted with vermilion, are often of the Ficus family. Medicinally, the fruit of figs have been used for their mild laxative action. As they are also demulcent, figs have been used to reduce catarrhal build-up in the nose and throat. The roasted soft, pulpy interior fruit have been used as a poultice for boils and abscesses. The milky sap of the stem can be used for removing warts.

The Essence:
Keywords: "Generator"; expression of needs; soul food; feelings of emptiness resolved; letting go; belly dancing; energy to achieve.

The fig tree has a tightly defined sphere of action: it echoes the moment of creation where a single burst of energy manifested the universe. It contains the compassionate energy of life and the awareness of dynamic love. It holds the understanding that all things exist as part of one single creative impulse, fragments of a single creativity bomb.

Fig tree will work very well whenever there is a healing required within the pelvic area of the body. It will be restorative and energising to the subtle flows here. It helps to energise areas of stagnancy and coolness, where the natural flow of energy has ceased to move in a normal way. The cause of this particular form of static energy will be the failure to express honesty – the inability or reluctance of the individual to maintain and uphold their own energy integrity, their own right to exist as a unique entity.

The Governor meridian along the spinal column will be given a boost of energy that may release pent-up and unexpressed feelings and ideas. With this there will also arise a clearer message to others of your personal need for space and freedom. There may also be a new ability to identify and resolve feelings of lack or emptiness. Perhaps there exists an inappropriate longing or even a greed to own or possess, or to be someone or something else. This is simply a misdirected attempt to restore balance and calm instead of achieving a real freedom in one's life. Fig tree will turn the attention back to the causes of discomfort within oneself and help to resolve it there where it started, instead of continually mirroring dissatisfaction outward onto the world.

240

The mind is helped to become calm and creative, allowing one to see what is needed to flow into harmonious living again.

At spiritual levels, too, fears are calmed and clarity increases. It becomes easier to communicate ideas and information. There may also arise the ability to access far memory – memory from deep parts of oneself or from the akashic records of creation once this new openness has cleared away the tensions and frustrations blocking personal energy.

Signature:
Fig arises from fertile and warm ground (the energy of creation); the flower within the fruit (the originating energy still existing deep within every aspect of creation, also, returning to the causes of discomfort)

FOXGLOVE TREE (*Paulownia tomentosa*)
The Latin name of the foxglove tree derives from the daughter of Tsar Paul I of Russia, Anna Paulowna, who became the wife of King William II. The tree was first discovered by Westerners in Japan, by a German botanist, E. Kaemfer, in the 17th century. It is native to China where it has been highly regarded as a bringer of health and longevity.

In May, before the very large, heart-shaped leaves open, upright bracts bear a loose pyramid of purple flowers that resemble, both in shape and size, the flowers of the foxglove. The tree is airy and open and grows up to 23ft (7m) in southern England wherever it can escape from the late spring frosts.

The Essence:
Keywords: "Harmonious flow"; ending of turbulence; strengthens aura and life-force; happiness, relaxation; sharpens mental focus; increases energy efficiency; quieten all systems; smooth waters.

Foxglove Tree

Foxglove tree has a powerful action on the underlying and fundamental energies of the body. It has the ability to help in the removal of emotional blocks – caused by emotional wounds, shocks and traumas – that can then lead to a profound healing of the self on many different levels. There is an integration of different systems and a smoothing of all functions, similar to the effect that removing debris from a river brings all dangerous turbulence to an end, restoring a natural, harmonious flow.

This effect begins at the level of the etheric body where many potential problems are located, and from there it flows through all the subtle levels of the system, especially the meridian system. In this way the entire aura of a person is strengthened and balanced. Creative energy becomes available at all levels and this naturally increases life energy. There is a relaxation of tensions and an ability to enjoy living and to be much happier with oneself, without any need for self-deception or pretence.

Indeed, at the Brow chakra there is an energy increase that produces a strong amplification of discrimination and clarity. So at the same time that feelings are heightened, the mental focus is also sharpened. It becomes possible to understand and release inaccurate and unsupported beliefs and fears. With this reduction of confusion it is much easier to express what is truly felt and understood in a clear way that people can understand. This would be not so much at the level of everyday or intellectual understanding but more at the empathic and intuitive levels going beyond the limitations of language.

Foxglove tree energy can be of great use in quietening a turbulent mind. Like those who continually have radio or television playing in the background suddenly feel uncomfortable when there is no noise, so the mind can feel unnerved when there is a reduction of background thought and it immediately 'turns up the volume' to familiar levels. Foxglove tree makes it easy to accept new levels of quietness in the mind – caused mainly through an increase in efficiency that has resulted from the reduction of turbulence and stress. In a noisy mind, silence is often equated with emptiness and a loss of individual identity. Here, silence is now experienced as a natural function of the easy flow of energy and so causes little concern.

A similar state of flow and intuitive understanding occurs within the emotions, which also naturally reduce their activity to levels appropriate to the time and place. Emotional states arise and are expressed in a natural, easy way. They are neither held onto beyond the time they are relevant, nor are they suppressed because of a belief that they might be wrong in some way. The ease and flow that this essence brings to the whole system ensures that a genuine expression of the individuality is maintained without creating turbulence or upset to those around.

At its finest level foxglove tree takes the harmonious flow of the individual's energy patterns and integrates them within a transpersonal, universal pattern. Support, integration and an ability to transcend personal limitations, however those may be conceived, is possible at this level.

Signature:
The open, spacious appearance of the tree. Large purple flowers (integration of energy creating silence in the system).

GINKGO (*Ginkgo biloba*)
The ginkgo, or maidenhair tree, is perhaps the most ancient of trees still in existence. It is the only species in its family and has been found as fossilised remains that are over 180 million years old throughout the world. Although it is deciduous, ginkgo is usually classed as a conifer, but in fact it

is even older than the conifers, that are considered to be the earliest of the flowering trees.

Ginkgo can be very long-lived. It is found in China and from there was taken to Japan where there are esteemed temple trees over a thousand years old. Ginkgo has a simple form with a single upright trunk and short branches growing out to make a narrow pyramidal form up to 40m (130ft). The leaves are unique and unmistakable. Fan-shaped with a deep central notch, they are thick and hairless, carried on long stems that spring from short nodes on the branches. In autumn the leaves turn bright butter yellow. The flowers of the male and female trees are budlike catkins in March. When planted nearby the female trees become fertilised and bear a fleshy, plum-like seed that has a strong and unpleasant smell. Leaves and fruit are rich in medicinal compounds. No wild trees are known to exist. Ginkgo remains in existence by virtue of its medicinal and spiritual values. It has become a common park and garden tree since its introduction to Europe by 19th century explorers of the Far East.

The Essence:
Keywords: "the Ancient Way"; harmonisation with the Universe; invisibility; flowing with the tides; smooth flow of emotions; internal harmonisation; regulation of internal and external Elements; neutralisation of deep stress and trauma; clarification and purification; contiguous flow; harmonious vessel; the Way of Power.

The main energy of ginkgo helps the internal flow of the feelings within the individual. It is concerned with relationship to the self, self-directed and self-motivated. Without an open, honest awareness of what one's own state of being is, it is pointless reaching out into the world. Everything we feel internally is expressed in how we behave with everything around us. We mirror in our lives how we feel, or do not feel, inside. Without knowing this as reality it can seem as if circumstances, events and people conspire to prevent us from achieving our goals, when in fact it is the way we interact – our expectations, our blocks, our problems, that often initiates the friction that prevents success. Ginkgo brings a deep relaxation, a release of emotional stress that allows us to enjoy simple pleasures. Where there is an overburdening of emotion it brings release and an acceptance of difficulties.

The solar plexus chakra is balanced at emotional and mental levels. Welling up of strong feelings like anger, fear and resentment are quickly brought to a state of peace. That energy is given creative pathways to revivify the life energy in the body, rather than dissipating in emotional outbursts. Thus the system is strengthened and empowered to act constructively for the benefit of the self. This internal revolution of energy patterns reinforces personal truth and helps to uphold beliefs without the need to force those ideas on others, or to be unsympathetic to the opposite viewpoint.

With this internal harmonisation of flow it becomes possible to have a better connection with others, to be more sensitive and to feel the flow of energy between yourself and others. This can help to balance those who find that they are overly sensitive to the energy of others or who feel they need to be isolated and cut off from the unbalancing influence of other people. Those suffering from chronic energy loss (like ME and CFS), would perhaps benefit from the stabilising effect of the ginkgo tree essence. The essence also helps to create a useful balance of energies in relationships so that personal boundaries are maintained without closing down necessary communications.

Very deep stresses are helped to clear from the most subtle layers of the body. Tendencies from other lives or from ancestral and genetic patterns begin to work free and loosen their hold on behaviour and belief structures. Traumas that

Ginkgo

have locked the body into working in a certain way are gently melted so that a more creative, stress-free flow of energy can be established.

With this tree's energy comes a profound cleansing and purifying that ultimately can link the flow of the individual's personal energy circuits to the energy circuits of the Universal tides. Although this potentially provided limitless energy and limitless potential for action, in actuality it creates a seamless flow between desire and fulfilment, where the only fulfilment required is that which furthers the harmony of the Universe. In this sense ginkgo creates a state of invisibility. The individual creates no ripples, leaves no footprints, has no power except the perfect amount required to complete each task.

Signature:
The fan-shaped leaves that create an even flow of energy between the inner and outer worlds.

JUNIPER (*Juniperus communis*)
The juniper has the widest distribution of any tree, growing right across Europe, Siberia, Asia and America, from Atlantic to Pacific coasts. In Britain its distribution is scattered, growing as a low shrub on chalk downland, on the limestone moors of Cumbria and Yorkshire, and in the native pine woods of Scotland where it forms a tangled understorey.

Juniper has a great many natural forms – it can resemble a gorse bush in shape, or can grow to become a neat conical tree up to about 20ft (6m). Male and female flowers grow on separate trees. In April and May they appear as small cone-like buds at the base of the needle-like leaves. Berries are dusty green and ripen to dark blue-purple in the second year. The berries are used to make gin and essential oils. The former uses the ripe berries whilst the latter produces a

Juniper

superior oil from the green unripened berries. The essential oil is used as an aid to kidney and bladder problems (though it can cause irritation and stress the liver in large doses). It is diuretic, disinfectant, warming and stimulating to the circulation and the immune system.

Juniper has been used worldwide as an incense and a purifier of sacred space. It is said both to summon the ancestors and drive away harmful spirits. In Scotland, juniper wood was burnt on the doorstep at Samhain (Hallowe'en) to keep spirits at bay. In the Highlands juniper was also called the mountain yew, whose form and energy it resembles.

Juniper was one of the first trees to colonise northern Britain as the ice caps retreated and it was a major part of the landscape until larger trees got established, cutting out the light that the juniper thrives upon.

The Essence:
Keywords: "Doorway"; increased life-force and personal power; renunciation of the past; generosity; relaxation; old stresses released; discrimination to see past, present and future; ancestral patterns; inner versatility.

Juniper brings a strength and revitalising energy to all levels of the body. It steadies the life-energy and allows it to move in those directions best suited to the individual. Sense of purpose and personal power to achieve goals is encouraged and this influx of energy naturally supports the immune system and the maintenance of life-force. It becomes easier to clarify intentions and make practical changes according to one's wishes.

Juniper essence helps to release us from the failures of the past. It relaxes the energy of the Circulation-Sex meridian, allowing us to accept and forgive mistakes and incorrect actions. Regret, remorse and jealousy are released. Those

250

things that are really important and relevant are brought into focus. There is more confidence in one's own abilities and the capability to achieve one's own happiness. There is a relaxation, an acceptance of things as they are, and an increase in happiness and joy. Freedom from the weight of the past means the possibility of a completely new start to living.

There is a huge release of stress that has accumulated at the level of the Sacral chakra. This is where stresses that cannot be immediately dealt with are buried. They result in long-term energy blocks that restrict creativity and lead to rigidity on many levels. All the inefficiencies in a body stem from this accumulation of unresolved events. Juniper has a strong cleansing and purifying action that helps to relax the tensions and releases the blocks wherever they have been stored. Emotional and physical release together with an increased sense of joy and pleasure come with this tree's energy. Tension is released from the areas of the head and spine and the Heart chakra is also cleansed of barriers that prevent growth.

At very fine levels of the self there is increased discrimination, an innate intelligence that is able to see the hidden beginnings of things. In practice, this helps to reveal the distant past and how it has come to influence the present. Juniper offers us a way to link to the flow of our ancestor's history without being swayed by those events in any negative way.

Juniper is able to help us, through its cleansing properties and through its ability to link with the past, to make use of, in a positive and truly personal manner, every sort of energy and experience that we might possibly come across in our lives. This naturally instils in us a great sense of safety and self-confidence. Having access to the great passage of Time, there is little that can come completely out of the blue at us. Everything can be seen in terms of its progress, its development, its conclusion. Change, the one thing we refuse to accept easily into our lives, becomes the pattern by which all things can be measured. It becomes possible for us to see equally clearly into the Past, the Present and the Future.

Signature:
The purifying smoke; the sharp pungent, perfume of the fruits that enlivens the senses.

LIQUIDAMBER (SWEET GUM)
(*Liquidamber styraciflua*)
This tree superficially resembles the Acer family, but its leaves are alternate rather than opposite. The leaves are strikingly large with five or seven distinct pointed lobes, the central, terminal lobe being a lot larger than the side lobes. Leaves are smooth and finely toothed turning to a range of magnificent colours in autumn, from oranges to reds to violets, purples and blacks. Liquidamber is broadly conical and densely foliated growing to about 40 – 45m (130 – 150 ft.) Small male and female flowers appear with the leaves in late spring.

Liquidamber originates from Mexico and the southern United States and is famous for its aromatic gum resin that exudes from the trunk. The resin is used as perfume, medicine and as a flavouring. The wood is known as satin walnut.

The Essence:
Keywords: "Sweet tongue". Self-aware dynamic energy; 'backbone'; personal energy integrity; release of emotional energy to care for self and others; involvement; loquaciousness of the bard; digestion of all creative states; passionate expression, calm mind.

The energy of liquidamber is dynamic and passionate. It works primarily with the emotional drives that it is able to direct and mould in compassionate and creative ways.

252

Liquidamber

Liquidamber moulds raw emotional energy to bring the individual maximum emotional support and positive life-energy. The force of this life–energy cannot be other than itself. It is strong and undiluted, yet it is the energy of life and so, when manifesting it automatically brings positive change. This tree energy frees core resources of dynamic self-awareness. At whatever level is needed, liquidamber can revitalise, rejuvenate and re-align the passionate will to live.

Liquidamber strengthens the Governing meridian parallel to the spine. It gives 'backbone' – the courage of one's convictions. It helps to maintain personal energy integrity in situations where there is opposition to individual's expressing their own needs and opinions. This also prevents personal energy from falling under the influence of strong forces in the surroundings, so there will be less likelihood of 'entrainment' at any energy level, physical, electromagnetic or subtle.

The second, sacral, chakra, is a focus for this tree's energy. There is an energising of creativity and an increase in the enjoyment of the experience of life. There is the desire to satisfy personal creativity, to manifest one's deepest wishes, to really get involved and dive into the fullness of living. Symptoms that express the blocking of the sacral chakra – emotional detachment, lack of feeling, boredom, rigidity, inability to relax - would all be eased with this tree essence.

Liquidamber also encourages a great ability to heal through communication. At the throat chakra (complementary energy centre to the sacral chakra), there is the possibility of using the voice with great skill – in such a way that a flow of loquaciousness, a 'sweet tongue', can heal the body, calm the mind and nourish the spirit. Such skills were recognised by our ancestors. The power of the musician Orpheus was strong enough to gather souls back from the dead. The Celtic bard was not just an itinerant folk-singer and messenger but often a magician who used sound. Taliesin and Amergin could control mood and intellect with their skills. Throughout the world shamanic healers and magicians use sound to heal and mend. Expressing the underlying emotional reality of a situation can prevent wars, can release pain, can bring understanding to the listeners. Liquidamber, whose leaves can resemble large, floppy, green tongues that turn rainbow-hued in autumn, shows its ability to reveal the creative essence.

Liquidamber also helps to balance the relationship of the individual to the object of love. It brings a flow of energy that reciprocates in a balanced way the need to be loved with the needs of the other. It also relaxes the natural fear of opening too much, of giving too much away, of risking failure, so that a more spontaneous behaviour is possible.

All types of energy can be used and it becomes possible to accept and transmute hidden, unusual or completely unfamiliar energy patterns. It enables the mind to see the underlying validity of the energy source free from preconceived notions or beliefs. Without judgements it is possible to access and make manifest a vast, creative potential within the mind. This can be further supported by a steadying influence on the fine spiritual states of awareness where liquidamber brings an even flow of self-knowledge – a constant self-referral that helps to calm the up-welling of doubt and fear as it smoothly communicates relevant information.

Signature:
The long, tongue-like leaves growing in profusion; their wonderful range of colours in autumn; the sweet medicinal resin.

Lombardy Poplar (*Populus nigra 'italica'*)

Lombardy poplar is a natural form of the southern European black poplar found in Northern Italy and first introduced into Britain in the middle of the 18th century by Lord Rochford who planted it at St. Osyth Priory, Essex. It is the male trees, bearing large red catkins in April, that tend to be planted in Britain. Lombardy poplar can reach 130ft (40m) with a sweeping, elongated oval profile. In the USA, where it is commonly planted, the hot autumns turn the trees into stunningly beautiful, golden towers. In Britain too, given the right seasonal conditions, the trees can be a wonderful sight, both in spring and autumn. The leaves are similar to the black poplar but the diamond-shaped leaves are even wider than they are long, with translucent margins of small, regular teeth. Lombardy poplar grows rapidly, as much as 100ft in the first forty years, though lightning strikes and storm damage can destroy the single crown, which nonetheless can re-grow with multiple crowns within twenty years. The trunk is largely covered by vertical shooting branches and is heavily buttressed. Like all poplars, the roots are strong and draw groundwater from a large area. The lifespan is around 150 years, though fallen trees can still send out suckers.

The Essence:

Keywords: "Aspiration"; discrimination; acts of unique creativity; carried by life-force; revealing sources of purpose; flow of peace through achievement of personal unique inheritance; understanding the currents and tides of your life; understanding deep drives; inspiration to aspire.

The main quality of this essence is the understanding of intuitive processes. It helps to discriminate between information from different sources, sharpening the intellect so that it can make sense of intuitive feelings.

The second, sacral, chakra is particularly energised so as to allow an expression of personal creativity that can release and

256

Lombardy Poplar

reveal one's personal goals and ambitions. The creative flow when released will then naturally follow a very individual and empowering path.

The subtle bodies, particularly the Causal and Spiritual bodies (both very fine, non- personality based aspects of the self), are also motivated along the same lines. The Causal body is enabled to access karmic influences that directly influence the current life. There are certain patterns of behaviour that we carry with us and, unless we consciously let go of them, they tend to become entrenched, even though they are outmoded or prove continually to be unsuccessful strategies. These patterns can be set up as our belief systems develop in early childhood, or they can be much older genetic or past life patterns. Knowing what motivates our instinctive and automatically accepted responses can help to clarify how we behave and how we help or hinder our real goals in life.

In a similar way Lombardy poplar essence works with the Spiritual body to bring us a better understanding of the illusory strength of emotional reactions. Not that emotions are not real – simply that they occur much like the weather in the world occurs. They are not indicative of much meaning except as expressions of the movement or restriction of life energy. Emotions have no intrinsic moral or intellectual value, but nonetheless they give flavour to our experience of living. Lombardy poplar can help to integrate the experience of these emotional tides into the spiritual reality of our self-awareness. Emotions can then be seen not as the measure of our existence, nor as a hindrance to our spiritual understanding, but as an enrichment of our senses and another tune in the symphony of our living.

Lombardy poplar essence can help to reveal the most profound levels of communication from deep time (the edges of space and time as we perceive them), through the unique expression of the personality. The essence can reveal what is

258

motivating our personal choices, our patterns of behaviour, and what activity naturally supports the flow of our unique life-energy. Aspiration derives from the same root word as "breath". Aspiration –our hopes and dreams, what we reach for - is what feeds our life energy in the same way that our breath feeds the living organism.

Signature:
Lombardy poplar is a visual fountain of green; an elongated, sky-reaching variation of the black poplar. Like a green flame, it curves up into space, always reaching upwards.

NORWAY SPRUCE (*Picea abies*)
Norway spruce is a mountain tree of highland Europe, growing from the Balkans to Scandinavia. Before the last Ice Age the tree grew in Britain but disappeared until it was reintroduced in the early years of the 16th century.

The young trees are familiar to us as the Christmas tree, but left to mature it can become a large timber tree up to 130ft (40m) living for about two hundred years. The leaves are bright green needles growing on all sides of the shoots. The fruit are large cones, hanging down like cigars, with rounded scales. Upper branches sweep upwards whilst the lower branches are either level or descending, both in graceful sweeps. During the 18th century Norway spruce was widely planted as a major forestry tree, but these days it is mainly limited to frosty or exposed sites where Sitka spruce does not do so well. Spruce is used for building timbers and makes good paper pulp. The resin can be made into turpentine and pitch, while the young shoots and leaves make a tea rich in vitamin C.

The Essence:
Keywords: "Trust"; understanding change; lightness; open to experience; seeing clearly; axis; beacon.

Change is the one fundamental quality of life. It is the one constant in the universe of energy. Understanding this allows change to happen, and along with it comes transformation and purification. Letting go and knowing that you will fall into something more interesting is the essence of Norway spruce. The acceptance that everything that happens is the potential for new beginnings helps us to focus on what we have rather than what we may lose.

The Triple Warmer meridian is particularly stimulated. This allows a flow of protecting energy to circulate through the main organs of the body. The reduction of fear and tension eases internal communication and so reduces wear and tear, as well as stress, on the physical body. There is an increased sense of hope and lightness and the feeling that it is possible to be much more self-sustaining.

With this tree energy comes delight in exploring new avenues. There is a sense of ease, a natural happiness and an ability to share at the level of the feelings and the senses. This change is focused on the activity of the sacral chakra. When unbalanced or over-energised, this energy centre can create a hedonism or profound selfishness, but with Norway spruce it is possible to remain true to one's own feelings without insisting that your point of view is the only right way to live. There is confidence to acknowledge personal experience without denigrating other's feelings. So there is a balance in the feelings – they are not given too much priority (hedonism) nor is there a suppression of emotional energy (puritanism).

The Etheric body, so important to the integrity of the body as a whole, is helped to remove the problems caused by aggressive emotional patterns. Fragmented parts of the self are unified in self-healing.

The mind becomes clearer and it is easier to communicate information. At the finest spiritual level comes the ability to

Norway Spruce

access deep intuitive flows of inspirational knowing. Possibly even the communication of profound teachings.

Norway spruce helps us to experience the nature of universal energy, and learning from this we are able to transmit it to others.

Signature:
Despite living in harsh conditions the tree is graceful and relaxed. The Christmas tree: a symbol of new starts, regeneration, transformation.

OLIVE (*Olea europea*)

The olive is the most important crop tree of the Mediterranean area. It is a cultivar that derives from its wild relative, *Olea sylvestris*, a smaller bushier tree with spiny stems and smaller leaves and fruits. Olive is a long-lived evergreen tree that grows slowly up to 15m. It has a broad, irregular crown and a short gnarled bole – often consisting of inter-grown, contorted branches and boughs of silver grey, slightly fissured bark. The twigs have four angles and carry opposite, sharply pointed leaves of leathery green grey. The flowers are green-white, fragrant and borne on long, open panicles in July and August. They ripen in the autumn into an oily green fruit taking a year to become mature. The wood is heavy in oil and a rich orange brown. It has distinctive patterning that reflects the contorted growth of the bole. The olive branch has long been the symbol of offered peace and prosperity.

The Essence:
Keywords: "Valour"; warmth; solar energy; truthfulness; motivation; passionate clarity.

Olive has an energy that will benefit those who have great passions and strong drives. It gives the ability to be able to direct these strong desires in a creative and life-enhancing

262

Olive

direction. Olive enables potentially damaging and self-centred behaviour to be mediated by wisdom and empathy. Energy that is so dynamic is neither inherently positive nor negative. Like fire, it simply exists until the fuel it uses is consumed. Like fire, such energy can be channelled to sustain life or to destroy life. With the help of olive essence the energy can be turned towards practical healing, of the self and of others, and to positive creative expressions.

Olive works on the meridian system in such a way as to encourage acting and living in a wholly truthful manner. The Governing meridian is strengthened and energised by the release of emotional tensions that were originally created by the inability to speak or act in a truthful way. Such situations can arise when one 'holds one's tongue' and 'knows one's place'. That is, when constraints are placed upon the individual by the beliefs of others and these are then accepted as 'proper' behaviour. Olive tree addresses this constellation of behavioural patterns, particularly when it deals with ideas about service and responsibility to others. It can be used for those who tend to put other's needs before their own, exhausting their own reserves of energy. Olive helps to balance one's needs with the needs of others in a more constructive and fair manner. The Triple Warmer meridian can be negatively affected by this suppression of personal desires and can become overwhelmed with underlying resentments and the heaviness of service.

With such a pattern of denial, self-righteous indignation can build up yet be suppressed and ignored. Olive is able to allow a positive flow of emotional energy so that it becomes possible to regain a personal sense of freedom and self-determination. Olive prevents a build-up of pent up emotion by releasing and expressing it truthfully in a natural and easy manner – rather than with explosive anger. Energy moves through the body and releases those knots of controlled passion, indignation and sense of unfairness in such a way that a person can become their own master again without the need to reject the established pattern of relationships with others. All the chakras are deeply energised, which strengthens the sense of self. Courage and motivation increase and energy is available to develop practical, down to earth solutions.

In the mind, there is an ability to heal issues of self-worth and sense of value. Such issues will very often be interwoven with the same constellation of beliefs to do with serving and helping others. Problems often arise from a false sense of inferiority or an egotistical altruism, both of which unbalance a proper perspective of how and why one acts as one does.

Emotionally, olive can be very good at healing and clearing self-issues in general. Whenever there is doubt about one's ability to get better, olive brings a positive and soothing energy that can help all forms of illness. Having energised and supported many different aspects of the self, olive allows a much more immediate and multi-level experience of spiritual states. This is partly because of its activating solar qualities and also because olive is so good at clearing away the limiting vision so that things can be seen much more clearly for their own true nature. Perception is largely a construction of the mind. If the mind is tightly bound by rigid belief systems it will be very difficult, if not impossible, to perceive something that contradicts, or lies outside of, these concepts.

Olive tree presents us with a powerful energy to free ourselves from the enervating presence of false boundaries and judgements, helping us to stand up as a unique individual in our own power and truth.

Signature:
The rich, warm, lubricating oil; the deep orange wood; its slow, steady growth and slow-ripening fruit (control of energy levels)

ROBINIA (LOCUST TREE, BLACK LOCUST, YELLOW LOCUST, FALSE LOCUST, FALSE ACACIA) (*Robinia pseudoacacia*)

The Robinia is an American tree native to the south-eastern States of the US where it can be found in woods and thickets in the Allegheny Mountains and the Middle Mississippi Valley. The tree was introduced into Britain by John Tradescant in 1638 and was championed by William Cobbett in the 18th century as a useful substitute for oak where the land was too dry for that native tree. His idea failed to take hold, mainly because the demand for timber declined with the development of the iron industry. Robinia prefers dry soil and a hot climate so really only prospers in the southern half of Britain. It does well as a city tree as it is resistant to heat and poor soil and its late leafing and early fall reduces the effects of pollution on it. When the weather is warm enough robinia flowers in midsummer with cascades of fragrant, white, pea-like flowers. When fertilised these flowers form dark brown seed pods, which originally reminded the American settlers of the locust beans, or carob, native to the deserts of the eastern Mediterranean.

The robinia grows to 80ft (25m) with an open crown of angular thorny branches bearing bright green leaves comprising eleven to fifteen oval leaflets. The Latin name derives from the French gardener, Jean Robin, who grew trees from seed in Paris.

The Essence:
Keywords: "Awakening"; calm mind; dissolving 'glamour' and obsession; "drama queen"; optimism; clearing emotional and mental clutter; open to larger reality.

This tree and its essence are cooling and calming. It allows the mind to flow in imaginative ways that inspire and create peace rather than, for example, becoming locked in fearful anxieties about future outcomes. A positivity and relaxation

Robinia

help the flow of energy through the body.

When there is some disparity between hopes, wishes, dreams and the actual reality of the situation, Robinia helps to bring a new clarity. Locked into imagination people can become isolated and withdrawn from those around them. This tree energy gently restores a balanced appreciation of interior imaginative worlds and external phenomenal experience. Obsessive behaviour, repeating mental anxiety, phobias, and what used to be called 'hysteria' – becoming locked into imaginative dramas, can all be relieved with the energy of robinia.

There is a general enlivening effect based around the throat chakra making it possible to really communicate one's own ideas and concepts and simply to be able to express one's own joyfulness. This subduing of fears and anxieties, focusing more on positive values gives a chance for a better under-standing of situations, better memory and clearer intellectual capacity. It creates a cleansing and purification of the mind, a clearing away of old emotional cobwebs.

This clearing has a further effect on how the emotions are experienced. There is an increase of balance and peace, an ability to take in a larger, less individualised viewpoint, to be able to understand things from a universal perspective where evolutionary forces and the very nature of matter and awareness expand and flow, in order to experience and relate in new, unexplored ways.

Robinia clears the mental and emotional clutter created by looking too closely at the details and allows us to get a spacious panorama, to take a deep calming breath, and to see that really things are flowing and that joy can be had in simply being real and paying attention to what is going on now.

When we know and see clearly what is really going on we can decide to act in appropriate ways. The more we become open to reality, the more our actions naturally follow the flows of universal energy. We do what we want to do, but what we want is also what the universe wants. This is how the enlightened person disappears into the universe. Nothing is sublimated, personality is not annihilated, desires are not squashed. Simply, the bit of awareness within the bit of the body, expands to encompass everything else as well. In fact, this is the situation that already exists. The idea of difference, separation and the existence of individuals distinct from an 'outside' is really an inaccurate assessment of the real state of things. Robinia helps to create the opportunity to expand into the universe a little more effectively.

Signature:
The cascades of pure white flowers. The acacia–like thorny twigs waking us out of our dream.

SEA BUCKTHORN (*Hippophae rhamnoides*)
Sea buckthorn was one of the pioneer species that re-colonised Britain after the last Ice Age. On poor, gravelly soils buckthorn quickly establishes itself by roots that sucker freely, binding the soil together. Like alder, buckthorn's roots fix nitrogen into the soil increasing its fertility and thus allowing other plants to grow. Sea buckthorn needs plenty of light and space and is soon crowded out by larger trees. Its natural habitat is now the poor soils of the seashore.

Sea buckthorn is a thorny, low-growing shrub, not usually more than 10ft (3m) in height, except when sheltered from the wind. The leaves are willow-like, though thinner and more convoluted, of a dusty green colour, with hairy undersides. Male and female flowers appear on different plants and are very small, appearing along with the leaf buds in spring. Female plants bear bright orange berries in great numbers that remain all winter on the branches. These berries have traditionally been made into jelly and are rich in vitamins and minerals. Sea buckthorn is known also as "sallow thorn" along the east coast of England. It is no relation to the common buckthorn or to the alder buckthorn, two shrubby trees with strong purgative actions.

The Essence:
Keywords: "Pioneer"; fresh perspectives; watching clearly from a distance; un-involvement; protection from harmful influences; understanding and dealing with emotions; development of subtle, spiritual perceptions.

The clearing away of confusing clouds of emotion is the key to sea buckthorn's actions. It brings clarity of mind and a certain detachment. Subtle perceptions become sharper and there is a distancing from the normal turmoil of the mind that gives some space to reconsider preconceived ideas and a willingness to accept new possibilities.

We can learn better to keep at an appropriate distance from others and remain in a calm, balanced state. Emotionally this can help with issues to do with pride, power hunting or grasping attitudes – where we seek to impose ourselves onto others. Sea buckthorn will also help to balance the opposite tendency to remain haughty or aloof by encouraging the ability to communicate feelings and wishes.

This re-balancing will benefit the Gall Bladder meridian if it is suffering from the effects of pride or haughtiness. Likewise, the Lung meridian is balanced with a more creative way of escaping from the established, unsuccessful, modes of communication with others.

In the subtle bodies it is particularly the Emotional and Spiritual bodies that are affected. With the Emotional body a protective barrier is established that helps to keep the

Sea Buckthorn

individual separate from the emotional energy of others. There is an ability to understand better the nature of emotional energies so that it is less likely that one will become entangled in them. There is also a quietening of the emotions within the self, which helps to clarify why emotions are arising and to distinguish where they have come from.

With the essence of sea buckthorn spiritual energies have access to the physical levels of the body, especially by way of the solar plexus and sacral charkas. In this way spiritual energies integrate with the physical to make it a real, powerful force. The world and the spirit are more easily experienced as inseparable, (which in truth they are). This allows a powerful, personal energy base for developing skills and achieving goals.

In spiritual practices, sea buckthorn brings a quiet mind. It subdues mental processes or creates a detachment from mental processes – including memories and belief systems. Because calm is experienced it is more possible to receive new information. This process favours listening instead of analysing. The use of mantra might also be enhanced with this essence.

Signature:
A small, defensive, withdrawn appearance, keeping itself to itself yet having bright orange fruit rich in nutrition (concentration of energies into the real world). Does well given room for itself.

SILVER FIR (*Abies alba*)
The firs have much softer, leathery foliage than the spiky spruces. The silver fir has a smooth light grey-green, neatly cracked bark heavy with resin from which turpentine is made. When given space to grow, the lowest branches can swing upwards to grow parallel to the main trunk.

Silver fir is the prominent native forest tree of the Central European mountains and it is the largest fir except for those growing in the American Rockies. The earliest planting in Britain was in 1603 and it became a significant forestry tree, only being replaced when American species with faster and hardier growth were introduced in the 19th century. The American silver firs – the grand fir and the noble fir – have largely replaced the European silver fir as a timber tree.

Silver fir can be recognised by the light coloured clean trunk and quite bright green clumps of foliage. The female flowers, green upright spikes, only grow near the tops of trees and become large, erect elongated cones that cluster together in dense rows.

The Essence:
Keywords: "Enthroned"; empowering; going with the flow; transformation; open crown; brightness; flow of healing and creativity.

With this tree comes the energy to empower and manifest one's desires with wisdom and skill. It is in essence, deeply protective because it gives practical expression to the individual's true nature. Going in harmony with one's inherent abilities and skills automatically ensures greater safety and success.

The Liver meridian is strengthened by this ability to follow the natural flow of energy, accepting the circumstances that arise in life and making changes to accommodate wherever necessary. This ensures that a positive attitude and cheerfulness are easily maintained, which allows for the maximum growth and transformation within the individual life.

Of the chakras, the crown is most activated by this essence. The effect is to firmly root and establish the individual into their universal context. The crown is counted as the seventh

Silver Fir

chakra, though in fact it functions more as a hologram for the complete human system, including within itself as it does every level and every function of the six body-based chakra centres, the subtle bodies and all other physical and subtle systems of the body.

As the root chakra at the base of the spine links us into the Earth's greater energy body, so the crown chakra above the top of the head links us into the universal energy web. Between these two links our energy flows as if within the wires of an electric circuit. Where one link is damaged the current of life-force is drastically reduced or stops altogether. When the crown chakra is not correctly related to the body it is as if a large shadow overhangs the person, cutting off nutrition from above. Isolation, alienation, dread and confusion are some of the main symptoms of this. Silver fir ensures that the crown is working in harmony with the body and that the personal awareness has maximum access possible to the seamlessness of the universe and to all of its sentient parts. Balance and security, wisdom and love, are the natural experience within this state.

With silver fir there is an increase in optimism and positive action. Impetus is given to those activities that bring personal happiness and contentment. Emphasis is given to doing things, to practical solutions and to dynamic expressions of joy in living.

At its very finest level silver fir enables creative visions to be rooted in practical reality. There is a better ability to achieve personal potential – largely through an increasing fascination in watching the ways that creativity unfolds within the mind and then moves out into the world.

This interest in the pathways of manifestation, in how energy moves, grows and changes, also teaches us the skills to maintain the balance within ourselves, allowing us to heal and protect our energy integrity and to work with the healing potential within other people too.

Signature:
The energy Silver fir brings to the crown chakra is reflected by the prevalence of cones at the very top of the tree.

WALNUT (*Juglans regia*)

The name of this tree derives from the Anglo-Saxon for 'foreign nut' and is probably a Roman introduction, possibly cultivated by the Romano-British tribes, hence named after them – 'walh, welsh, walls' being the Old English (Anglo-Saxon) name given to the native 'foreigners'. The Latin name 'juglans' means Jupiter's nut.

The natural range of walnut is from Central Asia and China, Iran, Asia Minor, to the Balkans. In Britain it is most found in the south and central areas but has been planted as a parkland tree in the north of Scotland. Walnut prefers deep fertile soils and warm summers. In Britain the fruit rarely ripens but can be picked green for pickling.

Walnut grows rapidly up to its maximum height of 100ft (30m) and then continues to spread outward, though it rarely lives beyond two hundred years. As a valuable timber tree mature individuals are rare to find.

The leaves are similar in structure to ash, with seven leaflets – three or four pairs plus a terminal leaflet – that get larger towards the tip of the branch. Leaves and flowers appear late in April or May. Male flowers are substantial greeny-brown catkins, and female flowers are feathered green capsules that ripen into the fruit that consists of the hard nut and its edible kernel. Walnut has a smooth grey bark with deep vertical fissures. It can be recognised by the smell of the leaves, reminiscent of boot polish.

Walnut

The black walnut, native to North America, is sometimes found in Britain but has delicate roots that make transplanting difficult. Black walnut, like the 'English' walnut, is an important tree for high quality furniture-makers.

The leaves and bark of the walnut are laxative and astringent and have been used for skin conditions and ulcers. Walnut oil is extracted from the edible nut and is used to polish the wood, as well as being an exotic cooking oil. The leaves give a brown dye and are repellent to all insects. Walnut, particularly the American black walnut has been found to be extremely effective at removing parasites from the gut.

The Essence:
Keywords: "Liberation"; purification and cleansing; sturdiness; removal of all sorts of intrusions; getting rid of unwanted influences; personal power and integrity; sense of security.

The clear, well-known property and effect of walnut essence is familiar from the Bach Flower Remedies, where it is characterised as a link-breaker. Walnut's energy is the protection of personal space. Dynamic energy is released that will directly effect the sense of personal power, stimulating the desire to grow and be free from any perceived restraints – especially with regard to spiritual goals (in contrast to practical ambitions).

There is a marked cleansing of the Heart meridian, which is linked to the emotional expression of love and forgiveness and, of course, their opposites, hate and blame. The clarity that walnut initiates here reveals a person's real motivations in life - where one has begun, where one hopes to be going - and this knowledge, even if it is on an unconscious, non-verbal level of awareness, gives a sense of security. Knowing oneself is really the only way to recognise and combat the influence of other people and other circumstances outside of oneself.

A similar action occurs in the Large Intestine meridian. Here walnut energy creates purification and cleansing. It becomes more possible to let go of things that are no longer appropriate or necessary. The sense that a new start would be a very good thing, that a willing release of outworn patterns of expectation and behaviour is easy to do, that one's potential is within one's own control, can all arise once this meridian is brought to balance. The Large Intestine meridian is affected by the emotions surrounding the concepts of worthiness, goodness and cleanliness. 'Not good enough', 'dirty!', 'bad!', 'unworthy', are all judgements that become lodged in the belief systems whilst still a young child. They limit our potential for growth and personal achievement, also lowering our life-energy sufficiently that negative energy patterns can make further inroads. When these false ideas are revealed and they begin to be purged from the body with the help of walnut we become much less susceptible to the energies of those who seem to know better or who seem more powerful than us.

Our natural flow of energy, the pleasure we feel simply existing and playing is intensely personal and can be very sensitive to the restrictions and rigid opinions of others. Walnut creates a sense of safeness, a self- containment of the sacral chakra that allows a grounding, centring and quietening to establish the fertile ground for personal creativity.

The Astral body, the fourth level of our energy makeup, is the holding vessel for our existence in time and space. It maintains a correct balance between the universal and individual energies, and likewise keeps a healthy balance between the influences of past, present and future existence. The Astral body keeps us in the universal web whilst still maintaining our recognisable personal boundaries. Walnut energy helps to strengthen this energy body so that we can be at peace within ourselves, and simultaneously, be aware of our links with other things. We can have a clear sense of separation, a distinct individuality that can maintain its equilibrium in the face of emotions and ideas from others.

Having established this safe definition of the individual and cleared it of intrusions that drain the life-energy, walnut allows a relaxation of the awareness at very subtle levels. Being less open to unwanted influences, knowing our own qualities, and accepting ourselves, it becomes possible to be really happy just as oneself, content to be a passionate human being, enjoying life and experiencing the spiritual energy of physical existence. Walnut shakes us awake from someone else's dream within which we find we have been living, tells us who we are and lets us fully experience and enjoy our uniqueness.

Signature:
The leaves drive off all insects (potentially harmful energies).

WESTERN HEMLOCK (*Tsuga heterophylla*)
The hemlocks are a small group of trees similar to spruce, native to North America. They were given this confusing name because the foliage was thought to resemble the rodent-like smell of Conium maculatum, the common umbelliferous hemlock that grows in European hedgerows. Whereas this herb is extremely toxic, the hemlock spruces are quite medicinal. The western hemlock is a narrow, conical tree to 200ft (60m). It grows quickly and is tolerant of shade. In young trees the leading shoot arches over, whilst the lower shoots tend to spread wide in graceful droops. The leaves are round-ended needles irregularly growing around the stems with smaller needles on the top surface. Male flowers are dark red buds in early spring, fertilising the green female buds, which become small, open, egg-shaped cones. Unlike the pines, the hemlocks do not have bud swellings from which the leaves and new twigs develop.

Western Hemlock

The Essence:
Keywords: "Open grace"; cleansing, clearing, quietening, focusing; serenity; new beginnings; acceptance; expulsion of old 'demons'; confusion and aggravation reduced; clean sheet.

One of the primary effects of Western Hemlock is its ability to bring quietness and clarity to the mind. Where there is the confusion of too many options, the potential of too many possible outcomes, western hemlock will reduce the noise so that what is really there can be clearly seen and be distinguished from the phantasm of speculation. Equally, when there seems to be an absence of options, where nothing seems to be acheivable, the essence can sharpen the insight to discover new possibilities. The energy is cleansing, clearing, quietening and focusing.

The crown chakra is brought into this process with an influx of serenity. Reducing unnecessary activity gives the flow of essential ideas a free passage into consciousness, where they can be turned to practical solutions. This clear state of calm awareness also benefits the whole of the energies of the body, helping to identify and remove energy intrusions that do not belong. Confusion and fear are good environments for negative entities to take advantage of. Reducing the levels of confusion and fear remove the camouflage from harmful energies and make it less easy for them to become established.

An aspect of the Heart chakra concerned with vengeance and forgiveness is activated with this tree energy. These feelings have to do with holding onto pain and letting go of pain. The pretence of forgiveness where none really exists, or giving in to the will of others for the sake of reducing conflict, is replaced with a real relaxation of acceptance – neither ignoring the hurt nor seeking vengeance for wrongs. The cleansing energy of western hemlock allows new beginnings to be simply that: starting with a clean sheet.

Aggravation and anxiety of the mind is calmed and peace increases. It becomes easier to understand the opposite viewpoint to the view that one holds true, and so the roots of selfish conflict can be more easily avoided. Acceptance and relaxation into an honest, open state quieten the mind and enables deeper spiritual insight to enter into more meditative states.

The emotions are calmed because the mind is prevented from building up its own fantasy scenarios. Instead, an even flow of balanced equilibrium enters the mind and heart. Like smoke that can obscure all reality where it becomes stuck in an airless, windless place, so western hemlock is like a fresh breeze that rapidly clears the misconceptions and false ideas around a problem to reveal what is actually there to be dealt with.

Signature:
The irregular placement and size of the needles on the twigs, reminiscent of too much going on in the mind and emotions.

WESTERN RED CEDAR (*Thuja plicata*)
The western red cedar is not a true cedar but is related to cypress and juniper families. Young trees form familiar compact cones of dense bright green foliage made from flattened rope-like leaves. This species can be identified by its pineapple-like scent and by its single upright leader stem.

In damp, cool climates western red cedar can grow rapidly, reaching about 80ft (24m) in thirty years with a full height of 160ft (50m). Western red cedar is native to the mountains of the west coast of America and was an important timber tree to the Indian peoples who found that its soft deep red wood could very easily be cleft into planks whose long fibres were water-repellent and so resistant to decay. Small flowers appear at the end of branches in early March with female

Western Red Cedar

flowers becoming small, papery brown cones that shed seeds in great numbers. It grows well in shade and so is planted as a protective tree for other species.

First introduced into Britain in the middle of the 19th century via Exeter, it soon became a popular planting in large gardens and parks. The other American thuja (*Thuja occidentalis*), known as the northern white cedar, is a much smaller tree (to 15m) and although possibly the first American tree grown in the Old World, introduced sometime in the 16th century, it rarely grows well in Britain. However, its twigs are the source of the herb used for coughs and for toning lower abdominal muscles. Externally it has been used for killing warts and it is effective for fungal infections of the skin.

The Essence:
Keywords: "Constancy"; underlying peace; play of emotions; belief in oneself; screening harmful influences; subtle tides of consciousness; steadiness.

The primary influence of this tree is the perception of the underlying silence, stillness or peace behind every possible experience; that there is a constant flow of energy and a connection beneath all the changeability of life. This is particularly focused on the experience of the ever-flowing and changing of the emotions. Whatever emotions are being experienced it becomes possible to see them as just another aspect of personal life as is a taste, sight or sound – that is, we do not become overwhelmed by a fleeting but possibly very strong emotional reaction.

With this alteration of perspective it becomes possible to see every experience - no matter what its quality - as a means to achieve one's place in the flow of life. The emotions are the wavetops of our awareness-ocean, whilst the deep flowing currents are the steady patterns of force that carry a consistent, sustaining energy. This tree essence will really help those who are continually carried away by strong emotional reactions – not by changing the emotional states but through revealing the underlying peace upon which the emotions ride, seeing emotions, like thoughts, as a natural way life expresses and enjoys itself.

Beliefs and attitudes that are to do with one's self-image and the ability to express love can affect the energy of the Heart meridian. This tree energy calms and soothes agitation from these sources that may otherwise impair the functions of this meridian.

The same process occurs at the level of the brow chakra where western red cedar can help to heal damage that has distorted the mental processes and the subtle perceptions. The strengthening of mental integrity brings back a belief in one's own mind and protects it from otherwise harmful mental influences – be they forceful thoughts of others, concepts, indoctrination or warping philosophies, or simply background psychic 'noise'. It is like a screen or visor that helps to filter out harmful frequencies, strengthening the mental immunity. With an increased feeling of one's own solidity, personal creativity can flow more freely.

At the crown chakra this process becomes the protection of one's basic energy patterns. The individual is able to act in accord with their own spiritual nature rather than being swayed by others. There is also an increased energy to allow change when it is necessary and to bring in dynamic activity to transform and grow.

This essence will help those whose relationships with others is unbalanced – either because they rely too much on the approval of others and who are continually drained emotionally by others, or, on the other hand, those people who do not register or ignore the feelings of others.

There is an openness to other levels of knowledge and experience that increases energy to the whole system and frees the individual up to new ways of perceiving and acting. This has an overall effect on the subtle anatomy of the body, helping it to relax into itself and accept new energies at the same time as being able to let go of inappropriate patterns and blocks from the past. This is invaluable in removing many of the underlying causes of disease so that actual illness is avoided.

A calm descends upon the mind when it turns to meditative and contemplative states. Western red cedar calms the physical activities of the body so that the awareness becomes more attuned to subtle tides of consciousness.

Signature:
The evenness of the leaf scales and their branching growth: the even experience of life in all circumstances.

WILD SERVICE TREE (*Sorbus torminalis*)
The wild service tree is a native of the British Isles but these days it is a rare sight, both because it favours ancient woodland and because it superficially resembles a small maple from a distance. The tree is similar to rowan in its shape and form. It is a fairly neat tree with ascending branches making a domed canopy at around 60ft (20m). The young bark is very similar to rowan but when mature the dark grey is broken by shallow cracks more like a maple. The leaves are closely alternate on the branches and so look clumpy from a distance. The leaves are a bright green, quite leathery and smooth, and resemble an elongated maple where the first lobes grow out close to ninety degrees from the leafstalk and become more acute as they near the leaf tip. In autumn the leaves turn a stunning ochre, copper and purple red.

Wild service tree flowers in May or June – around the same time as hawthorn whose flower heads it closely resembles. Fruit ripens into clusters of olive-brown or reddish-brown speckled berries. These fruits were a staple of the Neolithic peoples, having a sweet exotic taste after being 'bletted' by frost or left to mature once picked. A single tree can produce tons of fruit. The fruits also have a long history of use as a flavouring for alcoholic liqueur. In the far West the tree is known as maple cherry and in the South East as checkers or chequers, possibly after the speckled fruit.

The distribution of wild service tree is very localised in Britain, though more common on Continental Europe. It is found in the remnants of ancient woodland where it tends to spread by vigorous suckering and rarely by seed propagation. It favours clay and limestone and is most numerous on the Weald, reaching from Kent to Hampshire. It can also be found in the Severn and Wye valleys and in the Welsh Marches as well as ancient hedgerows and areas once covered by dense forest, such as the Forest of Arden in Warwickshire. It can be found in the North to about the edges of Cumbria and the Lake District.

The name of the tree some think derives from its Latin name 'sorbus', or from the Latin for beer 'cervisia'. Others reckon the name is probably derived from the Old English word 'syfre'.

The Essence:
Keywords: "Unfoldment"; expansion of awareness; understanding motives; past life healing; harmony and healing relationship with self and surroundings; quiet, alert, aware; foundation of awareness; source of personal perceptions; self-definition; where we have come from; navigation (knowing the tides and currents of existence); hidden currents.

Wild Service Tree

Wild service tree directs its energy to the expansion of awareness and the growth of clarity. There is a natural tendency to calm fears and restore the balance of mind. This naturally arises where there is a clearer picture about what is driving our behaviour – the reasons why we act or behave in the way we do. Understanding these patterns means they can be directed and controlled in the most appropriate directions.

This tree helps the Heart meridian to correct and balance for an effective deep healing of any long-standing emotional trauma. Such deep patterns or fractures of stress, unless released, set up permanent echoes which have a habit of repeating again and again, so that they can even become tendencies that are carried from life to life. Thus, past life issues and past life emotional trauma can be greatly alleviated by this essence.

Equilibrium and calm also infuses the Gall Bladder meridian and this clarifies our needs and desires. Here too, the essence helps to familiarise ourselves with our internal environment so that we can work more clearly in the external environment of the world.

Emotional stress at the sacral chakra is reduced. There is an increase in peacefulness, which allows personal creativity to emerge. There is also an increase in the ability to express oneself. Minor chakras at the ends of the fingers and toes help us to become more sensitive to the energies around us and allow access and use of healing energies. Wild service tree helps to activate these chakra points in a balanced way. Imbalances here may be indicated by a rejection of other people's energy or a tendency to unconsciously draw energy from others, leaving them feeling drained.

Wild service tree creates a degree of silence, like a blanket, over emotional noise. It doesn't prevent or sedate the flow of emotions or of thoughts, but it places the awareness in a state where these are no longer an obstruction to experiencing quietness. Having turned away from the usual noise of the conscious awareness, wild service tree brings a quietness and receptivity to spiritual states that allow a deepening of perception and insight.

Signature:
A retiring tree, quiet in the landscape, very sensitive and particular about its environment, but where it is established it sends numerous vigorous suckers from its roots. Knowing one's roots, establishes one's own firm awareness of place and direction.

As an indicator of ancient landscapes it suggests the remembrance of past structures that underlie the present.

WILLOW LEAVED PEAR (*Pyrus salicifolia*)
Willow–leaved pear is quite a common sight as a garden and park tree, particularly the weeping form 'Pendula'. It is a small, neat, domed tree to 10m with grey-green woolly leaves densely covering the main branches. The leaves are long and pointed, covered in a silvery down, especially when young. The flowers arrive with the leaves. They are quite robust with five white petals and very noticeable anthers of purple red.

Willow-leaved pear is native to Siberia, Persia and the Caucasus where it grows on woodland margins and in thickets.

The Essence:
Keywords: 'Dance of life'; security within the self; dance of joy; healing; cleansing; balanced relationship; personal power and vitality; acceptance; creative living; enjoyment of existence.

With the energy of willow-leaved pear comes a profound sense of security in oneself. This makes it possible to accept change

291

without upset. There is an increased contentment, ease and experience of joy. Better self-awareness and flexibility give a greater possibility to act with wisdom, attuning to circumstances as they present themselves.

Willow-leaved pear focuses some of its actions on physical processes that are clearing, detoxifying, healing and purifying. This makes it a useful essence during and after periods of illness.

The Governing meridian is given stimulus that results in a more joyous expression of energy. This provides the individual with greater dynamism, a confidence when action is required, and a sharper assessment of possible risks. It also helps to temper strong and inappropriate emotional reactions by reducing frustration and anger.

The Circulation-Sex meridian (also called Heart Protector or Pericardium meridian), deals with sexual security. Willow-leaved pear focuses energy here in such a way that whenever a new start is required, especially in an emotional relationship, there is a greater self-confidence and self-awareness that allows the change to be made wisely. Fears that arise from sexual and relationship issues are lessened.

The solar plexus chakra, in particular, is energised by this tree. The chakra deals with the understanding of personal power and how to maintain energy levels. With this essence there is an ability to access finer levels of perception and intuition that help to show up what is needed to achieve growth. It becomes much easier to communicate desires and wishes, ideas and instructions to others in order to achieve personal goals.

Minor chakras are stimulated that increase self-worth and the ability to stand up for oneself. Thus, this tree's energy would benefit those who feel inadequate and wish to

Willow-leaved Pear

withdraw from the company of others. Equally, it would be helpful for those who always need to be seen and heard and whose pride gets in the way of proper relationships. Tensions that show in the neck and shoulders often signal difficulties in communication and expression, and this essence may reduce these symptoms of stress. There is a greater ability to understand others and to create a loving and balanced relationship. Those who appear hard-hearted or insensitive, and those who feel they must please others at all times or who are very empathic, are both helped to achieve a more productive equilibrium in their emotional relationship to others.

Willow-leaved pear brings the mind to a better state of clarity and open-mindedness, cleansed of all unwanted thoughts. There is the ability to see things clearly for what they are, with no illusions.

At fine spiritual levels there is a greater integration of life-energy to personal creativity. This favours all creative actions and will help to disperse creative blocks, for example. More fundamentally, this creative energy feeds the unique expression of every individual and is essential to maintain health and vitality. It brings significant levels of protection and enhances the healing abilities of the body. The dance of life is felt within and is able to be expressed to others. Enjoyment of existence is vital to our continued existence, and this tree is very good at empowering the individual to release fear and get on with enjoying life.

Finally, willow-leaved pear brings a commitment to follow the flow of universal life, completely accepting the perfection of how things already are – in their own true states of being.

Signature:
The hairy leaves – a means of finding out what is going on in the world, communication, sensitivity.

Chapter 10

Tree Attunements

It could be said that the main lesson of the tree seer is 'paying attention'. All other techniques and practices are simply strategies to help us to pay attention in particular ways. There aren't really any extra-sensory perceptions – having a physical body all our perceptions rely upon the senses. (Even when we leave the physical body behind it is likely that we will have become so used to their mechanisms that we will interpret our experiences in terms of the familiar sense impressions we knew in life.) It is as well to include the mind along with the other sensing mechanisms of the human being, as in some of the systems of Tibetan and Indian philosophy. This avoids the huge Western assumption that the body and mind are separate and unrelated entities, or that one is a figment of the other.

The tree attunements that we have used for the last ten years provide a comprehensive set of means to engage the attention in ways that favour the experience of a tree's characteristic energies within the body and mind of the experiencer. Like changing the frequency of a radio, each process opens a new space in the personal awareness which, given the right time and place, will make tangible the unique awareness and consciousness-flavour of a tree and its spirit.

There are inherent problems with formulaic solutions and definitive explanations. They rarely provide the explanation as fully as hoped and they limit the actual experience by setting up boundaries of expectation. They are surprisingly and annoyingly self-fulfilling, and most frustratingly tend to be either 1) wholly dismissed or 2) wholly accepted as The Truth, end of story. All accepted truth usually starts off as a snappy idea, or something easy enough to be remembered and recounted by others. The source and path of this truth is very soon forgotten – especially if the original sources are not remembered or are purposely not mentioned. Oral traditions may have had safeguards to prevent such feedback loops, but modern reliance on the published word has no such safeguards. Without sources and references it is only guesswork as to whether the writer is thinking originally or is simply copying down the opinions of others.

Chasing sources can be illuminating. Very often a whole area of study rests upon one or two acknowledged texts to whom everyone else defers. Fine if the sources are accurate. There was a celebrated case a few years ago in anthropology where one researcher invented a complete tribe of dream healers in Indonesia. It became a classic reference for all those interested in the therapeutics of the dream state. Likewise, the Carlos Casteneda saga rumbles on even after his death. Some things need to be thought of as real and have real motivating power even though they spring from dubious sources. Not that it is all subterfuge. Ideas and notions have a life of their own and are picked up or forgotten in huge tides. Something that we may consider to be our original idea may, in fact, have been suggested directly or indirectly by others. Life is a web, mind is an ocean, memory is a creative invention. Our thought processes and conclusions are framed by the languages we have learnt to use. The assumptions of our ancestors are often buried so deep within the picture of the world that it is impossible to see their all-pervasive influences. It is the human intellect that plays with these nuances of belief and language but fails to see their limitations. Like a bee against a window-pane we react to something that we can't define but yet constrains our activities.

Open attention, presence within the body, disinterest in the rightness or wrongness of an experience, curiosity and a sense of humour all encourage us to be aware of the unexpected. Taking such a stance it is possible to use clear, simple instructions and not get shackled by their lack of ambiguity. These tree attunements are not Rules. In the years of study-ing this area of tree wisdom no rules have been uncovered at all – other than a similarity in using and opening the senses. These attunement techniques work because they can take your awareness directly to the tree spirits themselves. They have no other value if they cannot do this.

Life-energy is all-pervasive and expansive. It can be defined in limitless ways. These tree attunement techniques take certain parameters and define the tree energies in those terms. It's weird but it works – and works very well. It offers a framework of developing a relationship with the Tree Kingdoms that is of great potential, both for exploration and for healing work.

Working with Tree Mantra
1) Familiarise yourself with the sounds by reading them out loud. Find a comfortable rhythm and emphasis that suits you – but try to adhere to the pronunciation as closely as possible if guidelines are given. (The syllables are written as closely as possible to how they should initially sound).

2) If you plan to work with the mantra out loud get into a comfortable position where your breathing is not restricted in any way. Repeat the sounds at a speed that feels right for up to five minutes, then rest in silence for the same length of

time. Repeat this process for as many cycles as you wish. The silences are as much a part of the process as the sound making. Maintain your clarity and awareness. When you become distracted, simply return to the sounds.

3) If you want to work with the tree mantra quietly or silently begin in the same way to familiarise yourself with the sounds. Gradually reduce the volume of your voice until you are whispering and then just mouthing the sounds. Take the sounds internally and continue repeating them in your thoughts. Again, continue for up to five minutes followed by five minutes silence. Notice your body and mind activity. When you become distracted turn the attention to what each of your senses is experiencing in relation to the tree's energy. Repeat the cycles for as long as you like.

Working with the Note Sequence
1) Sing or play the note sequence on an instrument. Stick to the sequence for a while until it is fully in your memory. Begin with notes of even length but allow them to fall into their own rhythm.

2) Listen out for underlying tunes, counterpoints, harmonies. Allow the notes to develop into a living expression of the experience of your awareness meeting the energy of the tree spirit.

3) Return to the theme note sequence throughout the process, especially if you feel a loss of connection or a lack of inspiration.

Working with the Colour Sequence
1) Imagine that the air all around you turns to the colours of the sequence one by one. With each breath, breathe in each colour deeply into your body. Allow time for the process to

build up its own momentum and energy. Repeat breathing the colour sequence as long as you like.

2) In a similar way, imagine that with each breath you are drawing towards you a sphere of each colour from the distance. Allow it to enter your energy field and settle within you.

3) Use the colours of the sequence to make patterns and designs. Allow free play of the senses. Keep the intellect as far from the process as possible.

Working with the Trance Position

1) Familiarise yourself with the placement of the hands and feet and the posture of the body. Make sure you can adopt the position as exactly as possible and that you are able to relax into the pose.

2) You will need to have someone who can drum or rattle for you, or have a recorded journey drum session of about 15 to 20 minutes in length. The speed of the rhythm should be moderate to fast.

3) Prepare yourself and the space as you would for any other work, take up the trance position and signal for the drummer to begin. Breathe easily and take time to relax into the position. Once in the position all your experiences are modified by the tree energy you are using. Do not dismiss any experience, nor expect any type of event. It may take several sessions to begin to gauge what is happening, or you may find yourself immediately in a recognisable trance state. Make sure that you don't slip from the exact trance position. If you do, simply reposition yourself and continue. Keep your awareness alert and open.

4) Some positions may give you the opportunity to add some of the other attunement techniques such as the tree mantra or colour sequence. A few moments of integrated practice at the beginning may steady and deepen the experience.

Working with the Energy Net

1) If possible use a single coloured cloth that is large enough to lie upon. Lay it on the floor so that when you lie down your head will be to the north (unless instructions are otherwise).

2) Make sure that you will not have to be disturbed during the process. Deep states of awareness can occur quite rapidly in a crystal net.

3) If the crystals are all placed around the body, put them in place and then lie within them. If some stones are on the body, have them to hand so that they can be easily reached and placed or taped in position. Someone else to place the stones and to watch the timing can be useful if it doesn't feel intrusive.

4) Crystal nets tend to act in four or five minute periods, at the end of which time there is usually a significant deepening of awareness and relaxation. Time your session so that you end it before the next dive occurs. The optimum maximum time is twenty minutes, which will need a safe recovery time of forty minutes before resuming normal activity. Regular periods of five or ten minutes (with a recovery time of ten and fifteen minutes respectively), can be more useful than an occasional longer period within the energy net.

5) If there is any discomfort in the net simply roll out from the crystals and take time to compose yourself. Continue from the beginning or leave it until another time. Use grounding procedures if there is any difficulty in re-establishing normal perceptions. Remember that you are modifying the body's

energies to become closer to the tree spirit. It is likely that normal sensing mechanisms will not work as you expect, and that your experience of space and time will be altered.

Attunement to the Spirit of Aspen

Mantra (sound spell): CHOO TOE TIE TEA VOO

Note Sequence: D F# D C# Eb Eb C#

Colour Sequence: Blue - white - indigo - white - dappled vibrations of light (as seen through closed eyes at sun and leaves)

Trance Position:

1. Standing, feet together

2. Arms straight, hands about 30 degrees from body

3. Head up, eyes closed

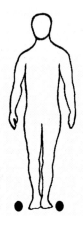

Energy Net:

1. On a white cloth

2. An amethyst placed beside the left foot

3. An amethyst placed beside the right foot

Attunement to the Spirit of Atlas Cedar

Mantra (sound spell): YEE OO BAY BAY BAY

Note Sequence: G B G B C# C# B A B

Colour Sequence: Red - green - indigo - gold - red

Trance Position:

1. Lying on back,
legs straight and together

2. Left arm by side,
palm up

3. Right arm 45 degrees
from body, palm down on
ground

4. Head turned to
the right

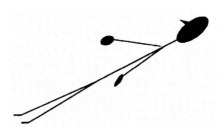

Energy Net:

1. On a white cloth

2. A smoky quartz by the
left side of the neck

3. A smoky quartz by the
right foot

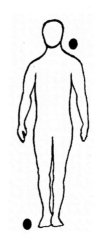

Attunement to the Spirit of Bird Cherry

Mantra: GIY'EE GIY'EE (the G is hard. This mantra rhymes with an elongated sigh - s-igh)

Note Sequence: G D C E G D D C

Colour Sequence: Orange - blue - pink.

Trance Position:

1. Sitting on floor, body upright sitting on hands, so that they cover are in contact with CV1 GV1(over the perineum and base of spine covering genitals)

2. Position of the legs isn't important

Energy Net:

1. On a gold cloth

2. Clear quartz on the right hip, level with the second chakra

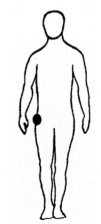

Attunement to the Spirit of Blackthorn

Mantra: JIM OO KO JEE JEE DAY

Note Sequence: C# E F A C# Eb D (the last D is an octave lower that the other notes)

Colour Sequence: Yellow - yellow plus pink - violet- white

Trance position:

1. Lying on back

2. Left leg straight

3. The sole of the right foot placed against the kneecap

4. Both arms and hands held close to sides

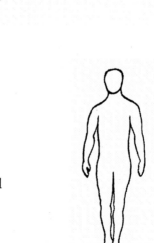

Energy Net:

1. On a white cloth

2. A black obsidian between and just below the level of the feet

Attunement to the Spirit of Black Poplar

Mantra: J'HAY YAA ROO D'HOO HOO RNAA

Note Sequence: F# D F F# G

Colour Sequence: Dark blue - dark red field with gold sparkles - violet

Trance Position:

1. Lying on back, legs wide apart

2. Arms wide apart above head, palms up

3. Mouth wide open

Energy Net:

1. On a dark red cloth

2. In each hand a dark green jasper

3. A dark green jasper taped to the top of each instep

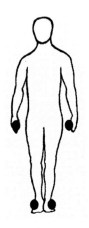

306

Attunement to the Spirit of Box Tree

Mantra: NYER LERT. YERRRU YERRRI

Note Sequence: Ab C#

Colour Sequence: Blue - green - pink - indigo - black

Trance Position:

1. Upright,feet shoulder width apart

2. Palms of both hands facing backwards by the neck and ears

3. Upper arms close to body, lower arms bent upward

4. Eyes closed but turned slightly upwards

There seems to be no energy / crystal net, but attunement is enhanced by placing a piece of boxwood near the medullar oblongata / base of skull / top of neck area. This is also a good placement for the tree essence

Attunement to the Spirit of Catalpa

Mantra: J'HAY

Note Sequence: G C# C# G

Colour Sequence: Yellow ochre - red ochre - dark brown

Trance Position:

1. Standing, with a wide stride

2. Both feet pointing forward

3. Arms away from body,
forearms held up and crossed mid arm

4. Palms open facing to the back,
near the shoulders

Energy Net:

1. On a white cloth

2. Yellow jasper beside left ear

Attunement to the Spirit of Cedar of Lebanon

Mantra: TUSS EYE TUH GHEE SIGH

Note Sequence: * A *E G A B G* E* (* denotes lower octave if before the note, upper octave if after the note)

Colour Sequence: Orange - green - blue

No trance position found as yet.

Energy Net:

1. On an orange cloth

2. Labradorite placed beside the right side of the body between the second and third charkas

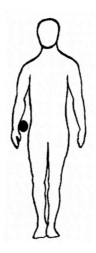

Attunement to the Spirit of Cherry Laurel

Mantra: SHOE INGOO HOO. ING (uh) ING (ih)

Note Sequence: F# *G Bb* C# *F#

Colour Sequence: Blue - indigo- orange - pink with yellow sparkles

Trance Position / Meditation:

1. Fingertips together making a hollow V - shape with your palms

2. With your eyes open, visualise the colour sequence occurring in that space between your hands

3. When complete, close eyes and relax, continuing to hold your hands in the same position

Energy Net:

None yet found.

Attunement to the Spirit of Cherry Plum

Mantra: VRR... DUH DRR... KEH LUH

Note Sequence: G A F C# C C#

Colour Sequence: orange - white

Trance Position:

1. Seated on a chair, thighs apart, lower legs coming together with feet parallel but not touching

2. Hands open resting palms down over the knees

3. Head relaxed backwards resting on the back of the neck

4. Mouth open, jaw relaxed

5. Back relaxed

Energy Net:

1. On an orange cloth

2. Below the feet, on the middle axis, a carnelian

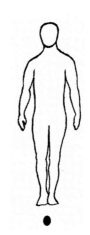

Attunement to the Spirit of Copper Beech

Mantra: DOO VAA TEA.. TEA BUY D'HEE

Note Sequence: E F D E G

Colour Sequence: Brown - orange - play of dark rainbow tones

Trance Position:

1. Lying on left side

2. Knees to chest

3. Head and eyes looking to the east

Energy Net:

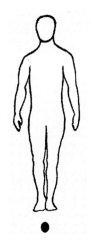

1. A violet cloth

2. Below and between the feet on the mid - line, a piece of copper

Attunement to the Spirit of Douglas Fir

Mantra: SAY GEE B'HAA TOO GEE B'HAA HRRR (uh)
(all the 'g' sounds are hard, as in good)

Note Sequence: Ab G D D Eb D

Colour Sequence: Blue - yellow - flashing black and white - gold (repeated sequence)

Visualisation:

A single star in a deep night sky

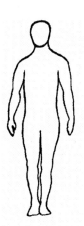

Energy Net:

1. On a pale yellow cloth

2. A golden topaz placed
3 ft. below the feet

Attunement to the Spirit of Eucalyptus

Mantra: CH'RRR (uh) KOO G'HAY

Note Sequence: G A *G * F *E *G *Ab *F *Ab *Ab

Colour Sequence: Orange - green

Trance Position:

1. Standing, feet on ground, facing forward, one foot apart

2. Spine bent backwards a little

3. Hands : left over right behind and supporting the neck

4. Facing west

Attunement to the Spirit of Field Maple

Mantra: TRRRIH VOO HRRRUH VAY

Note Sequence: F# Eb F#

Colour Sequence: Brick red - indigo - white

Trance Position:

Imagine that you are suspended vertically in the air, high above the ground, with your arms and legs spread like a pentacle.

Energy Net:

1. On a white cloth

2. Soladite placed beside the right arm

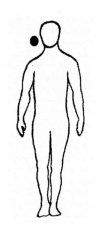

Attunement to the Spirit of Fig

Mantra: VRRRUH VRRRIH VO VOW

Note Sequence: F E C *D *D *F *C

Colour Sequence: Darkness - red - orange - green - darkness

Trance Meditation:

No forms, simply a visualisation of the colour sequence.

Energy Net:

1. On a blue cloth

2. Two red rubies placed beside the right hand

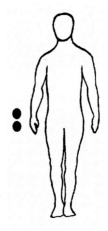

Attunement to the Spirit of Foxglove Tree

Mantra: GAA CHAI GAA GHAI CHAI

Note Sequence: E C C C C C F D D

Colour Sequence: Indigo

Trance Position:

1. Seated on a chair, left foot on floor

2. Right foot crossed over left ankle

3. Hands held wrist to wrist, fingers straight, left over right

4. Arms held close to body

Energy Net:

1. On a white cloth

2. Level with the heart chakra on the left side, a milky quartz

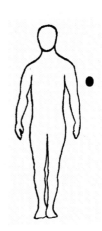

Attunement to the Spirit of Ginkgo

Mantra: TIE. RNUH. BHAA

Note Sequence: G E C D F E D E D

Colour Sequence: white......

Trance Position:

1. Standing, feet slightly apart

2. Bend forward with hands (palms) placed on the ground in front of the feet

Energy Net:

1. On a white cloth

2. Beside left knee, a white agate

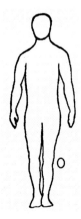

Attunement to the Spirit of Glastonbury Thorn

Mantra: SH'TOO ING INGGUH MAA VOO

Note Sequence: Eb D F Eb C D F D

Colour Sequence: White - violet - black and white - violet - black

Trance Position:

1. Standing, leaning on a staff, planted to your right

2. Both hands on staff, left hand lower than the right hand

3. Staff placed just outside of the right foot

4. Head looking forwards

Energy Net:

1. On a violet cloth

2. Ruby at the heart chakra

3. Twelve clear quartz points evenly spaced around the body, points outward

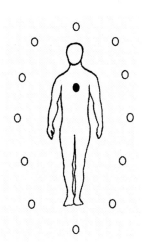

Attunements to the Spirit of Gorse

Mantra: ING UH KOO SHOWCH AAAA

Note Sequence: F

Colour Sequence: Blue - white - yellow-gold

Trance Position:

1. Standing with feet slightly more than a shoulder width apart

2. Left hand on the inguinal canal (groin)

3. Right hand held ninety degrees to body, straight out, palm upwards

Energy Net:

1. On a gold cloth

2. On the left side of chest, over the heart, a sugilite

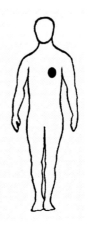

Attunement to the Spirit of Holm Oak

Mantra: KOO REE COW KOO

Note Sequence: C Eb *A *G *B Eb D

Colour Sequence: Black - green - white - blue - red - black

Trance Position:

1. Lying on back

2. Legs open, bent at knees, feet symmetrical but not touching

3. Same position for the arms, above the head, hands not touching

4. Mouth wide open

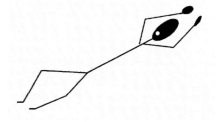

Energy Net:

1. On a green cloth

2. A green aventurine on each groin point (lower front of pelvis)

3. A green aventurine on the front of each arm pit

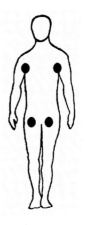

Attunement to the Spirit of Hornbeam

Mantra: SHO CHEE BAA CHEE G'HUH'LUH SHO

Note Sequence: C B C# C# B B B C

Colour Sequence: Like a dark night - turquoise - blue - concentric rainbow colours (non-defined darkness)

Trance Position:

1. Lying on back

2. Arms 45 degrees from the body resting with palms down

3. Heels on the floor, legs 45 degrees apart

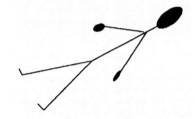

Energy Net:

1. On a dark cloth

2. A milky white calcite placed on the midline of the body, one ft. above the head

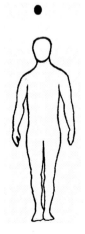

322

Attunement to the Spirit of Italian Alder

Mantra: EYE JEE DHOO YO

Note Sequence: A B Eb* A

Colour Sequence: Turquoise - orange - rainbow spectrum

Trance Position:

1. Kneeling on left knee

2. Right foot, with sole on the ground, knee bent

3. Hands held up in front of the eyes, palms inward

4. Eyes closed

5. Chin tucked in, neck stretched

Energy Net:

1. On a turquoise cloth

2. Rose quartz by the right hand side of the body, level with the knee

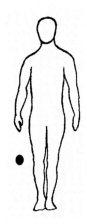

Attunement to the Spirit of Judas Tree

Mantra: GO PUH KAY DIE

Note Sequence: Eb D D C# C# C# E

Colour Sequence: Magenta - blue - orange

Trance Position:

1. Lying on back, knees raised, legs together, feet on floor

2. Arms above head, palms upward

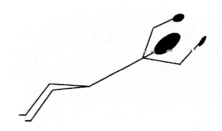

Energy Net:

None yet found

Attunement to the Spirit of Juniper

Mantra: CHOO PIE MOW DHAA

Note Sequence: F# E Eb Eb D Eb *Eb

Colour Sequence: Green - indigo - blue - turquoise - green

Trance Position:

1. Lying down on back

2. Knees bent, soles of feet on floor about one ft apart

3. Arms at 45 degrees from body on floor, palms down

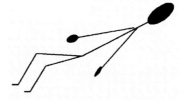

Energy Net:

1. On an indigo cloth

2. Citrine on the forehead

3. Amethyst between the feet

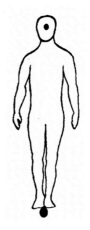

Attunement to the Spirit of Laburnum

Mantra: G'HUT RRRI BHAA GAA SIGH

Note Sequence: C C C C# C C# C C# C# C C# C

Colour Sequence: Orange - white - yellow - green - red

Trance Position:

1. Standing, feet shoulder width apart

2. Forearms held across body (chest / solar plexus)

3. Hands holding the sides of lower ribs

Energy Net:

None yet found

Attunement to the Spirit of Larch

Mantra: KEY BOO GO CHAI SO

Note Sequence: Eb F# Eb C Eb C#

Colour Sequence: White - blue/green - indigo - violet - white

Trance Position:

1. Walking along the line of a circle (like a tightrope)

2. Arms held straight, pointing to the line of the walk

3. Hands are fists except the 1st and 2nd fingers which point down to the line

4. Thumbs are straight, right thumb on left thumbnail

5. Each step say one sound of the mantra (KEY...BOO..etc)

Energy Net:

1. On a brown cloth

2. Clear quartz beside the right hip

Attunement to the Spirit of Leyland Cypress

Mantra: DEE RAY KEY TOO D'RR SHUH PIH

Note Sequence: F# C# F# F#

Colour Sequence: Violet - blue - gold - white

Trance Position:

1. Standing, legs together, heels together, feet splayed apart slightly

2. Arms held away from the body out to the side at about 30 degrees

3. Hands with palms outward

4. Head looking straight forward

Energy Net:

1. On a green cloth

2. A white topaz near the top of the arm on the left side

Attunement to the Spirit of Lilac

Mantra: CO SHU KI....CO SHU KI....CO SHU KI..

Sound Sequence: B C D F E D F

Colour Sequence: Indigo - blue - green - orange - pink

Trance Position:

1. Lying down on back

2. Head looking up, eyes closed

3. Hands together, palms touching

4. Fingers folded over other hand (at 90 degrees)

5. Hands over heart centre on chest

6. Legs straight, slightly apart

Energy Net:

1. On an indigo or dark blue cloth

2. Beside right hip - azurite

Attunement to the Spirit of Liquidamber

Mantra: TUH LUGOO TIT OW TU LUH

Sound Sequence: G *Eb *F# *Eb

Colour Sequence: Blue - yellow - indigo - black - indigo

Trance Position:

1. Lying on the right

2. Curl into a foetal positions

3. Hands clasped behind back

Energy Net:

1. On a blue cloth

2. Left side, beside ear - dark blue quartz/ aventurine and a yellow calcite

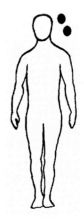

Attunement to the Spirit of Lombardy Poplar

Mantra: BEE PIE GHOO JOE FUH VOO

Note Sequence: Ab C# E C Ab E

Colour Sequence: White - yellow - black - indigo - orange

Visualisation:

1. Seated within an indigo blue fountain of water

2. Outside the cascade of water is visible the darkness of space illuminated by stars

3. At the highest point of the fountain (above it) is a brilliant golden sun around which are flying white, birdlike beings

Energy Net:

1. On a pink cloth

2. Lapis lazuli on the left side below the left foot

3. Just below the lapis, a carnelian

O

331

Attunement to the Spirit of Lucombe Oak

Mantra: PODE H'RRRRUH K'RRRRUH K'RRRRUH

Note Sequence: C *F# *G C C# Eb Eb *G

Colour Sequence: Yellow - orange - yellow - white - turquoise - red with green flashes

Trance Position:

1. Standing, legs wider than shoulder width

2. Right hand, palm to heart chakra (centre of chest)

3. Left upper arm, tight into side, lower arm at 90 degrees with palm upward

Energy Net:

None yet found

Attunement to the Spirit of Manna Ash

Mantra: JAY GURRA JEE TOO BURRA GUH' GURRA

Note Sequence: G C C C G E F E D C

Colour Sequence: Green - fading to darkness

Trance Position:

1. Kneeling upright

2. Left arm held out straight in front, palm outward and fingers turned to the right (elbow to outside of arm)

3. Right arm in the same position, right hand placed over the back of the left hand

Energy Net:

1. On a violet cloth

2. Beside the right ear, ruby in zoisite

Attunement to the Spirit of Medlar

Mantra: BUY NYEE SHA HUW NYEE

Note Sequence: F# C E C *F

Colour Sequence: Blue - pink - white - dark turquoise - yellow - indigo

Trance Position:

1. Sitting back on heels

2. Hands over navel, right over left

Energy Net:

1. On a pink cloth

2. Yellow citrine above the top of the head

3. Above the citrine, a clear calcite (Iceland spa)

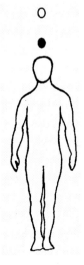

Attunement to the Spirit of Midland Hawthorn

Mantra: D'HAA

Note Sequence: Ab G Eb F# G Ab

Colour Sequence: White - violet - blue - orange - yellow - black

Trance Position:

1. Lying down on right side

2. Knees bent, thighs 90 degrees to body, legs together on top of each other

3. Arms straight above head, fingers outspread, palms outward

Energy Net:

1. On a white cloth

2. A rhodonite centrally placed above the head

3. An ametrine placed beside the right foot

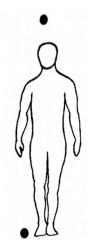

Attunement to the Spirit of Mimosa (Silver Wattle)

Mantra: RNAA SHAY BOO, RNAA SHAY BOO.

Note Sequence: D *G G A

Colour Sequence: Green - blue - blue with white veining - yellow

Trance Sequence:

1. Lying on right side

2. Knees slightly bent

3. Chin bent down to chest

4. Use an arm or a cushion to support head

Energy Net:

1. On a white cloth

2. A tiger's eye at the throat chakra

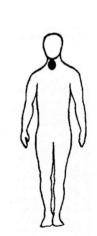

Attunement to the Spirit of Norway Maple

Mantra: SHIK EYE RIP AY RIH

Note Sequence: F Ab Ab F# F# G G F

Colour Sequence: Green field with slow pulsing pink points
- yellow -white

Trance / Meditation Position

The same position as one's physical body is in but visualised
inside the sacral chakra

Energy Net:

1. On a black cloth

2. A rubellite (pink or red
tourmaline) on the right side level
with the hip / sacral chakra area

3. Yellow calcite on the left side
level with the heart chakra

Attunement to the Spirit of Norway Spruce

Mantra: D'HIH HURAT. BOW BAA

Note Sequence: B A G* G* G*

Colour Sequence: Yellow - gold - white - green

Trance Position:

1. Standing, or sitting, feet together

2. Right hand crossed over left hand covering the top of the forehead / front of skull

3. Shoulders and elbows relaxed

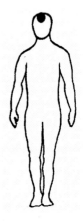

Energy Net:

1. On a white cloth

2. Any orange stone, such as carnelian or amber, placed on the middle of the hair - line (front of cranium)

Attunement to the Spirit of Olive

Mantra: MRRUH TOO J'HEY TOO

Note sequence: A Bb Eb D D Eb C

Colour Sequence: Gold - blue - white - red

Trance Position:

1. Seated with knees, legs and feet together

2. Hands held flat against the sides of the thighs, upper legs

3. Head and eyes turned down, looking at the floor just in front of your feet

Energy Net:

1. On a white cloth

2. An amethyst placed on the top of the arch of the left foot

3. A red garnet centrally placed above the top of the head

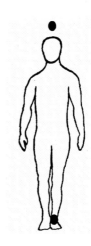

Attunement to the Spirit of Osier

Mantra: CHAA J' FAA CHAA

Note sequence: Ab. Ab. C. A. *C. * Eb. *F. C*. Eb*. F *. Ab. Ab. C A (second section 3 notes lower octave, next 3 upper octave)

Colour Sequence: Orange - white

Trance Position:

1. Seated cross-legged, body upright, head to front

2. Left hand held off body, palm toward heart chakra

3. Right hand, at same level as left, but at 90 degrees, in line with the right arm, which is held against the side of the body

Energy Net:

1. On a violet cloth

2. A moonstone held on the heart chakra

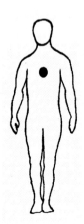

Attunement to the Spirit of Pear

Mantra: DAY SHIH SHIH DAY

Note Sequence: G F B * Bb *G *F *G *E *D *D

Colour sequence: Pink - yellow - orange - lime green

Trance Position:

1. Standing upright, feet a little apart, parallel but turned to the left

2. Hands and arms relaxed by the sides

3. Head turned to look to the left

Energy Net:

1. On an orange cloth

2. Carnelian by the left side of the neck

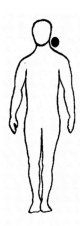

Attunement to the Spirit of Pittospora

Mantra: K. G. G. G. (No vowel sounds nor aspirates, just plosives at the back of the palette whilst breath is held)

Note Sequence: F# G Ab Ab

Colour Sequence: Pink

Trance Position:

1. Sitting on floor cross - legged

2. Hand placed under each buttock

Energy Net:

1. On a blue cloth

2. Five rhodonites placed around the body in a shape of an inverted pentagon. (Stones beside the shoulders, beside the hips and below and between the feet)

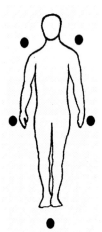

Attunement to the Spirit of Privet

Mantra: JOWE DOUGH JUH
(JOWE rhymes with how, DOUGH rhymes with go)

Note Sequence: F* * A *A# *G *F

Colour Sequence: Black - gold - pink - indigo - black

Trance Position:

1. Kneeling, thighs upright

2. Hands and arms in 'orans' position, palms outward, fingers splayed at shoulder level (arms bent, upper arms close to body)

3. Mouth kept wide open

4. Hands tilted up slightly

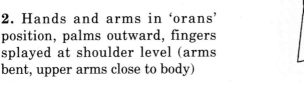

Energy Net:

1. On a black cloth

2. A red garnet on the left abdomen, level with the navel, above the hip.

Attunement to the Spirit of Red Oak

Mantra: TAY K'HOO PAA KAA GHEY AAA

Note Sequence: B A F F Eb Eb Eb D C

Colour Sequence: White - turquoise - magenta - green - turquoise

Trance Position:

1. Sitting on ground, knees up, crossed legs, arms around legs

2. Head straight forward

Energy Net:

1. On a white cloth

2. A red garnet between the knees

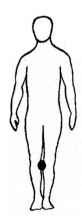

Attunement to the Spirit of Robinia

Mantra: B'HRRUH HIGH. B'RRUH HIGH. B'RRUH HIGH

Note Sequence: D D C D E C# C

Colour Sequence: Pink - white - gold - green - pink

Trance Position:

1. Lying on front, legs together

2. Head straight down

3. Hands on skull above ears (parietal bone), middle fingertips touching over the top of skull

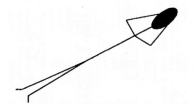

Energy Net:

1. On a pink cloth

2. Lapis lazuli on right frontal eminence (bump at side of forehead)

3. Citrine on left side at the bottom of the ribcage

Attunement to the Spirit of Sea Buckthorn

Mantra: VOH SAY JAI JAY SAY

Note Sequence: C C B *G *G

Colour Sequence: White - green - yellow - white...(repeating)

Trance Position:

1. Visualising the body sitting above and within sea spray (not actually in the water)

Energy Net:

1. On an indigo cloth

2. Rose quartz beside the left hand side at knee level

3. Rose quartz at right side at eye level

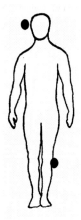

Attunement to the Spirit of Silver Fir

Mantra: RAYII HUH HAA J'HAA

Note Sequence: G A E A G D

Colour Sequence: Green - red - blue with interlocking white starlight

Trance / Meditation:

1. See energy descending to the top of the head from above and spreading downward in concentric green cones.

2. See this being mirrored from below also.

3. As you do this a white light begins to glow at the solar plexus gate (bottom of ribcage). A light also begins to glow at the base Chakra (base of the spine), and then also at the top of the head

4. These three lights form a space within which interaction with spirits can occur.

Energy Net:

1. On an indigo cloth

2. A clear white flourite at the crown chakra

3. A gold citrine at the solar plexus gate

4. Aquamarine at the base of the spine

Attunement to the Spirit of Spindle

Mantra: HOO P'HAA HOO P'HAA

Note Sequence: E E F# F# E

Colour Sequence: Orange - yellow - red - pink - orange

Trance Position:

1. Kneeling upright

2. Hands together, left over right, at hara. Holding them to the body.

3. Head down, chin to chest

Energy Net:

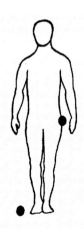

1. On an orange cloth

2. Gold citrine by the right side, level with the foot

3. Black obsidian on the right side, level with the hara (sacral chakra)

348

Attunement to the Spirit of Strawberry Tree

Mantra: KEEN YEAR KOO SHAA. KEEN YEAR SHOO SHAA.

Note Sequence: F# D G E A F# F#

Colour Sequence: Blue - yellow

Trance Position:

1. Lying on right side

2. Knees drawn up as if in foetal position

3. Right hand over eyes

4. Left hand on heart

Energy Net:

1. On a red cloth

2. Sodalite on brow chakra

3. Clear quartz beside left hand

4. Jet beside right hand

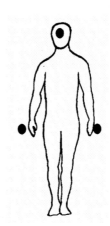

Attunement to the Spirit of Sweet Chestnut

Mantra: DIRREL DOW RAITH

Note Sequence: C# F# C D D C* E E C#

Colour Sequence: Magenta - dark green - black - blue - red - magenta

Trance Position:

1. Standing straight, chin to chest

2. Left hand held to heart chakra but kept away from the body

3. Right hand held to second chakra but kept away from body

4. Finish by holding hands, palms outward in 'orans' position

No Energy Net found

Attunement to the Spirit of Tamarisk

Mnatra: TOO

Note Sequence: Eb G Bb D* Eb G G * F# *E

Colour Sequence: Slate blue/grey - blue - red - colour of sunlight on water

Trance Position:

1. Lying on back

2. Soles of feet together, legs apart (relaxed to floor)

3. Arms straight, 30 degrees from body, on floor, palms upward

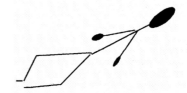

Energy Net:

1. On blue/grey cloth

2. Citrine midway between feet

3. Opal on left side by ankle

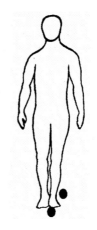

Attunement to the Spirit of Tree of Heaven

Mantra: D'H....B...D'HAY RUH

Note Sequence: G C# *G *D

Colour Sequence: Red - blue - gold - black

Trance Position:

1. Lying on back

2. Soles of feet together, knees apart

3. Upper left arm 90 degrees to body axis, lower arm parallel to body, facing down the body, palm down

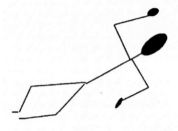

4. Upper right arm 90 degrees to the body axis, lower arm parallel to body, facing up the body, palm upward

Energy Net:

1. On a white cloth

2. Yellow beryl (helidior) by the left side level with the navel

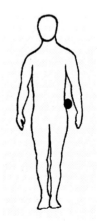

Attunement to the Spirit of Viburnum (V. Tinus)

Mantra: DRRR UNG IH J'HER UB

Note Sequence: F# G G D D E

Colour Sequence: Pink - sensation of light (no specific colour, nor white)

Trance Position:

1. Lying on front, body straight

2. Arms straight above head, palms held together

Energy Net:

1. On a dark pink cloth

2. Amethyst at the solar plexus

3. Lapis lazuli touching the right elbow

Attunement to the Spirit of Walnut

Mantra: SHAY SHL' SHAY NOO

Note Sequence: F# G Ab C# Eb C

Colour Sequence: Turquoise - red - white - orange - red - white

Trance Position:

1. Lying on back, legs bent, soles of feet towards each other but not together (like a frog's legs)

2. Arms bent at elbows, upper arms at right angles to body, lower arms making a right angle (parallel to body axis) palms down)

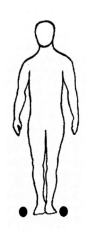

Energy Net:

1. On a turquoise or orange cloth

2. Green aventurine by the left foot (to the outside)

3. By the outside of the right foot, a red garnet

Attunement to the Spirit of Wayfaring Tree

Mantra: T'HOO CHEE S.... T'HRR RRUD HIH

Note Sequence: D *F G * F

Colour Sequence: Magenta - magenta centre expanding outward to turquoise - gold

Trance Position:

1. Lying down on right side

2. Right knee brought up to chest

3. Left leg straight but brought forwards from spinal axis

4. Fingers interlocked and folded over each other (prayer like), held close to sacral chakra

Energy Net:

1. On a red cloth

2. Six Lapis Lazuli, arranged as a hexagon (one above the head, one below the feet, two at shoulder level, two at thigh, mid-leg level

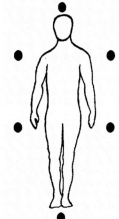

Attunement to the Spirit of Western Hemlock

Mantra: OOO.....PHOO.KO

Note Sequence: C# Bb Eb Eb F# Eb

Colour Sequence: Yellow - red - magenta

Trance Position:

1. Sitting cross legged

2. Left hand on top of left thigh/knee

3. Right hand resting on top of head

Energy Net:

1. A white cloth

2. Labradorite at the top of the head

3. Azurite between the feet

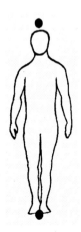

Attunement to the Spirit of Western Red Cedar

Mantra: SO GUY G'HUU DRRRUH

Note Sequence: *Eb *C *C F F D C Eb Eb *C.

Colour Sequence: Violet - yellow - magenta - gold - white

Trance Position/Meditation

Imagine having a straight body, rapidly moving upward into space, continue this upward sensation

Energy Net:

1. On an orange cloth

2. Two iron pyrites placed level and beside the hips

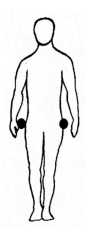

Attunement to the Spirit of White Willow

Mantra: TAANG UH TA' UNG UH

Note Sequence: D E D G B G D *B *E

Colour Sequence: Gold - turquoise - red - infinitely fast vibration

Trance Position:

1. Sit on bottom, knees to chest, hands around legs (left on left leg, right on right leg)

2. Visualising moving forward very quickly

Energy Net:

1. No stones and no cloth; body bathed in light of gold, turquoise and red

Attunement to the Spirit of Wild Service Tree

Mantra: AAA CHAY

Note Sequence: G D G B

Colour Sequence: Green - violet - yellow - blue - green

Trance Position:

1. Standing, eyes closed, hands cupped behind ears

Energy Net:

1. On an indigo cloth

2. A bowl of water by the right side, level with the navel

3. A candle midline beneath the feet

4. A piece of wood by the left side, level with the heart

5. An image of the letter K by the right side, level with heart

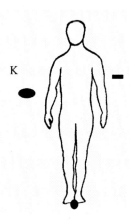

Attunement to the Spirit of Willow - Leaved Pear

Mantra: AY TOO   (AY rhymes with 'hay')

Note Sequence: F# D Eb F#

Colour Sequence: Cream white - blue - orange

Trance Position:

1. Lying on back, legs together

2. Arms lying straight out from body at about 20 degrees

3. Left hand, palm up

4. Right hand, palm down

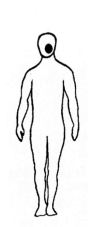

Energy Net:

1. On a magenta cloth

2. Clear quartz by left nostril

Attunement to the Spirit Wych Elm

Mantra: PRRRUH GHAY TOE MOON GOO VO

Note Sequence: E C# F D G

Colour Sequence: Indigo - white - pink - black - indigo

Trance Position:

1. Standing with hands and arms relaxed

2. Body weight on left leg (making a contraposto position)

Energy Net:

1. On a blue cloth

2. Clear quartz at the top of the head touching the crown

3. Amethyst placed beside the left hip

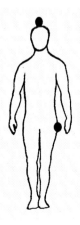

Attunement to the Spirit of Yellow Buckeye

Mantra: DUS HUH YIH RRNUH (all short vowel sounds)

Note Sequence: E C G D A

Colour Sequence: Red - gold - blue - violet - deepest midnight blue

Trance Position:

1. Sitting on hands (palms down)

2. Back straight, head tilted back

3. Position of legs not important

Energy Net:

1. On a blue cloth

2. Black obsidian centrally placed below feet

3. Red garnet beside left ear

4. Iron pyrites level with the heart chakra on the right side of the body

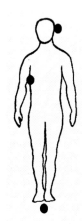

References and Sources

Barnard, Julian "*Bach Flower Remedies: Form and Function*" Flower
Remedy Programme UK, 2002

Bear, Jaya "*Amazon Magic: The Life Story of Ayahuascero and Shaman
Dan Agustia Rivas Vasquez*" Colibri Publishing Mexico, 2000

Bown, Deni "T*he Royal Horticultural Society Encyclopaedia of Herbs
and Their Uses*" Dorling Kindersley UK, 1995

Buhner, Stephen Harrod "*The Lost Language of Plants*" Chelsea Green
Publishing Canada, 2002

Conway, David "*The Magic of Herbs*" Jonathan Cape, 1973

Conway, Peter "*Tree Medicine*" Piatkus UK, 2001

Cowan, David and Girdlestone, Rodney "*Safe as Houses? Ill-health and
Electro-stress in the Home*" Gateway Books UK, 1996

Cowan, Tom "*Shamanism as a Spiritual Practice for Daily Life*" The
Crossing Press USA, 1996

Danielou, Alain *"The Myths and Gods of India"* Inner Traditions Canada, 1991

Darwin, Tess *"The Scots Herbal: The Plant Lore of Scotland"* Mercat Press Edinburgh, 1996

Devereux, Paul *"Stone Age Soundtracks: The Acoustic Archaeology of Ancient Sites"* Vega UK 2001

Goodman, Felicitas D *"Where the Spirits Ride the Wind. Trance Journeys and other Ecstatic Experiences"* Indiana University Press USA, 1990

Gore, Belinda *"Ecstatic Body Postures. An Alternate Reality Workbook"* Bear & Co USA, 1995

Grieve, M and Leyel, C.F. *"A Modern Herbal"* Jonathan Cape 1931, Tiger Books, 1994

Gurudas *"Gem Elixirs and Vibrational Healing Vol I"* Cassandra Press USA, 1989

Harner, Michael *"The Way of the Shaman"* Harper Collins, San Francisco USA, 1990

Hume, R.E (trans) *"The Thirteen Principal Upanishads"* Oxford University Press UK, 1934

Lilly, Simon & Sue *"Crystal Doorways"* Capall Bann Publishing UK, 1997

Lilly, Simon & Sue *"Tree: Essence of Healing"* Capall Bann Publishing UK, 1999

Lilly, Simon & Sue *"Tree: Essence, Spirit & Teacher"* Capall Bann Publishing UK, 1999

McTaggart, Lynn *"The Field"* Harper Collins UK, 2001

Mulchahy,S (trans) *"Macdonald Encyclopaedia of Medicinal Plants"* Macdonald & Co Ltd, 1984

Naddair, Kaledon *"Keltic Folk and Faerie Tales: Their Hidden Meaning Explored"* Century Paperback (Rider) UK, 1987

Narby, Jeremy *"The Cosmic Serpent. DNA and the Origins of Knowledge"* P Tarcher/Putnam USA, 1999

Thurnell-Read, Jane *"Geopathic Stress"*, Vega UK, 2001

"Shaman's Drum – A Journal of Experimental Shamanism and Spiritual Healing" PO Box 270, Williams, OR97544 USA

"The Foundation for Shamanic Studies Newsletter" PO Box 1939, Mill Valley, California 94942, USA

FREE DETAILED CATALOGUE

Capall Bann is owned and run by people actively involved in many of the areas in which we publish. A detailed illustrated catalogue is available on request, SAE or International Postal Coupon appreciated. **Titles can be ordered direct from Capall Bann, post free in the UK** (cheque or PO with order) or from good bookshops and specialist outlets.

A Breath Behind Time, Terri Hector
Angels and Goddesses - Celtic Christianity & Paganism, M. Howard
Arthur - The Legend Unveiled, C Johnson & E Lung
Astrology The Inner Eye - A Guide in Everyday Language, E Smith
Auguries and Omens - The Magical Lore of Birds, Yvonne Aburrow
Asyniur - Womens Mysteries in the Northern Tradition, S McGrath
Beginnings - Geomancy, Builder's Rites & Electional Astrology in the
	European Tradition, Nigel Pennick
Between Earth and Sky, Julia Day
Book of the Veil , Peter Paddon
Caer Sidhe - Celtic Astrology and Astronomy, Vol 1, Michael Bayley
Caer Sidhe - Celtic Astrology and Astronomy, Vol 2 M Bayley
Call of the Horned Piper, Nigel Jackson
Cat's Company, Ann Walker
Celtic Faery Shamanism, Catrin James
Celtic Faery Shamanism - The Wisdom of the Otherworld, Catrin James
Celtic Lore & Druidic Ritual, Rhiannon Ryall
Celtic Sacrifice - Pre Christian Ritual & Religion, Marion Pearce
Celtic Saints and the Glastonbury Zodiac, Mary Caine
Circle and the Square, Jack Gale
Compleat Vampyre - The Vampyre Shaman, Nigel Jackson
Creating Form From the Mist - The Wisdom of Women in Celtic Myth and
	Culture, Lynne Sinclair-Wood
Crystal Clear - A Guide to Quartz Crystal, Jennifer Dent
Crystal Doorways, Simon & Sue Lilly
Crossing the Borderlines - Guising, Masking & Ritual Animal Disguise in the
	European Tradition, Nigel Pennick
Dragons of the West, Nigel Pennick
Earth Dance - A Year of Pagan Rituals, Jan Brodie
Earth Harmony - Places of Power, Holiness & Healing, Nigel Pennick
Earth Magic, Margaret McArthur
Eildon Tree (The) Romany Language & Lore, Michael Hoadley

Enchanted Forest - The Magical Lore of Trees, Yvonne Aburrow
Eternal Priestess, Sage Weston
Eternally Yours Faithfully, Roy Radford & Evelyn Gregory
Everything You Always Wanted To Know About Your Body, But So Far
    Nobody's Been Able To Tell You, Chris Thomas & D Baker
Face of the Deep - Healing Body & Soul, Penny Allen
Fairies in the Irish Tradition, Molly Gowen
Familiars - Animal Powers of Britain, Anna Franklin
Fool's First Steps, (The) Chris Thomas
Forest Paths - Tree Divination, Brian Harrison, Ill. S. Rouse
From Past to Future Life, Dr Roger Webber
Gardening For Wildlife Ron Wilson
God Year, The, Nigel Pennick & Helen Field
Goddess on the Cross, Dr George Young
Goddess Year, The, Nigel Pennick & Helen Field
Goddesses, Guardians & Groves, Jack Gale
Handbook For Pagan Healers, Liz Joan
Handbook of Fairies, Ronan Coghlan
Healing Book, The, Chris Thomas and Diane Baker
Healing Homes, Jennifer Dent
Healing Journeys, Paul Williamson
Healing Stones, Sue Philips
Herb Craft - Shamanic & Ritual Use of Herbs, Lavender & Franklin
Hidden Heritage - Exploring Ancient Essex, Terry Johnson
Hub of the Wheel, Skytoucher
In Search of Herne the Hunter, Eric Fitch
Inner Celtia, Alan Richardson & David Annwn
Inner Mysteries of the Goths, Nigel Pennick
Inner Space Workbook - Develop Thru Tarot, C Summers & J Vayne
Intuitive Journey, Ann Walker Isis - African Queen, Akkadia Ford
Journey Home, The, Chris Thomas
Kecks, Keddles & Kesh - Celtic Lang & The Cog Almanac, Bayley
Language of the Psycards, Berenice
Legend of Robin Hood, The, Richard Rutherford-Moore
Lid Off the Cauldron, Patricia Crowther
Light From the Shadows - Modern Traditional Witchcraft, Gwyn
Living Tarot, Ann Walker
Lore of the Sacred Horse, Marion Davies
Lost Lands & Sunken Cities (2nd ed.), Nigel Pennick
Magic of Herbs - A Complete Home Herbal, Rhiannon Ryall
Magical Guardians - Exploring the Spirit and Nature of Trees, Philip Heselton
Magical History of the Horse, Janet Farrar & Virginia Russell
Magical Lore of Animals, Yvonne Aburrow
Magical Lore of Cats, Marion Davies
Magical Lore of Herbs, Marion Davies
Magick Without Peers, Ariadne Rainbird & David Rankine

Masks of Misrule - Horned God & His Cult in Europe, Nigel Jackson
Medicine For The Coming Age, Lisa Sand MD
Medium Rare - Reminiscences of a Clairvoyant, Muriel Renard
Menopausal Woman on the Run, Jaki da Costa
Mind Massage - 60 Creative Visualisations, Marlene Maundrill
Mirrors of Magic - Evoking the Spirit of the Dewponds, P Heselton
Moon Mysteries, Jan Brodie
Mysteries of the Runes, Michael Howard
Mystic Life of Animals, Ann Walker
New Celtic Oracle The, Nigel Pennick & Nigel Jackson
Oracle of Geomancy, Nigel Pennick
Pagan Feasts - Seasonal Food for the 8 Festivals, Franklin & Phillips
Patchwork of Magic - Living in a Pagan World, Julia Day
Pathworking - A Practical Book of Guided Meditations, Pete Jennings
Personal Power, Anna Franklin
Pickingill Papers - The Origins of Gardnerian Wicca, Bill Liddell
Pillars of Tubal Cain, Nigel Jackson
Places of Pilgrimage and Healing, Adrian Cooper
Practical Divining, Richard Foord
Practical Meditation, Steve Hounsome
Practical Spirituality, Steve Hounsome
Psychic Self Defence - Real Solutions, Jan Brodie
Real Fairies, David Tame
Reality - How It Works & Why It Mostly Doesn't, Rik Dent
Romany Tapestry, Michael Houghton
Runic Astrology, Nigel Pennick
Sacred Animals, Gordon MacLellan
Sacred Celtic Animals, Marion Davies, Ill. Simon Rouse
Sacred Dorset - On the Path of the Dragon, Peter Knight
Sacred Grove - The Mysteries of the Forest, Yvonne Aburrow
Sacred Geometry, Nigel Pennick
Sacred Nature, Ancient Wisdom & Modern Meanings, A Cooper
Sacred Ring - Pagan Origins of British Folk Festivals, M. Howard
Season of Sorcery - On Becoming a Wisewoman, Poppy Palin
Seasonal Magic - Diary of a Village Witch, Paddy Slade
Secret Places of the Goddess, Philip Heselton
Secret Signs & Sigils, Nigel Pennick
Self Enlightenment, Mayan O'Brien
Spirits of the Air, Jaq D Hawkins
Spirits of the Earth, Jaq D Hawkins
Spirits of the Earth, Jaq D Hawkins
Stony Gaze, Investigating Celtic Heads John Billingsley
Stumbling Through the Undergrowth , Mark Kirwan-Heyhoe
Subterranean Kingdom, The, revised 2nd ed, Nigel Pennick
Symbols of Ancient Gods, Rhiannon Ryall
Talking to the Earth, Gordon MacLellan

Taming the Wolf - Full Moon Meditations, Steve Hounsome
Teachings of the Wisewomen, Rhiannon Ryall
The Other Kingdoms Speak, Helena Hawley
Tree: Essence of Healing, Simon & Sue Lilly
Tree: Essence, Spirit & Teacher, Simon & Sue Lilly
Through the Veil, Peter Paddon
Torch and the Spear, Patrick Regan
Understanding Chaos Magic, Jaq D Hawkins
Vortex - The End of History, Mary Russell
Warp and Weft - In Search of the I-Ching, William de Fancourt
Warriors at the Edge of Time, Jan Fry
Water Witches, Tony Steele
Way of the Magus, Michael Howard
Weaving a Web of Magic, Rhiannon Ryall
West Country Wicca, Rhiannon Ryall
Wildwitch - The Craft of the Natural Psychic, Poppy Palin
Wildwood King , Philip Kane
Witches of Oz, Matthew & Julia Philips
Wondrous Land - The Faery Faith of Ireland by Dr Kay Mullin
Working With the Merlin, Geoff Hughes
Your Talking Pet, Ann Walker

FREE detailed catalogue and FREE 'Inspiration' magazine

Contact: Capall Bann Publishing, Auton Farm, Milverton, Somerset, TA4 1NE